The Japanese Social Crisis

Jon Woronoff

First published in Great Britain 1997 by
MACMILLAN PRESS LTD
Houndmills, Basingstoke, Hampshire RG21 6XS and London
Companies and representatives throughout the world

A catalogue record for this book is available from the British Library.

ISBN 0–333–65024–7 hardcover
ISBN 0–333–65025–5 paperback

First published in the United States of America 1997 by
ST. MARTIN'S PRESS, INC.,
Scholarly and Reference Division,
175 Fifth Avenue, New York, N.Y. 10010

ISBN 0–312–17261–3

Library of Congress Cataloging-in-Publication Data
Woronoff, Jon.
The Japanese social crisis / Jon Woronoff.
p. cm.
Includes bibliographical references and index.
ISBN 0–312–17261–3 (cloth)
1. Japan—Social conditions—1945– 2. National characteristics,
Japanese. I. Title.
HN723.W673 1996
301'.0952—dc21   96–46623
                                                            CIP

This book is printed on paper suitable for recycling and made from fully managed and
sustained forest sources.

10   9   8   7   6   5   4   3   2   1
06   05   04   03   02   01   00   99   98   97

Printed and bound in Great Britain by
Antony Rowe Ltd, Chippenham, Wiltshire

Contents

Foreword

When the predecessor to this book, *Japan: The Coming Social Crisis*, was published back in 1980, it met with even more incredulity than *Japan: The Coming Economic Crisis* which had appeared the year before. Everybody knew, or thought they knew, that Japan's society was one of the most harmonious, dynamic and in many ways admirable societies that ever existed. True, the economy might slow down. But what could possibly disturb this extraordinary society?

Among the Japanese, admittedly, there were already some who realized that the country was headed in the wrong direction. The political scene was increasingly corrupt and the ruling party was running out of ideas and ideals, if less so than its ineffectual rivals. Education had already become more a question of cramming than learning and many felt that 'lifetime employment' was closer to 'lifetime enslavement' than happiness through work. But any complaints were either not heard or not heeded by foreigners. For the 1980s was the decade of Japan as Number One in one sector after another as Americans and Europeans tried to 'learn from Japan' with regard to education, management, law enforcement and even social relations, and Asia decided to 'look East.'

The events of recent years have blown away the froth and uncovered many serious weaknesses. This discovery was punctuated by happenings that no one, including myself, could ever have dreamed of. The great economic upswing of the late 1980s turned out to be partly a financial 'bubble' whose bursting has depressed the economy for years. The ruling Liberal Democratic Party was not only voted out, it split and turned into rival parties which, if necessary to gain power, joined with erstwhile rivals. The Kobe earthquake not only tore up parts of that city, it showed that the Japanese authorities could not even mount a proper rescue operation. Then, in March 1995, that most precious of illusions of a calm and secure Japan was shattered by not one but a series of poison gas attacks by a rogue religious sect.

At this point, it does not take much courage or imagination to write about a social crisis. It is plain to see. Or is it? Perhaps not. For the exceptional happenings just mentioned are only the beginnings and in some cases just surface phenomena or 'accidents' which might not have happened. The true crisis reaches much deeper and the rot is spreading more rapidly than most observers realize even now. At present, virtually all social institutions are being undermined in one way or another and they could easily collapse, one after the other. With this, the whole superstructure of Japan could be left without solid foundations and a crisis far more damaging would ensue. These deeper, broader and usually also less visible manifestations must be carefully examined.

When the first social crisis book was written, the trends were already negative on the whole, although many sectors were still flourishing. Sad to say, the trends have remained negative over the past decade-and-a-half and there are no real signs that any of them are taking a turn for the better. What Japan will be like in another 15 years is impossible to say. But, if it is not to turn into something very considerably worse than at present, it is necessary to focus on the underlying problems, understand them better and, if possible, take measures to solve or contain them. I do not expect this to happen. But I would be pleased if it does.

For the purpose of this book is not to boast that 'I told you so.' I was among the very few who were critical. I am among the very few who could claim to have predicted the future with the slightest degree of accuracy. And the 'reward' was to be criticized and condemned by my peers, especially foreigners like myself, although the Japanese grasped much better what I was getting at. This book is written in the perhaps futile hope that in the future I may say 'this time I was wrong.'

Jon Woronoff

1

The Present

(The Crisis That Came)

It is, indeed, an ill wind that blows no good. Certainly, no one would have wished the series of misfortunes that occurred during the 1990s upon Japan. But they did serve the purpose of awakening the Japanese to the fact that their society and economy were not as miraculous as claimed and that there were deep-rooted problems that had to be solved. It has also stopped foreigners from proclaiming Japan as number one, at least for the moment, and insisting that it had achieved more than the rest. In this new atmosphere, perhaps both Japanese and foreigners will look more closely and see more precisely what the problems are.

For me, the good is that I can finally describe Japan's problems frankly and openly without being taken for a crank. Everybody now knows that something is wrong, so criticism is no longer off limits. It is permissible to suggest just what might be wrong and also why, although this may be embarrassing to some. It is also a relief that every negative comment does not have to be carefully prefaced with a reference to the misleading words of praise of one apologist or another, which must then be disproved so that, with luck, the criticism will register. By now, most of the vacuous claims of the Japanapologists appear patently absurd and can be readily dismissed, although that is not always the case. In some areas, the Japanese still maintain a better reputation than they deserve.

Let us also hope that this new mood will incite a serious reassessment among the Japanese as to what is good and bad in their society, what should be preserved, what should be changed and what should be discarded. And then, making an exceptional effort, they may actually do something for once in addition to just talking about it and creating a consensus. This last hope is probably ill placed, but it is nonetheless sincere.

1

Facing Facts

When giving a speech, the Japanese nearly always start from some decisive date which appears almost as the beginning of a new era. Most formally, they count the years as of the start of a new imperial reign, finally passing from the 63-year long Showa era in 1989 to the present Heisei era. But they also used the end of the war in 1945 as a marker, or the merger of the Liberal and Democratic parties in 1955, or the oil crisis in 1963. Then there was the first yen crisis of 1971 and several others thereafter. More recently, they could start with the puncturing of the 'bubble economy' in 1991 or the demise of the Liberal Democratic Party in 1993. Yet nothing has marked the recent past more than the Kobe earthquake and especially the poison gas attacks by the Aum sect in 1995.[1]

Coming on top of the most serious postwar economic crisis, and then the most serious postwar political crisis, this social crisis dissipated any feelings the Japanese may have had that they were somehow more dynamic, more harmonious, more law-abiding and, in short, more everything good and noble than other peoples. This was no easy concession for, during more than four decades after the Pacific War, the Japanese had been restoring their self-confidence and generating a bit of hubris as well. They were encouraged in this by endless compliments and applause from abroad. Book after book, article after article were written to praise one aspect or another of postwar Japan. While this was not generally known, some of these books and articles were inspired more by financial than moral concerns and a few were paid for outright. But much of the admiration was genuine.

Thus, the letdown, the return to reality, the final admission that Japan was not truly superior came as a shock. Now, and hopefully before it is too late, the Japanese are engaging in some much needed soul-searching in order to find out when and where they went wrong. And more authentic foreign friends, not the flatterers and apologists but the critics, are doing the same.

In order to do so, however, it is necessary first to get beyond the various traumatic events which have grabbed the headlines. They are significant, they are symptomatic, they are stunning, but they are also too specific. There are many more phenomena which are broader and deeper and will be the undoing of Japan if they are not corrected. So, even these terrible events must be seen in their context.

For example, it was not the rise of a financial bubble that was so alarming as that it was not only allowed but encouraged by a supposedly omniscient bureaucracy and that even supposedly hard-headed businessmen engaged in 'financial engineering.' It was not only the collapse of the LDP that was nasty but also how it happened, through personal ambition and opportunism rather than for reasons of policy, showing just how shallow the party had always been. Obviously, an earthquake cannot be predicted with any great accuracy. But it was more than foolish of the Japanese authorities to pretend that they could do better than others and then, once it occurred, not even be able to mount a decent rescue operation. No one could prevent the Aum sect's guru from hatching evil plans, but surely the police should have been aware of what was in the offing and acted faster and more effectively.

It would therefore be pointless to devote more time than necessary to such glaring events, happenings and other surface phenomena rather than the less visible but more worrisome trends which are occurring in nearly all the fundamental institutions. The ones dealt with in this book are fairly broad and cover much of Japan's society. They include the educational system, the company, the state (parties, bureaucracies and business organizations), the family, religions, established society and the nation. Last, but sadly not least, there is the individual. For I now realize that I made a major mistake in the first social crisis book. I thought that the individual was, as largely in the West, the source and basic element of each of these institutions. In Japan, the individual is much more a residual, the result or product of these institutions, shaped and controlled more than shaping and controlling.

In order to see what is happening in each of these institutions, and to the individual, it is indispensable to follow the trends. That was already done in *Japan: The Coming Social Crisis*. This time the trends have been extended much further. Naturally, they have been updated since 1980, where the previous book left off. But they has also been traced further back into the past. Only thus can one see how truly sweeping the social trends have been in Japan. Only thus can it be grasped

that Japanese society, far from being stable and immutable as
so many claimed, has actually been undergoing almost constant mutation and transformation during the modern period,
if most intensively over the past half-century.

While extensive, this change has been much less noticeable
than elsewhere for various reasons, some of which will be elucidated later on. The Japanese have a great respect for precedent and do not vary traditions readily, at least on the surface.
And they pay endless tribute to time-honored customs and
practices, so much so that they may seem to exist when there
is nothing more than the form left and the essence has long
since disappeared. More important, the older generation still
dominates society to the extent that younger generations have
little choice but to pay lip service to antiquated ideas and
ideals. Consequently, to know what is going on, it is essential
to ignore ritual and ceremony and focus on action, to judge
people and institutions by what they do more than what they
say and not take anything for granted. To know where Japan
is headed, it is essential to pay more attention to the younger
and youngest generations than their elders do.

This is not easy in any society. It is particularly difficult in
Japanese society. But the effort must be made. Even if there
is no reason to expect that each and every trend can be perceived and interpreted, at least the broad currents can be
charted and the general direction can be indicated. That is
certainly better than sticking to old concepts and inherited
ideas which have lost all meaning. Also, by stating which category behaves in which way, whether men or women, old or
young, of higher or lower status, we can at least break away
from the inanity of braying 'the Japanese do this . . .' and 'the
Japanese do that. . . .'

This does not imply a leap into nothingness or pure speculation, although certainly some interpretation is necessary. For
there are ample pointers and indicators that are readily available for anyone who cares to use them. There is no shortage
of serious studies of different social categories, there is plenty
of anecdotal evidence, and there are many polls and surveys
which ask people what they think and want. Some of these
surveys have been undertaken periodically over the years and
decades, some actually stretch back to prewar days. True, none
of these things can be used in isolation. But, when they coincide

with one another, when the responses point strongly in one direction or another, when the trends are significant and steady, it is justifiable to draw conclusions.

What Is A Crisis?

One reason so many foreigners, and also many Japanese, did not see the crisis coming is that a crisis tends to take very different forms in Japan from other places. In the West and much of the Third World, the word 'crisis' conjures up images of mounting anger and resentment that finally burst loose with crowds forming in the streets and mobs crying for the heads of the hated leaders. There is sound and fury. There is also violence. Armed groups form and attack public buildings, one former or putative leader after another is assassinated, ordinary citizens cower within their homes and only walk the streets if they are armed. We have seen so many scenes of CRISIS in the television news that we have become experts.

And we know that, even with Kobe and the Aum sect, nothing like that has occurred in Japan. But there are some, mainly Westerners, who think it could and who imagine a crisis in Japan in similar terms. One is Brian Reading, author of *Japan, The Coming Collapse.* He provides an intriguing scenario.

> The nation is again economically threatened. There are deep divisions within it that can no longer be papered over. There is a similar concentration of wealth and power in few hands. There are gangs who extort, intimidate and murder. Politicians are corrupt and self-seeking, in league with big business, finance and the criminal yakuza organisations. As political paralysis and social disorder mount, will some group akin to the inter-war militarists be able to take hold of power and form a fascist dictatorship?[2]

No, thank goodness, he thinks not. But before we utter a sigh of relief, let us read his prognostication: 'anarchy, not tyranny, is the danger.'[3] This is cold comfort. Whichever way Japan goes, it is bound to be messy and perhaps bloody. Only, both tyranny and anarchy – although they have occurred in Japan's past history – are very unlikely outcomes for present-day Japan. It is a very different society from the West, and the

Third World, and olden-day Japan. So the denouement will most probably come about in very different ways.

My understanding, which has been relatively correct thus far, is that Japan's ultimate collapse will assume almost the opposite form. There will not be an explosion but an implosion. No group, let alone any individual, is strong enough to dominate Japanese society and impose its will. And no group, let alone any individual, is strong enough even to attack that system and tear it apart. The people as a whole are dissatisfied, and many are disgruntled, but rather few are desperate. And even the dissatisfied, disgruntled and desperate are not in an aggressive mood. They are not turning to violence; they show no inclination to tear society to bits.

But they are unhappy enough that they are no longer willing to give the same allegiance and support as in the past. They will no longer go out of their way to hold up various institutions on which society rests. This is crucial. For that can also result in a collapse. To undermine a political party, you do not have to rebut its ideas or assassinate its leaders, it is quite enough to stop voting for it. And democracy can be sapped by not studying the issues or, more simply, not voting for any party. Family members have certain moral and legal responsibilities and, by neglecting the former and violating the latter, they can seriously weaken the family which, by the way, can be undone by divorce. It is harder for employees to cease supporting their work unit, but they can work less diligently. Students can study less meaningfully. Members of religions can neglect the precepts and visit the temple or shrine on fewer occasions. And so on.

Most of this can be done casually and unobtrusively with no resort to violence. No one really has to break the law. Indeed, nobody even has to declare openly that he is dissatisfied with the existing state of these institutions and that, for such and such a reason, he is withdrawing his support. He can just turn away from them as many Japanese are doing, and go his own way. If this way involves the creation of other, viable institutions that could substitute for the present ones, perhaps the collapse would not even take place. But most Japanese are not turning toward something else, but retreating into their own private worlds. The institutions could become hollow and brittle and, one by one, they could come tumbling down and Japan with them.

When I initially suggested that Japan's crisis would take the form of implosion rather than explosion, it was basically because the trends pointed in that direction. There had as yet been no sign of implosion. Indeed, it hardly looked as if an implosion, or anything particularly dire, was likely to occur. That was expressed in one of the hatchet jobs done on my books and which, although amazingly vulgar, appeared in the highbrow, academic *Journal of Asian Studies.*

> In true Cassandra-style, Woronoff ends his book by suggesting that Japanese society is moving toward decay and collapse, which he thinks will come not with a bang (another war) but a whimper. . . . My own reaction to Woronoff's pronouncements about Japan was to recall an old joke about a man who proposed killing his wife with a surfeit of sex. Several months later the man looked wan and ill while his wife appeared to be thriving. When friends pointed this out to the husband, he merely cackled and said, 'Little does she know she's going to collapse tomorrow.' Japan may be headed for a similar fate, but the country surely doesn't look it right now.[4]

At present, it is hard to imagine anyone sharing the views of the reviewer, Sheila K. Johnson. For there have been notable cases of implosion. The most extraordinary, and entirely unexpected (not even by me), was the collapse of the Liberal Democratic Party. It was almost a textbook case of implosion. There was no attempt by an ambitious politician to hijack it, resisted by others who fell out. There was no quarrel over policy between politicians of contending views, who then broke away. There was no commitment to some principle that was so strong the party would accept defeat in the elections to maintain it. Nothing so dramatic. Some politicians, and factions, simply thought they might get more ministerial posts faster outside the party rather than within and just left it, tying up on occasion with former opponents, who also thought so little of policy and principle that they too allowed their parties to dissolve.

Although less visible, there have been many other instances of implosion, some of which may ultimately be even more fateful. The family is obviously collapsing, with more divorces, fewer and later marriages, and less children. Many companies have lost their drive and, more seriously, lost their hold on employees, who think more fondly of switching jobs or, if they stay, still refuse to give their all. The formal schools and colleges are losing their ability to teach and do little more than apportion diplomas to students who care only whether they can pass entrance exams and get into suitable companies. Mainstream religions are stagnating, but even new religions, whose membership may be boosted for a while, ultimately lose out to yet newer religions as fashions change. Here too families, companies, schools and religions have been imploding and will continue to do so.

This would not have happened if the Japanese were able to define their problems, discuss them openly and freely and then seek solutions. Some of this process exists. The Japanese have, not once but repeatedly, indicated what the problems and grievances are. Indeed, they have gotten so far as to seek essential reforms: educational reform, electoral and political reform, economic reform, reform of relations between the sexes and generations, you name it. They have even adopted pronouncements and programs that should bring about reform. But they have hardly moved an inch closer to solutions.

The process of change and reform has always ended in gridlock. On the way to consensus, there was not enough imagination and ingenuity, not enough trust and confidence, not enough give and take to achieve, then implement, compromises. In particular, the powers that be, which varied from case to case, were not willing to renounce their advantages and those who sought change were not strong enough to impose it. The most common outcome has thus been immobilism. And immobilism could only contribute to further dissatisfaction, alienation and implosion.

So, in order to fathom what is wrong with Japan, it is not terribly useful to consider sporadic happenings and acts of violence, one has to look beneath them where the movement is barely perceptible. Japan's predicament is not typified by the rise of a tiny, if dangerous sect, but the fading of 'established' and 'mainstream' religions and religion per se. Its economy is not threatened so much by the bursting of a financial 'bubble' as that an economy which once served it well cannot be adapted even after the negative aspects outweigh the positive.

Most strikingly, Japan has not been weakened so much by the demise of the LPD as by the spreading dis-affection with all parties and politics as such.

If not enough is done to change, adapt, update, modernize and reform the schools, companies, parties, bureaucracies, families, society and nation, let alone the individual, then the process of decay and implosion will continue and tomorrow's crisis will be many times more debilitating than today's. Few will see it coming. It will not be featured in the television news. Yet, this different kind of crisis will be as devastating as the more visible and violent ones abroad.

Since a Japanese crisis can assume very different forms, I will periodically refer to it as a Japanese-style crisis. And I will use similar formulations in many other contexts, for Japanese-style schools, Japanese-style companies, Japanese-style politicians, Japanese-style families and so on. This is not just a matter of semantics. For the essence of so many Japanese personae and institutions is so different from those familiar to us in the West, and many other places, that most descriptions and analyses would be meaningless otherwise. Admittedly, this may become boring, so the qualification will not always appear, but it should always be understood.

This is most obvious in politics. For the Japanese-style politician usually does not pursue policies, nor does the party he belongs to have a program, nor does the electorate vote for him (rarely her) to attain political goals. Indeed, aside from 'pork barrel' politics, there are not many other concerns. The bureaucrats provide the policies, draft the laws and execute them. But they are not elected, or removable, at the behest of the people. So, it would also be best to speak of a Japanese-style bureaucracy and Japanese-style democracy, and so on. But even simpler things like a family, a husband and a wife, marriage, divorce, etc. have their own distinctive characteristics and, without knowing them, it is impossible to grasp what the problems are and why they are not being solved.

I apologize for any tedium that may arise from use of the term Japanese-style and periodic digressions to show what the differences are. Still, nothing that is happening in Japan would make any sense without it. And the crisis, which to many outsiders would otherwise pass unnoticed, could be mistaken for relative peace and quiet.

Japanapologetics

There are other reasons why foreigners, more so than locals, did not see the crisis coming and were completely perplexed by the more lurid happenings that signaled its arrival. One is that the Japanese did a fairly good job of covering up any problems. Some of this was clearly deliberate. The Japanese government, among other things, produces promotional material on Japan which might, were it an enemy and not a friend, be regarded as disinformation and propaganda. The bureaucracy generates statistics which, as we know, can lie. And, in Japan, statistics tend to be particularly untrustworthy when they reflect on Japanese performance, such as unemployment, income distribution or trade. The business community is also a prolific source of statements and papers, many of them glossy magazines that depict a society almost as idyllic as that of the People's Republic of China.

Another portion was unintentional, more or less. It can be traced to a cultural tick whereby the Japanese distinguish between two modes of presentation. One is *tatemae*, which involves a more positive, appealing, idealized version of things. The other is *honne*, in which more unpleasant aspects may appear. The two can be regarded as the ideal and reality, things as they should be and things as they are or, if you are so inclined, falsehood and truth. What is most disconcerting is that the Japanese not only regard *tatemae* as about as good as *honne*, in many cases they prefer it. They prefer it especially when dealing with outsiders and foreigners are, by definition, outsiders. So any foreigner should immediately ask himself whether something he has been told or read smacks of *tatemae* or *honne*.

This does not imply that the Japanese are the only ones who adopt such behavior. Many Asian and Middle Eastern societies make similar distinctions and have an equally pronounced preference for the rosier version. Even in the West, one tends to get the *tatemae* (party line) from officialdom of all sorts, be it politicians, bureaucrats, company executives, principals and teachers, pastors and priests, and so on. One might also not confide the strict truth, about grandma's cancer, sister's pregnancy or dad's affair to all and sundry. A handy Japanese example should suffice, this borrowed from a speech by former Prime Minister Ohira.

We stand on the threshold of a new age transcending the age of modernization; we have moved from an economic-centered age to a new age with its emphasis on culture. The new society which is our goal is one in which distrust and confrontation are overcome and understanding and trust are cultivated in pursuit of the truly worthwhile life in all its aspects, home, community, state, and global society. It is a society in which the individual's creativity is welcomed, his labor is justly rewarded, there is respect for law and order, each is true to his own responsibilities and restraints and there is ample understanding and consideration for others.[5]

Isn't it lovely! No wonder the Japanese prefer *tatemae* to *honne*. And, if you did not know it stemmed from a Japanese prime minister, you might have mistaken it for the words of an American president, a French premier, even an Arab sheik or a Latin American caudillo for that matter. But this sort of thing gets in the way when one is seriously interested in examining realities, in particular unpleasant realities. So, it must be remembered that there is a *tatemae* for virtually everything and many are harder to refute than this one. They must be sorted out in the realm of politics, labor relations, schooling, family ties, everywhere. Take one on the truly proverbial work will, this coming from an authority on industrial relations.

The Japanese have not put a high, positive value on rest and respose. In fact, they have always felt somewhat guilty about resting. It is true that a great many contemporary Japanese have begun to think about leisure. . . . However, leisure remains no more than a diversion. Leisure is unable to fill their lives with meaning and purpose. It is when they work that the Japanese feel they are really alive. The Japanese work ethic remains vigorous.[6]

The business community is also a prodigious generator of *tatemae*, some spread informally, others in official resolutions like this one from the Federation of Economic Organizations (Keidanren).

Our goal is to create a kinder and more harmonious society where businesses full of vital energy and consumers comfortably coexist. Both management and employees must pool their experience and energy and work together to build a new social order and a promising future. Business too must change, guided by the norms of a new vision of the business enterprise as a free and creative entity and a new relationship between it and society.[7]

Once again, this sort of thing exists elsewhere at higher levels. What is different in Japan is that countless ordinary folks will mouth exactly the same slogans and echo the same pious sentiments even when they know these are not true. Yet, unlike people living in dictatorships who are afraid to tell the truth, the Japanese are under no compulsion to do so. They just feel more comfortable uttering a *tatemae* than a *honne*, especially to someone who is not in the know and thus should not be treated to the truth. The only way to get the truth out of these quite ordinary Japanese is to force it out of them, by rejecting the *tatemae* and intimating one is already privy to the *honne*. And even then it certainly helps to ply them with liquor. Under these circumstances, there is reason to question the veracity of the Japanese even if you are willing to consider this just a quaint social custom.

That the Japanese so glibly repeat the *tatemae* does not mean that they actually believe them. Among insiders, the *honne* is discussed frankly and openly and only a fool would believe anything else. Even outsiders are no fools. If something sounds too positive, promising or optimistic, they realize it is a *tatemae* although they may not know what the *honne* is, so they assume something considerably worse. The truth, or a reasonable facsimile thereof, also appears in many newspapers, magazines and books. Those who seek can find. Even foreigners can have a good idea of what is going on by reading English-language dailies, weeklies, magazines and book translations. At least, like the Japanese, they can distrust anything that sounds too positive, promising or optimistic and assume the truth is considerably worse.

A third reason so few foreigners were aware of the gradually worsening social situation is that they counted mainly on other foreigners to inform them. These foreigners were diplomats, journalists, businessmen, academics and assorted specialists. But, one way or another, most of them got it wrong. One of the more comprehensible explanations is that many of these foreigners only remained a short time in Japan and never sifted out the *honne* themselves, good-naturedly passing along the *tatemae* as if they were meaningful. Others were constantly surrounded by Japanese whose role it was to feed them the good news and make them feel happy during their stay. Then, admittedly, Japan is a hard place to figure out and the people are as inscrutable as any, especially if you are confused by the difference between what they say and what they do. If you stick to the latter, they are much more scrutable.

Alas, there were other explanations as well. The diplomats, particularly the Americans, felt it was their function to maintain harmonious relations and saying nice things made them particularly *grata*. The businessmen wanted to sell as much as possible and found this easiest with Japanese partners with whom they closely cooperated. The journalists sought to grab headlines and that was simplified by writing about the latest Japanese miracle, of which they invented vast quantities. The academics, however, were the most disappointing of the lot. Many knew the country, knew the people, knew the language and probably even knew the truth. But they still wrote fantasies and figments. Why? Some liked Japan and felt they should be kind. Others realized that propounding on one prodigy or another could also help their career. Then there were enticements like invitations to conferences with all expenses paid and local sales of their books. There was also good money to be made by saying the right thing.

There was one last explanation. During the 1970s and 1980s, until the sorry debacles of the 1990s, the vast majority of foreign observers tended to praise Japan and things Japanese almost indiscriminately. Anyone who went against this tide would be in trouble. Diplomats could become *non grata*, businessmen could lose contracts, journalists might have their articles scrapped or relegated to a back page, academics found it harder to get teaching positions and specialists were simply deemed wrong. Those who did criticize Japan suffered for it; their books were condemned and banned from reading lists (if not actually burned), they were not invited to conferences on Japan and jobs as consultant were restricted. There was very great pressure to marginalize them and, in some cases, outright attacks were launched on the so-called 'revisionists' as if they were actually guilty of more heinous crimes than just providing an alternative view, one that was often closer to the truth.

Thus, there was no end to the statements that mirrored Japanese *tatemae* emanating from the foreign 'experts.' Just a few samples need be quoted here since many others will be encountered further on in this book. Obviously, one must start with Edwin O. Reischauer, the most eminent Japanologist ever, professor at Harvard University, where he trained successive generations of Japanapologists, and then ambassador to Japan, the most *grata* they ever had. He could claim that 'political corruption is not widespread in Japan' and that 'the national bureaucracy has been entirely untarnished by scandal' and, even more audaciously, that its system of democratic rule 'was not notably inferior to those of the West and perhaps stronger in some respects.'[8] Not many Japanese would dare utter such mendacious *tatemae*. But the master was clearly outdone by his pupil, also professor at Harvard, Ezra F. Vogel. Showing that foreigners can not only turn fine *tatemae* but actually spin them into a best-seller, he produced *Japan As Number One*. This far no Japanese were willing to tread.

> The Japanese have been on the forefront of making large organizations something people enjoy. . . . Japanese from an early age are taught the value of group life. They learn to make school life and the life of work organizations more pleasurable. Japanese are uncompromising in requiring individual performance, but they can then take this performance for granted and concentrate on camaraderie, games, ceremonies, parties, and celebrations. Employees come in to their workplace on vacation and weekends in large part because they enjoy the cameraderie.[9]

Obviously, the recent difficulties and mishaps in Japan make it harder for foreigners to foster such *tatemae* nowadays. But they have not quite given up, as subsequent quotes will show. And, when they cannot safely present Japan as number one, they do the next best thing by insisting that for all its faults it is still better than most other places and, while things may look bad today, there is no doubt that the Japanese will improve the situation for tomorrow.

Even being understanding and lenient, it is extremely difficult to regard this as just a quaint custom, for these foreigners were brought up to distinguish truth from falsehood and some were actually committed to telling the truth by their professional code of ethics. Yet, time and again, they made comments which could most generously be regarded as exaggerations but were usually just outright lies. They were not *tatemae!* They were lies, namely statements that could be readily disproved by reference to existing and known facts. Consequently, faced with a barrage of *tatemae* from the Japanese, which were then consecrated as realities by hypocritical foreigners, it was extremely hard for outsiders to know what was going on in Japan and certainly to realize that things were bad and getting worse.

Thus, knowing the pitfalls, rather than just having my say and getting it over with, I will repeatedly have to scrutinize the *tatemae* presented by the Japanese and the pseudo-realities presented by the Japanapologists to show that they are illusions. Only then can I try to define the actual situation or *honne.* Again, it may be tedious, but it is still indispensable. The only relief is that things have gotten so obviously bad that now I am likely to be believed more readily than before.

2

The Company
(Fraying At The Edges)

Unquestionably, the most significant social institution in Japan today is the company. The term 'company' should be understood here more broadly as the employer and workplace, whether a corporation, a private company or a government department, whether a factory, an office or a store. The model, naturally, is the big Japanese corporation with tens of thousands of employees and branches throughout Japan and around the world. But the system they have developed and the practices they engage in are emulated, consciously or unconsciously, by even the smallest units in certain ways.

The importance of this relationship is recognized clearly by the employees. Many of them wear the company badge, some dress in the company uniform, and when introduced to outsiders they are presented not as individuals but as emanations of the company, Toyota's Mr. Such-and-so or Mitsubishi's Miss What's-her-name. This goes even further: when speaking of the company, they refer to it as 'us' and when speaking of other companies they sometimes attach the honorific *san*. To the company, they give their primary allegiance, higher even than any allegiance to society or the state. And, for the company, they are willing to make sacrifices they would not even consider for any other social institution, be it association, religion or family.

The idea of the company as a surrogate family is not a terribly old one and, in fact, the company as an institution has only been around for about a century. In the early days, the company was certainly not the principal building block of society, it was just a place to earn money and most workers showed little loyalty. They would work for a while, earning what they needed, and then move on, perhaps back to the farm, perhaps

16

to a stint in another company that paid higher wages. The only ones who stayed were young girls, often hired out to textile mills by their parents or middlemen, and who sometimes were locked up at night so they could not run away. The company's exploitation was crude and the workers' responses were often brutal, until the government sided with the employers and used the state's power to keep the workers in line.

Eventually some managers realized that a smoother, more harmonious relationship could be more effective. They improved working conditions, raised wages, reduced working hours and provided some fringe benefits. They offered relative job security to key personnel, and this gradually spread to others, who reciprocated with a degree of loyalty. This was all embellished with a philosophy of familism, with the company's founder or boss appearing as the stern but kindly father who has the responsibility of caring for the company's employees, its children. To anchor this philosophy more solidly, its sponsors worked back, claiming it arose out of time-honored Japanese customs of cooperation, mutual help and, especially, harmony. Thus, a tradition was invented.[1]

This tradition had to be reinvented after the Pacific War when compulsion was the more common practice. For the workers were angry about how they were being treated, they could not get by on the pitiful wages paid for endless hours, and they were finally able to organize freely. Individually, by moving from job to job, or collectively, by carrying out strikes and sometimes more violent actions within and outside of the trade unions, they made their dissatisfaction felt. More enlightened managers again realized that a new social contract was necessary and they salvaged it from the prewar heritage. Employers offered better conditions, wages and hours. Above all, and this was crucial at a time of widespread unemployment, they promised job security for ever larger segments of the workforce. This was dubbed 'lifetime employment' by some, an alluring *tatemae* that conceals a less attractive *honne*.

Thus was familism reborn. Yet, as in earlier years, it was propagated more actively by company executives and other 'fathers' than by their 'sons' and 'daughters' in the offices and factories. One of the better descriptions comes from Akio Morita, founder and leader of Sony, among the most enlightened and articulate of Japan's new breed of managers.

There is no secret ingredient or hidden formula responsible
for the success of the best Japanese companies. No theory or
plan or government policy will make a business a success,
that can only be done by people. The most important mis-
sion for a Japanese manager is to develop a healthy relationship with his employees, to create a familylike feeling within
the corporation, a feeling that employees and managers share
the same fate. Those companies that are most successful in
Japan are those that have managed to create a shared sense
of fate among all employees. . . . [2]

The Company 'Family'

This vision of corporate harmony appealed not only to Japanese managers, it also struck a chord with dozens, then hundreds and now probably thousands of foreign management
'experts' and gurus. This seemed to fulfill the undying wish
for a humane form of management that not only took the
workers' interests into account but allowed them to participate
in determining their own fate. Broader notions like 'lifetime
employment' and 'bottom-up management' were soon joined
by more specific techniques like quality control, zero defects
and just-in-time delivery as part of a vision of how a company
should be run. But they never lost sight of the underlying ethos,
the bonding of company and worker in something resembling
a family. One of the earliest renditions came from Robert J.
Ballon, whose words I actually believed when I first arrived in
Japan and did not know better.

The lifetime employment system makes the working group
the most important group in life. After school or college the
new employee joins such a group. . . . He will be closely connected with it for years after and, because he will always
remain with the company, he will personally identify himself
with the progress and success of his particular group and
the larger organization of which it is part. In return for
being looked after and protected he gives complete loyalty
and devotion. The Japanese company man does not think of
his relationship with the company in contractual terms as is
usual with the western employee. It is more like belonging

to a family to which by far the most important part of his life will be devoted.[3]

There is no doubt that the company has become a substitute family. But the question is, what sort of family? Many (especially foreign) admirers of Japanese management tend to picture it in rather idealized terms as a happy family in which the boss is a doting father who looks after the best interests of his employees who, in return, devote themselves to the success of the company of which they feel they are a cherished part. Alas, the company family is not an idyllic family but a grubbier real-life one, and it does not follow any Western model but a Japanese one. In such a family, the roles are carefully allotted and reveal, on closer scrutiny, definite distinctions in status and advantages. Moreover, in addition to just the nuclear family, there are all sorts of relatives and in-laws, with differing statuses and advantages, and also what could be regarded as domestics and even serfs.

First of all, it is necessary to separate out the women, all the women, who are active in the economy. Women most definitely do not enjoy the same benefits as men.[4] For some four decades after the war, this was blatantly evident. Men and women lined up at different doors and were interviewed by different personnel officers when they were recruited by the company. They were then allocated different tasks, mainly relatively menial ones for women, for which they were paid differently: that is, less. But that was to be changed with the introduction of the Equal Employment Opportunity Law of 1986.[5] This law, by the way, was not a spontaneous act of Japan's Diet but a face-saving measure adopted after much hemming and hawing following the United Nation's Decade for Women.

As of then employers had to be more subtle. Within just a few years, however, the problem had been solved. Women lined up with men and were interviewed by the same recruiters. Then, just like the men, they were allowed to choose between two basic options. They could pick either a general-track (*ippan-shoku*) or a career-track (*sogo-shoku*) status. The former resembled the old, relatively servile tasks women had done before. The latter implied a genuine career, such as was offered mainly to men previously. It just happened that most women chose the former and most men the latter, the onus was thus on them.

But it is known that women who hesitated, or preferred the more challenging option, were solemnly warned of the rigors involved and sometimes told that such a career would make it impossible for them to raise a family.

Thus, post-1986 as before the law was passed, most women were given subordinate positions in the company. For the blue-collar workers, the differences were not quite as noticeable since they would also end up on the assembly lines or in other factory jobs. But the women tended to be used for their dexterity while men had the harder, heavier tasks. In fact, it is only quite recently that women were allowed into such masculine preserves as automobile production. For white-collar staff the differences were more conspicuous, sometimes even grotesquely so. Men were holding real jobs while the women engaged in petty chores such as typing, answering phones, delivering messages, cleaning up and serving tea. Such was the career of the 'office lady' or OL.[6]

The male-female divide is not the only one, even if it is most visible. There is also a fairly strict division between the jobs landed by college and high school graduates. Those with a college (even a junior college) diploma usually get a white-collar job and become a 'salaryman' (*sarariman*). They work in offices, in reasonably pleasant surroundings, and are part of the potential managerial elite. While women rarely rise very far, college graduates do get office jobs. High school graduates almost invariably end up in factories as blue-collar workers or with more lowly positions in the services and trades. In addition, while most college grads enter larger companies, high school grads and dropouts are often shunted into medium- and small-sized firms.

These four categories (male and female white-collar and blue-collar) basically make up the 'regular' staff of the company, especially the large company. But they are not the only ones employed. While they are recruited straight from school and accepted, in theory at least, for a 'lifetime' stint, others are hired here and there as needs arise. Many of these mid-career hires are employed on a contractual basis with a contract that has to be renewed periodically. Others are employed on a part-time basis, working so many hours a week, often referred to as *pato*. Although just casual or temporary labor, in practice they frequently spend many years with the company.

So much for the nuclear family and relatives, now let us turn to the domestics and serfs. Some are employees of outside service firms which send them in to handle specific assignments as and when needed. Others are attached to subcontractors and work on the company premises, often side by side with regular workers, but have no status in the company. Meanwhile, large companies tend to farm out work to smaller subcontractors which produce assorted parts and components and sometimes even finished articles. While the products bear the company name, those making them do not enjoy any of the perks of company employees, having to settle for the much less generous treatment of the subcontractors. It might be added that the subcontractors often enough have sub-subcontractors working under them and the arrangement can reach down five, ten and even more levels. The further down you go, the smaller and weaker the firms tend to be.

Thus, it can be seen that the Japanese company family actually consists of a core surrounded by several layers. Obviously, being in the core or one of the external layers involves more than just where one appears on an organigram. The more distant an employee is from the core, the fewer advantages he or she has. This affects virtually every facet of the person's work life. Only some more significant aspects will be mentioned here, namely tenure, promotion, remuneration, hours, working conditions and status.[7]

There has been much loose talk of 'lifetime employment' ever since that misleading concept was introduced in the theoretical literature by James Abegglen.[8] Within the core system the only ones who benefit in practice from an implicit guarantee (this is never mentioned in the contract) are the 'regular' male white-collar and blue-collar employees. They are recruited straight from school and often stay with the same company until retirement. Women, on the other hand, are usually discarded much sooner. Those who accept the general track are edged out most easily. But even those on the career-track come under substantial pressure to retire voluntarily, if not at marriage then certainly with childbirth. For then it is obvious that they could not, at least not without considerable trouble, meet the demands made on them by the company.

However it is done, whether by verbal pressure of higher-ups or fellow colleagues or finding some pretext, most women

Figure 2.1. *Women's Work-Force Participation by Age, 1993*

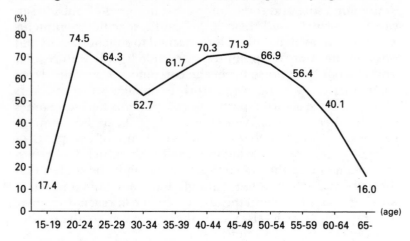

(%)

Women's uneven career path: in, out, in again, out again.

Source: Ministry of Labor, *Hataraku josei no jitsujo* (Facts on Working Women).
Credit: *Fact and Figures of Japan*, 1995, p. 56.

leave their jobs within five or ten years. But a large number of them return to work after raising a family. This will explain the M-shaped graph of women in the labor force, with a first bulge for the early twenties, when nearly 75 per cent of women work, a sharp dip to about 53 per cent by the early thirties, when some 'retire,' followed by a new bulge in the forties when many return to work. All in all, women only have 7.3 years of service against 12.4 years for men on the average.[9] (Figure 2.1)

It is extremely hard to speak of 'lifetime employment' for contractual employees or part-timers. They are deliberately hired with short-term contracts, sometimes very short-term, so that they can be dismissed whenever the company wants. This can be done on fairly short notice and simply by failing to renew the contract. The position of employees of subcontractors is equally tenuous, if in a somewhat different manner. The company can usually drop the subcontractor at rather short notice, again merely by not renewing the contract. It is then the subcontractor's problem to get rid of the workers. Since subcontractors are much smaller on the whole, they do not even claim to provide job security and quickly fire or otherwise dispose of excess labor.

When it comes to promotion, once again the possibilities

are infinitely greater for men. In fact, larger companies have what is called a 'career escalator' that almost guarantees this for those who stay with the company. Employees who are recruited directly from school rise from year to year automatically. Almost as automatically, by dint of seniority, they become *kacho* (section head), then *bucho* (department head), and so on up. Indeed, they may eventually become higher executives, vicepresidents, perhaps presidents and chairmen. This, at any rate, is the somewhat theoretical but nonetheless conceivable ascent of the male salaryman.

Blue-collar workers have a less glorious, if still reasonably encouraging, prospect. They too can rise from year to year and can become supervisors, foremen and so on in the factory. But it is exceedingly unlikely that they would rise above that level and become important executives in the company outside of the factory. As for women, whether white- or blue-collar, they are usually sidetracked. They rise more slowly and uncertainly, with few ever becoming middle-managers or supervisors, and then only after putting in many more years. In fact, even now, very few women have reached any managerial position, a mere 2 per cent being *kacho* and 1 per cent being *bucho*.

Not surprisingly, wages, perks, retirement benefits and other forms of remuneration parallel this. Women tend to earn considerably less than men, even when their starting salaries were rather close. From year to year, the gap grows. Overall, women only earn 56 per cent as much as men. Part of the difference can be traced to the fact that many women retire young and few hold executive posts. But early retirement and lack of promotion is not their fault. Morever, while a male-female gap exists in every country, it is much larger in Japan than in any other advanced country. And Japan is the only OECD member where the wage gap actually grew over the past decade or so at a time when it was shrinking elsewhere.

More surprising is the wage gap between white- and blue-collar staff. Starting salaries are much higher for the former and annual increments keep the gap large, with factory workers earning about two-thirds as much as salarymen in the same company. Naturally, part-timers and contractual workers earn less than regulars. Employees of subcontractors, and the subcontractors thereof, earn even less. The actual level tends to correlate to the size of the firm, with the personnel of companies with 1,000 or more earning 18 per cent more than those of companies with 100–999 employees and 26 per cent more than those of companies with 10–99 employees.[10] This applies also to overtime payments, fringe benefits, bonuses and pensions. Indeed, those whose positions are most tenuous would probably end up with no pension at all.

While all Japanese work quite long hours, there are clear differences here as well. The regular staff of larger companies, according to all the statistics, work fewer hours than the personnel of smaller companies. In fact, the smaller the company, the longer the hours. Larger companies also offer more paid holidays, longer vacations and more weekends off. This rule applies less to part-timers, who are not expected to work full hours. But, in Japan, they often do work as long as regulars and many put in a 40-hour week or more, so the expression 'part-timer' is a bit of a misnomer.

Working conditions also vary greatly. The regulars naturally get the most challenging and rewarding jobs, with the life of the salarymen considerably more agreeable and less strenuous than that of the factory workers. Admittedly, they often put in longer hours. But they get more perks and more respect. Most women are relegated to dead-end jobs. Aside from that, white-collar employees work in more centrally-located, smarter premises while increasingly factories are out in the sticks. This is nothing, however, compared to the hovels that masquerade as factories for some subcontractors. The jobs allocated to part-timers and temporary workers are frequently dull or unpleasant, the tasks regular staff shun. And those chores taken on by subcontractors are even dirtier, more dangerous and more demanding.

With differences in tenure, promotion, wages, and so on it is impossible to avoid differences in social position. These are more acute in Japanese society, where the requirements of status, hierarchy and even linguistic protocol place so much stress on higher and lower. There is no doubt that blue-collar workers (*koin*) are regarded as inferior, on the whole, to white-collar employees (*shokuin*) despite any amount of formal praise and *tatemae* in favor of this backbone of industry. That is obvious enough from the fact that blue-collar workers are high school graduates while white-collar employees are college graduates. There is a definite ceiling keeping factory workers from rising too high in the company. These differences are shown, for anyone with eyes to see, by the way factory workers – even supervisors – bow and scrape to visiting executives.

The relations with women are even more remarkable, especially in the office. While both may be college graduates, and the woman may actually be smarter, he takes the decisions and she backs him up; he deals with outside suppliers and clients and she stays in the background; he is treated as a somebody while she serves tea. In the factories, women try to be as meek and unobtrusive as possible, more successfully for the fresh young things, less so for the mothers and grandmothers who have returned for a second stint. Linguistically, the men ordinarily talk down to the women. And it is this very problem, namely that women are not used to talking down to or even as equals with men, that makes it so hard for them to act as superiors when the need arises.

In all this, 'regular' workers, both men and women, and even some of the contractual workers and part-timers, find it perfectly natural to treat employees of subcontractors as their social inferiors. The former are part of the company, the latter are not. Indeed, they are members of quite an inferior firm, to say nothing of the fact that they probably also have lesser academic credentials. And so it goes, from prime contractor to subcontractor, to subsubcontractor and on down.

All these people may be part of the company family. But it is hard to regard this family as particularly admirable, as so many foreigners do.

For one, it centers on an amazingly small core. The core employees, for all practical purposes, are the male 'regular' white-collar and blue-collar staff. Women, even if officially 'regular' employees, are not part of the true core. Yet, women now make up some 41 per cent of the labor force. The contractual and part-time workers are only marginal members at best. Yet, fully 13 per cent of Japanese workers are now part-timers and 26 per cent are regarded as non-regulars.[11] The personnel of subcontractors are most assuredly not part of the core. Yet, subcontracting accounts for about a third of many companies' value added and as much as 90 per cent in certain industries. It would seem that the core could be as small as 5 per cent of the workforce for companies with substantial subcontracting and some 25–30 per cent for other manufacturers. In services, the level would be somewhat higher. But only in a minority of cases could it represent more than half.

Secondly, it is considerably less than admirable in that the core employees obviously enjoy better tenure, promotion, earnings, conditions and status than those in the external layers. This introduces an invidious differentiation that is extremely hard to justify rationally. It can hardly be argued that men are inherently better workers than women, although they may appear so when the women are never given a decent chance and face so many difficulties and disadvantages. It may seem that college graduates are better educated than high-school graduates, although it is known that a college degree means rather little in Japan. And it is even harder to claim that blue-collar workers are somehow inferior to salarymen when it is Japan's factories that are highly productive and its offices that are so inefficient.[12] As for employees of subcontractors, or small firms in general, being less valuable than those of larger companies, that seems unlikely since they produce the essential parts and components or provide precious services without which larger companies could not function.

What is most unpleasant about this arrangement, however, is that far from being mutually beneficial to all family members it is clearly tilted in favor of the core staff. Women do the work men do not want to do; part-timers and contractual employees do the work that regulars do not want to do; and subcontractors are stuck with jobs that are either particularly painful or barely bring a profit. For this, the men are paid substantially more than the women, regulars earn considerably more than part-timers and those who work for large companies do better than the employees of smaller ones, especially subcontractors. Similarly, regulars have shorter hours and better conditions than peripheral staff. Thus, the prosperity of large companies is directly related to the fact that smaller companies, their suppliers and distributors, do less well. And, when a recession hits, it is the latter who are forced to lower their prices and, in serious cases, shift for themselves. This smacks of domination and exploitation.

Whose Company Is It?

Not content just to depict the Japanese company as one happy family in which the boss looks after the employees, some management 'experts' have claimed that any distinction between the two is increasingly irrelevant because the interests of employees and employer merge to such an extent that it becomes 'their' company. Peter Drucker, so harsh on Western management, has been particularly indulgent with regard to Japanese management. He claimed that Japan pursues 'employee capitalism,' in which employees come before shareholders, while America applies 'shareholder capitalism,' in which employees are subordinated to shareholders. James Abbeglen, despite decades working with Japanese corporations, went a step further and pretended that the company (*kaisha*) somehow 'belongs' to its personnel.

The *kaisha* becomes in a real sense the property of the people who make it up. It will not be sold, in whole or in part, without specific approval of all its directors, acting on behalf of all its employees. Earnings of the company go first as a return to investors with the entire balance going to ensure the company's future and thus ensure the future of its employees.[13]

Unfortunately, this premise cannot be borne out in practice either. The most glaring weaknesses relate to the idea that the company belongs to its workers who are its lifeblood and among its stakeholders, and therefore get priority over shareholders (as in the materialistic West). The fact of the matter is that the vast majority of Japanese companies, nigh on 99 per cent, are owned lock, stock and barrel by individuals. These are, admittedly, mainly the smaller and medium-sized firms but – as noted – they are the overwhelming majority. In these companies, all key decisions are taken by the owners directly or with their hired managers. The interests of, and effect on, the workers are doubtless considered. But the workers have no share in basic policy-making.

The only companies which, to some extent at least, might fit the ideal model are the larger, older and more bureaucratic ones which supposedly do not have 'owners.' Shares are traded on the stock market and ownership is widely dispersed. They are the remaining one per cent of companies. Yet, even in this category, there are many where one person, a family or a small circle of shareholders maintain a dominant position. This includes many of the construction, retailing and service companies as well as some in manufacturing. This influence is most obvious where the founder is still active, as for Matsushita, Honda and Sony in earlier years, or has been succeeded by other family members, as for the Toyodas in Toyota, the Mitarais in Canon, the Nakauchis in Daiei and the Tateishis in Omron.

Of course, in the larger companies and even some smaller ones, there is a degree of internal democracy, if you will. This has been summed up by fans of Japanese management under the expression of 'bottom-up management,' supposedly in contrast to 'top-down management' in Western companies.

One feature of this, much praised and admired because it is palpably indigenous, occurs through the *ringi* system where personnel at lower levels work out proposals (called *ringisho*), which are passed up through the hierarchy and, once approved, can be put into effect. Alas, as Japanese salarymen know only too well, this is a slow and cumbersome process. So many superiors must be convinced, and so many stamps affixed, that it is very time-consuming. Anyone against it can effectively block the proposal by sitting on it or show disapproval by not affixing a stamp. Since personnel transfers occur every few years, a proposal can be killed by holding off final approval. Yet, even when such lower-level intiatives are approved, most relate to relatively secondary matters affecting largely subordinate staff.

There is not much bottom-up management of this sort in the factories, where things are most cut-and-dried. Workers have specific tasks which must be accomplished. But, at least, they are encouraged to understand these tasks better and contribute to shaping them through Quality Control Circles. These do, indeed, make working life somewhat more interesting and can bring about changes, as long as they contribute to productivity. Still, it would be hard to call this 'democracy.' Workers are expected not only to attend QC meetings, but to participate actively, and if they do not this is held against them. The same applies to the apparently more spontaneous use of the suggestion box, since most companies expect a certain number of suggestions from each and every worker and failure to provide these would also have a negative effect.

While these forms of internal democracy are welcome, and certainly positive, they do not show that Japanese companies are so very different from Western ones. There too there are suggestion boxes, and increasingly QC Circles, and useful proposals can be initiated from below without anywhere near as much formality.

More striking is the fact that, while foreign management 'experts' praise Japan's bottom-up management, the bulk of Japanese executives, especially at higher levels, insist that they are top-down managers. This has been shown by repeated polls. And anyone working in a Japanese company knows that such things as wages, conditions, working hours, promotions, costs of inputs, pricing of finished products, profits, use of specific suppliers and so on are the prerogatives of those higher up. The same applies to relations with other companies in the same group (*keiretsu*), relations with politicians and bureaucrats, decisions on foreign investment and subsidiaries, and so on. Again, not so different from the West.

Of course, within the Japanese system, it is possible for those lower down to climb to the top. There is a definite appearance of this with the 'career escalator.' From year to year, employees do rise. Periodically, they are appointed to managerial positions. Indeed, this is almost automatic for lower-level posts. When it comes to higher ones, however, the situation is quite different. In privately-owned companies, members of the owner's family have clear priority. In larger, more bureaucratic ones, appointments result from arrangements between rival factions and it is often a question of connections and luck – far more than ability – that one does get a higher post. If there is any issue on which the top managers have the last word, it is their successors.

True, some Japanese companies (but far from all) try to induce a feeling of equality within the company's personnel or at least to avoid more invidious distinctions. Everyone in the factory wears the same uniform, they all eat at the same canteen, there is no executive section in the parking lot, and so on. But these features have been greatly exaggerated. For example, while everyone wears the same uniform, superiors have special badges which indicate their ranks. While they may all eat in the same canteen sometimes, it is clear that the executives often eat in fancy restaurants away from work, while ordinary employees consume company meals. There is no reserved parking for executives, but then again they don't need it. Many of them have chauffeur-driven cars provided by the company and are dropped off at the front door. In fact, if you look closely, the distinctions may be greater than in the West.

And that is quite natural. For one of the abiding characteristics of all Japanese institutions is hierarchy. How could it be
otherwise? Employees are recruited each year and rise from year
to year. Thus, someone who entered the company a year earlier
has more seniority. And someone who got in a decade earlier
has much more. The latter, according to linguistic protocol,
speak down to the newcomers and their juniors in general. Men
speak down to most women, aside from the rare ones who become managers or even executives. To know who your superiors
are is quite simple, just look, they are the older males. And a
junior who would not speak up to a senior, even out of ignorance,
would be in deep trouble. Thus, in addition to just distinctions
by rank, as in the West, Japanese employees have to pay attention to distinctions as fine as one more year with the company.

What is intriguing here is that foreign admirers of Japanese management rarely refer to the one institution that could
give the employees a share in decision-making, especially as
regards those decisions most important to their own welfare.
That is the trade union. This is normally the body in which
employees get together to present their wishes, perhaps even
demands, to management. But Japanese unions are very weak.
They are limited largely to blue-collar workers, yet run by white-
collar employees, who do not really have their interests at heart.
They are relatively small and fissured, a union not grouping all
workers in the sector but only those at a given company or
even factory, which means that they can be played off against
one another. And management is much better organized,
through bodies like Nikkeiren, and enjoys more support from
the government.

While the trade unions do have peak bodies for each sector
and these together form huge national federations, they have
been amazingly timid. The once impressive *shunto* or 'spring
offensive' has gradually degenerated into a charade where the
unions make demands they know will not be accepted and
gradually align downward on what the employers are willing to
pay. The result has been wage hikes which, in better times,
exceeded inflation slightly and, in worse, did not keep up with
it. Bonuses were also cut in harder times. Under these conditions, many working families could not make ends meet unless
the workers put in overtime or their spouses got a job as well.
Compared with other countries, while Japanese wages appear

high they cannot buy that much and the share of value added going to labor is unusually small showing that, on the whole, they have benefited less from Japan's economic progress.

If the contrast between the interests of the workers and management is notable for wages, it is even more striking with regard to working hours. Japanese workers put in something like 2,000 hours a year in the early 1990s, one of the heaviest schedules in the OECD. Officially, they worked some 100 hours more than Americans and 200–500 more than Europeans. But even this underestimates the gap, because it is widely admitted that many Japanese also have to do unreported (and unpaid) overtime which could amount to several more hundred hours a year. Shorter hours (*jitan*) have been a goal of the trade unions for decades and, since Japan was seen in a bad light and criticized by its trading partners, even the government made this a priority. Yet, while the time worked has decreased gradually over the years, it remains uncommonly high for an advanced country.

The situation for holidays and vacations is even worse. Many Japanese companies still work Saturdays, so the weekend is not even universally accepted. And summer (let alone winter) vacations are exceptionally short. In theory, most workers are granted at least two weeks. But they are under great pressure not to use the whole allotment and vacations only average some 6–8 days, brief compared to two weeks in the United States and ludicrously so when compared to three, four and five in parts of Western Europe. This is a particularly sad outcome when you consider that countless surveys have shown that the highest priority for the Japanese is more leisure. And many workers are even willing to accept lower wages if they could get shorter hours, some 41 per cent in a government survey of 1991 compared to 27 per cent in 1986.[14]

If Japanese companies will not give in to their employees on the most essential items, namely wages and hours, it is hard to see how they could be depicted as lavishing special care on their personnel. And, if Japanese workers find it so hard to impress management with their concerns, let alone impose their will, it is hard to see how one can refer to them as stakeholders or claim the company 'belongs' to them in any real sense. If anything, the truth is the exact opposite of what the system's supporters claim. It gives management relatively more power than elsewhere although there are some vents left for frustration and some compensations for those who can use them.

When you know the *honne*, the *tatemae* seems absolutely grotesque and you wonder how anyone who pretends to be an 'expert'. could possibly write such things. Yet, the flow of disinformation regarding Japanese management never ceases. Each new would-be guru builds on the nonsense compiled by his predecessors, erecting a tower that will hopefully collapse under its own weight one day. While waiting, one can muse on the words of Robert Ozaki, who proposed 'the Japanese enterprise system as a world model' in a book modestly self-advertised as 'a new inquiry into the nature and causes of the wealth of nations.' It is titled *Human Capitalism*, which the Japanese system purportedly is. Under it,

> . . . management and workers identify with their firm and with each other. They act as though they own the firm where they work. To them, the notion that shareholders are the legal owners of their firm is a meaningless technicality. Management does not perceive itself as representing the owners' interests. Both management and workers view themselves as one group jointly striving for the prosperity and growth of their firm, that is, for themselves.[15]

Work Ethic And Loyalty Revisited

Foreign observers, especially the more superficial or gullible ones, are immensely impressed by the sense of loyalty and work will of the Japanese labor force. It is known that there is relatively little job-hopping and most workers stick with the company through thick and thin. They put in long hours and make extraordinary sacrifices. This human aspect, more than management techniques or business strategies, is what many seek. According to Dr. Mahathir, the Malaysian prime minister known for his 'look East' policy, 'What we are interested in is your work ethic. That is what we are after. . . .'[16]

There is no doubt that Japan's work ethic was quite remarkable, at least right after the war. Employees did support their company and do whatever was necessary to get it going again. They accepted long hours, harsh conditions and – then, at least

– rather meager wages. They proudly sported the company badge and modestly referred to themselves as Mr. Such-and-so of Such-and-such Company. While they naturally had personal interests and goals that did not always coincide with those of the company, they repressed them and behaved like good soldiers, a not inappropriate comparison after the war when engaged in the overriding task of reconstruction.

Workers in the early postwar period were regarded as company 'warriors' and the toughest were known as *moretsu shain* (aggressive employees). Under their supervision, and subjected to their discipline, young recruits were encouraged to give their all for the company and many of them also became 'workaholics.' But this was increasingly less of their own free will than because they had little choice. Gradually, however, new classes joined the company who were brought up in the laxer atmosphere of economic recovery and who were not willing to accept the necessary sacrifices. What they really wanted was a comfortable home and a happy family life. They were known as the *mai homu* ('my-home') and *nyu famirii* ('new family') generations. Their deeper desire was to work only as much as required and then get away to their home and family. By now, those who claim that their private lives take precedence over work more than double those for whom work comes first.[17]

This trend would have been less significant if at least while at work company employees were willing to give their all. That was no longer the case either, as one class of fresh recruits followed another. The reasons for working were increasingly hard-headed. Already in the mid-1980s, one survey by the Ministry of Labor found that youngsters worked 'to earn a living' (36%) or 'upgrade their living standard' (36%) as opposed to 'fulfilling the purpose of life' (10%) or 'doing their duty as a citizen' (10%). As for willingness to work, about 60 per cent said they would like to work 'just as much as other people' while only 20 per cent responded that they would like to work 'more than other people.'[18]

Of course, most Japanese do not openly claim they dislike hard work (although there are more and more who do), but they show it through their actions. Thus, part of the urge to attend college has nothing to do with education but rather that this is the best way of getting a white-collar and avoiding a blue-collar job. When choosing companies, candidates place ever less stress on the prospective employer's contribution to national development or even future prospects and instead consider how comfortable life will be there. Companies known to demand less overtime, drive their workers less hard and offer more leisure find it easier to recruit. As a Hitachi executive conceded, 'Society now operates on the three principles of good fun, leisure and style. Hitachi cannot afford to be the only one which continues to be prim and proper.'[19]

More broadly, prospective employees have been turning away from manufacturing companies, especially in smoke-stack industries, and giving preference to financial and service companies. Work there is regarded as more comfortable and fashionable. Within industry, they particularly avoid the so-called 'three-K' jobs, those which are *kitanai*, *kiken* and *kitsui* or dirty, dangerous and demanding. Instead, they seek jobs that are more appealing and provide three other Ks: *kankyo* (pleasant environment), *kaiteki* (comfortable conditions) and *kyuka* (plenty of paid vacations). There is one other thing they want, indicated by many surveys and an abundance of magazines comparing company salaries, namely *kane* or money, a fourth K.

Another trend heading in roughly the same direction, but in some ways directed even more against traditional practices, is the growing unwillingness to sign on for a 'lifetime' job. As of the 1970s, a new category of worker arose which preferred temporary jobs or *arubaito* (from the German word for work). This attracted many workers who could not assume or find a full-time job but also a growing number of youngsters, fresh from college, who wanted to move from job to job, earning what they needed and then taking a break. By the 1980s, these people were known as 'freeters' or *furita* (from the English word 'free' and the German word 'Arbeiter'). While relinquishing job security, employee benefits and better pay, they found compensations. 'Unhampered by company employment regulations and labor contracts, they can consult directly with the employer about their working hours and quit whenever they want. They do not have to dress up for work, and they need not grovel before their superiors.'[20]

Even those joining large companies, and accepting 'lifetime employment' were increasingly different from their predecessors. Some accepted the need to work long hours, and devote themselves seriously to the company's success, but they did not seek or sometimes even accept promotions, which implied too much sacrifice and dedication. And they refused transfers, even if this further hurt their chances of success. As if this were not disconcerting enough, employees even insisted that they not be forced to work overtime and that they be allowed to take their full vacation. If the company refused, or tried to get rid of them, some turned to the (not very effective) trade unions or sued.

But at least, or so one would assume, when the Japanese work, they work hard. That is certainly the conclusion of most foreigners, although not all are quite as ecstatic as this American visitor after his first trip to Japan.

What I saw in Japan was a lean people yearning to produce. There were millions of industrious workers seeking efficiency, quality and production advantage. The so-called miracle is a product of working smart, working hard and working more than everybody else. Awareness began from the moment of arrival. On the bus from the airport, we wove through the inner-city of Tokyo that allowed us to look into upper levels of office buildings. It was late, very late, and yet the offices were filled with people. What in blazes were they doing there this time of night? My companion suggested that since they do business over the world, they must therefore work at odd hours. . . . No, I said to myself, there is more to it. . . . Perhaps it is nothing more than a yearning to be whatever they can be; to move on every detail, in every sphere, into every opportunity as soon as possible. That is what I think drives them.[21]

Actually, when it comes to work, there is no doubt that most factory workers are extemely diligent. They keep plugging at it from before offical starting time to after official closing time. They have very specific tasks to do, which must be accomplished within a specific time, and they get them done. After all, they are basically tied to the pace of the assembly line and they have to keep up. Moreover, they are constantly supervised by their superiors, who know exactly what they are doing and how hard they are working. Thus, in the factory, workers are busy, busy, busy.

The same does not apply to the offices. Salarymen and office ladies have rather poorly defined tasks which must be accomplished in due course but without too much precision as to deadlines. It is hard to know exactly what they are doing when they are at their desks and even harder when they move about. Their supervisors, who have their own job to do, cannot keep as close watch. Thus, many office workers just shuffle papers, some even read magazines and comics, while the office ladies serve tea. Staff at all levels participate in countless meetings and consultations, some essential, others less so. And they also spend a lot of time out of the office, busily commuting from one meeting to the next but occasionally slipping into a coffee shop for relaxation. If they do stay late at the office, it may be to accomplish more work. It may also be to chat with colleagues or wait out the evening rush. And they would not dare leave before their superiors, who in turn would not go home too early as this would hurt their own chances of promotion.

Not only is the work ethic weakening, another cornerstone of the system is under more stress, namely loyalty to the company. Over the years, Japanese employees have been thinking ever more of changing jobs. This too was revealed by endless polls. In a somewhat theoretical *Yomiuri* survey, over half the employees responded that they would change jobs *if* they could make better use of their abilities and earn more by doing so.[22] When asked more pointedly whether they expected to leave the company, even many managers (*kacho*) indicated that they wanted to set up their own company or change jobs one day.[23] Admittedly, job-hopping is still less widespread in Japan than in the West, but the level is rising, reaching 9 per cent by the 1990s.

If so many are thinking of switching jobs, or just day-dreaming about the possibility, it must be fairly obvious that they are not as loyal to the company as thought. In addition, they are hardly as emotionally attached to the *kaisha* as so many foreigners claim. In fact, repeated polls show that increasingly the principal reason for working is 'to earn income.' That was the choice of 57 per cent of the Japanese youths in a recent comparative study, somewhat below many Western countries but well above other Asian ones.[24] Further polls reveal that many Japanese do not particularly like the company they work for, which is unusually irksome if they have to spend their whole career with it. Most astonishing, even surveys of retiring salarymen indicated that, if they could do it over again, most of them would probably want to work for a different company.[25]

With this changing raw material, companies had to react. Initially, efforts were made to force the new workers into the same molds as the old. This was done by increased insistence on both discipline and financial incentives. But those were most effective for the 'my-home' and 'new family' generations which were still open to moral appeals and needed money for a house and schooling. Their successors could not be manipulated so readily and what they wanted most was less demanding or unpleasant work and more free time. At least, some in these cohorts did desire more independence and a chance to display their initiative. That could be harnessed to the company's good.

Still, by the 1980s, companies had to concede that it was just impossible to turn many of the fresh recruits into old-style company 'warriors' and 'workaholics.' Employees were thus given a choice, the one referred to previously, of following two different tracks. While most men still opted for the 'career track,' an increasing share preferred the 'general track.' They knew the chances of promotion were reduced, earnings would suffer and they might eventually be dumped, but this was all preferable to the alternative of selling their soul to the company, as it were.

This naturally shrank the core, and put greater pressure on the remaining core members. The biggest strain was felt by middle-managers, especially the *kacho*, who were in direct contact with young employees and had to urge them to strive harder for the company. Since such a response could not be forced, many adopted the tack of making friends and inviting younger colleagues out for a drink after hours, so they might be seduced or shamed into doing more. But this did not always work and, since the *kacho* was responsible for the performance of his section, his own hopes for promotion, earnings and tenure were on the line. Many could not take the strain and there was much talk of the spread of *kacho byo* (*kacho*'s disease) from which many suffered, this taking especially the form of ulcers, loss of weight and nervousness.

That ailment was already spreading in the 1970s and 1980s. By the end of that period there appeared something even more ominous, namely 'sudden death' and *karoshi* (death from overwork). The latter was rather loosely defined and hard to prove legally, but it was claimed that between 10,000 and 30,000 victims died of it each year. In most cases the medical cause was apoplexy or heart attack. That it was induced by overwork seemed rather obvious when, for example, the victims worked 3,000 hours a year, repeatedly went without weekends and vacation, had no time for meals or relaxation and were under pressure to perform. While these were extreme cases, almost half of those asked in a *Yomiuri* poll felt concern that either they or a member of their family might fall victim to *karoshi*. As one mother said, 'every morning I feel like I am sending my son off to war or something.'[26]

If Japanese employees are becoming less loyal to the company and less emotionally attached, why do so many stick with it? There are very good reasons. Some of them are positive. There are still workers who are grateful to the company for providing them with a decent living, giving them a chance to rise through the ranks and, in some cases, climb rather high. They are proud of what their company (and they themselves) have contributed to Japan's economic progress. But these workers, as noted, can be found more among the older generations. And even they are bound to the company by the same links that predominate for younger groups.

These have little to do with anything so high-sounding as 'loyalty.' Under the conditions of Japanese management, where most workers are recruited on graduation and rather few are taken in later, it is quite simply hard to find another job. Each large company already has its full complement of workers and only rarely accepts outsiders. This is not due only to the system, Japanese bosses have tacit non-poaching arrangements whereby they would not take on employees who had quit another company. Under these conditions, if someone wants to leave the company, where would he go?

Another serious impediment is that most Japanese company-men do not possess any special knowhow. They were trained to work for their company doing things it wanted and which other companies might not need. They were given enough skills to handle whatever task that was, but had no general skills that were transferable. This means they have precious little to offer another employer. They could not even become free-lance specialists since most large companies train their own internally.

Meanwhile, the longer an employee stays with the company, the more benefits he has. Gradually, from year to year, he rises in rank, earnings and status. This may not be much at first, which is why young recruits are more tempted to change than old hands. By the time they have been with the company for a decade or more, what can be lost by switching jobs is usually considerably more than what can be gained. Added to this, there are the bonuses which are granted twice a year, and would be missed. There is increasing entitlement to pensions and other retirement benefits. The company may even have guaranteed a housing loan. This is a lot to give up for the uncertainties of life in another company (whose own staff would certainly not welcome a newcomer).

Thus, job-hopping is most noticeable among the young and in a second group, those working for small firms. For, in small firms, wages and retirement benefits are smaller, the career escalator is flatter and 'loyalty' is not inculcated as assiduously. Indeed, the situation is pretty much one of hire and fire in keeping with the needs of the company and workers do not hesitate to quit if they can find something better elsewhere. So, anyone in a large company looking for another job would most likely find it only in a smaller or foreign company. And this sort of change is often risky and brings fewer gains. Rather than take a step down, unlike the step up that exists in Western countries, most Japanese would prefer to stay put. For such reasons, many Japanese employees call the system not 'lifetime employment' but 'lifetime enslavement.'

Within this context, it is possible to answer the question of the novice-cum-expert who wondered why so many Japanese employees were working late while refuting the conclusion of the expert-cum-novice who claimed that 'people still work long hours and for no extra reward other than the knowledge that they are a worthwhile member of the group.'[27] The *honne* is that the younger staff members do not dare leave until their superiors have gone home, and these superiors know it would be unwise not to stay late to show their devotion, and they all assume this will pay off in terms of promotions. Even if it does not, they know that leaving earlier would certainly result in slower promotions and possible dismissal. But the *honne* within the *honne* is that, while they do stay late, they rarely accomplish any useful work that could not have been done during the day.

Out Of Tune With The Times

When the admirers of Japanese management describe this
wondrous system, they often intimate that it has deep roots in
Japanese society. The company is like a customary family, the
huge corporate groups (*keiretsu*) bear a resemblance to the
feudal clan, relations between the boss and his core employees
are not unlike those between a lord and his *samurai* and those
between a main company and its subcontractors are comparable to a fief and its vassals. Throughout there is much appeal
to time-honored traditions of mutual support, correct relations and, above all, loyalty. Alas, as we saw, that is not the
case. The current system was artifically created by postwar managers to hold on to their workers and subcontractors at a time
of rapid expansion. That is, at a time when the companies
desperately needed the workers and the workers also needed
the companies.

Thus, if the circumstances were to change, or if employers
and/or employees were to adopt other goals, the management
system could very well change. Any changes could be for the
better as they could be for the worse. Alas, it seems that the
renowned Japanese management system has come unstuck and,
while some changes are seen as improvements, others are a
cause for concern. Only on the surface may it still appear that
all is well. Deeper down, everybody (aside from the foreign
'experts') knows that this is a time of crisis.

As noted, the core of the company is getting proportionately smaller. Within the staff, it now only consists of some
regular employees, and not all. This contrasts with earlier years
when every man was expected to stick to the company and
progress upward on the 'career escalator.' Now many get off
by opting for the 'general track.' Others stay on but, as we
have seen, they are far less willing to give their all. They have
not been replaced by women to any great extent, because it
has turned out to be terribly difficult to integrate them and
few enough are willing to make the sacrifices.

The core is shrinking in another way, too. Previously, most
of the subcontractors and suppliers were local firms which
could be integrated to an amazing degree in the company's
overall operations. Relations were close and personal and, while
there was more give for the subcontractors and more take for

the core companies, they were a team. However, as costs have risen in Japan, more and more large companies are shedding their local subcontractors and suppliers and taking on foreign ones. Most of them already have considerable numbers of subsidiaries abroad. The core company finds it much harder to integrate these foreign elements, which are also less willing to sacrifice for a distant and sometimes suspect 'boss.'

The problem is not only that the core is losing supporters at the periphery, it is also alienating them, accelerating any disintegration in this direction. For Japanese managers no longer like the old system as much as before. As noted, it was introduced in the 1950s and 1960s when expansion was rapid and it was essential to hold on to workers and suppliers. Not only that, with constantly rising turnover and profits, it was possible to reward them. Such a system functions much less well under conditions of relative stagnation and, worst of all, when certain sectors actually shrink. At such times, rather than hold on to workers and subcontractors, bosses want to get rid of them.

Because of the residual effects of the system, and the continuing lip service to 'lifetime employment,' large companies find it more difficult to cut back on personnel. This has to be done more slowly and subtly, but it is far from impossible. In fact, the first phases are rather simple under the core arrangement. The contracts with contractual workers, part-timers and others are simply not renewed. Women are encouraged more vigorously to retire on marriage or childbirth or harassed more stridently until they give up. Since much of the company's work is done by subcontractors and suppliers, these are just dropped and the work taken in-house to keep the remaining employees busy.

In certain branches, and at certain times, that is still inadequate. And even Japanese bosses refuse to carry employees who are not making a reasonable contribution whatever their position or hopes of tenure. Thus, for example, managers who no longer perform are given a title, and a desk near the window, but have no subordinates and no work. Eventually many in this 'window-sill tribe' (*madogiwa-zoku*) resign out of humiliation. More broadly, companies periodically suggest that those who cannot make the necessary sacrifices should retire voluntarily, with a small bonus, hinting that the next time around they will just be dismissed with no bonus. Most get the message.

Another tactic is to send managers and other employees to work in subsidiaries, often quite remote from the head office (and their own home). Or they may be seconded to subcontractors, suppliers or distributors. If that is not enough, companies may create special subsidiaries or help workers set up small firms, which are at first supported and subsidized, but later left on their own. The company has not fired them, heaven forbid, but it is no longer responsible if the subsidiary or supplier fires them or their new firm goes bust. In such firms, by the way, the work is usually harder, the hours longer and the wages lower.

At the same time, Japanese companies are increasingly demanding that workers do more than just stand on the 'career escalator.' There are proportionately fewer managerial posts open and, to get one, employees are expected to prove themselves through more active participation and loyalty. Ordinary workers are also supposed to contribute more and, increasingly, any rewards are tied to performance. If the performance is inadequate, employees will earn less and become managers later, if ever. Those who cannot hope to become managers are encouraged to develop useful skills and then shunted onto some slower track. More strikingly, instead of insisting merely that the staff be disciplined and hardworking, appeals are made for imagination and initiative. These new demands, and the screening process related thereto, also separate out those whom the company no longer really wants as part of the core.

These are very substantial changes for a supposedly immutable and mutually beneficial system. Some of the 'reforms' were made necessary by employees who just could not stand the old system. But far more came from employers who wanted to shape the system in ways that were more advantageous to them. Yet, while the system is becoming more and more 'Western' in some respects, with workers doing a specific job and being paid for that job, and also being discarded if they are no longer useful, it has remained different – or 'Japanese,' if you will – in others. Most workers are still recruited directly after graduation, they do ride a somewhat bumpier 'career escalator' and they are tacitly expected to stay with the company indefinitely (unless the company decides otherwise). And, of course, the core imposes its will on the periphery.

With so much general dissatisfaction with the company, and

most alterations in the postwar system being to the advantage of the employers and disadvantage of the employees, one would think that Japan's workers might do something about it. In a certain sense, perhaps they have. They are more cautious about which company they join, they are less willing to trust it and they are more willing to leave it if something can be gained. But these are again individual solutions to individual problems. Workers do not unite to make their company a more congenial workplace, let alone push the whole system in the directions that they want.

This could be done through existing institutions, namely the trade unions. Workers would simply have to participate more actively and reinvigorate the existing unions or, if worst came to worst, create more independent unions to replace those that are too dependent on the company. That has not happened. If anything, trade unions have become increasingly ineffectual and achieve little for their members. They are also run by bureaucracies and workers at the base have very little impact on officials at the top. Thus, the workers have turned away from their unions even more than from their companies. This is particularly true of young workers. Whereas once Japan could boast a very high unionization rate, as much as 56 per cent in 1950, the level has fallen to a more normal 34 per cent in the 1970s, and continued dipping to a low of 24 per cent in 1994. And a large percentage of this was in the public sector. Unlike the companies, the trade unions do not seem to have any strategy to reverse the trends.

Summing up, the archetypical Japanese-style management system that so many 'experts' purvey never actually existed except in their imagination. In practice, it was completely different from the theory. And even that system is being gradually transformed, here and there, in bits and snatches, for the simple reason that neither the employers nor the employees are very satisfied with it and it does not meet present needs. Under these conditions, it would seem that the gurus should stop preaching it as a panacea for all the abuses of the Western system. But that is most unlikely to happen as long as they find enough suckers not only to believe them but to pay them for their wisdom.

3

The School
(Education Runs Amuck)

Of all Japan's social institutions, none has generated such rave reviews as its educational system. It was singled out for praise by Edwin O. Reischauer, scholar and diplomat, or diplomat and scholar.

High literacy rates and excellent educational standards are also major reasons for Japan's success in meeting the challenge of a technologically more advanced West in the nineteenth century and for its subsequent achievement of a position of economic leadership. Nothing, in fact, is more central in Japanese society or more basic to Japan's success than is its educational system.[1]

This positive view was steadily built upon by successive generations of Japanapologists. Ezra Vogel listed the high quality of education and the high standard of literacy among Japan's greatest successes.[2] And literally dozens of 'experts' have analyzed the educational system, some going so far as to recommend it as a model for the West (or, indeed, the world).

But it is hard to define just what makes Japan's educational system distinctive, let alone superior, because the system itself is undergoing rapid change. And many of the changes are not for the best. Nor is the system itself always what it seems. For example, Japan's early advances were traced back to the 'educational system' which existed prior to its opening and was credited with instilling a disposition to learn and a high degree of literacy. There were, in fact, schools. Samurai children were taught in *hanko* schools while village children picked up the rudiments of reading and writing in *terakoya* or temple schools. More generally, Confucianism supposedly inculcated

44

a respect for knowledge. This does sound impressive. Except that the contents of the 'education' were Chinese classics and Buddhist scripture, of little use to a modern country, and the primary technique was memorization, especially of material needed to pass tests to enter the bureaucracy.

With the Meiji Restoration, it was realized that Japan needed a more 'scientific' or 'Western' educational system and as of the 1870s extensive reforms were launched. Alas, the initial steps were simply to reconvert the former samurai and temple schools into 'modern' schools, this conversion frequently being no more than a change of name. The same teachers stayed on, using the same methods, although new batches of trained teachers eventually replaced them and the system was gradually modernized. However, with the rise of nationalism, anything Western – including Western education – was condemned and then outlawed. And schools became a primary source of indoctrination.

After the war, at the urging of the American occupation authorities, the schools were democratized and the American structure was adopted, on the surface at least. Again, while the exterior changed radically, internally the changes were mitigated. In keeping with the tradition of renaming things, many high schools were upgraded to colleges and primary schools to secondary schools, whether they fit the bill or not. More seriously, democratization in the classroom was left to school teachers and administrators whose commitment to democracy was not always genuine. And the Ministry of Education remained particularly retrograde and eager to reimpose its control over the educational establishment.

Yet, try as they could, the old-fashioned administrators and bureaucrats could not dominate the younger teachers, many of whom were leftists or at least more liberal. Over the years, with new generations of youngsters, there was a certain loosening of the system. But the biggest changes were wrought, not by students, teachers or administrators, but businessmen who wanted to make money out of education as it existed in Japan. They created their own parallel educational system which at first just supplemented the official one, then began replacing it. The results were not expected by the Americans or the Japanese, but they could not be escaped.

Cramming Overwhelms Schooling

Like so many things in Japan, if it is merely viewed from without, the Japanese educational system resembles many other systems around the world. In fact, on the surface, it looks rather like the American system from which it was copied after the Pacific War with assorted German aspects at higher levels, those adopted about a century ago. Compulsory education covers elementary and lower secondary schooling. But many children already attend kindergarten and most continue on to higher levels.

Presented in purely numerical terms, the progress appears very impressive. By now, virtually all children complete their nine years of compulsory education and 95 per cent go on to upper secondary (compared to only 52 per cent in 1955). More than 38 per cent of the boys, and 43 per cent of the girls, then attend colleges or junior colleges, again a vast improvement over the early postwar years when the average intake was under 10 per cent. While the basic educational system is public, some of the primary and secondary schools and many kindergartens and colleges are private. The growth in attendance and the opening of more schools is often seen as a response to the supposed urge for learning to which the Japanese allegedly attach exceptional importance.

Admittedly, even in this context, there are some notable differences with other systems. One, at the base, is apparently positive. More and more children are going to kindergarten at ever younger ages. At the summit, the deviation is less positive, for there are very few graduate schools, certainly not enough given the large number of college graduates, many of whom must go abroad to have advanced training or obtain a doctorate. Also, at the college level, many of the women are attending not four-year but two-year colleges which offer considerably less education. And, even in the genuine colleges, women tend to take less demanding or useful courses. Thus, some of them never get a degree. (Figure 3.1)

While the number of schools and students is high compared to other countries, it is surprising to note that Japan's educational budget is relatively small. Japan only spent 3.8 per cent of GNP on education recently compared to 4.1 per cent in Great Britain, 4.9 per cent in France and 5.0 per cent in the United States.[3] That shows. The schools are often ramshackle affairs,

Figure 3.1. *Organization of the Present School System*

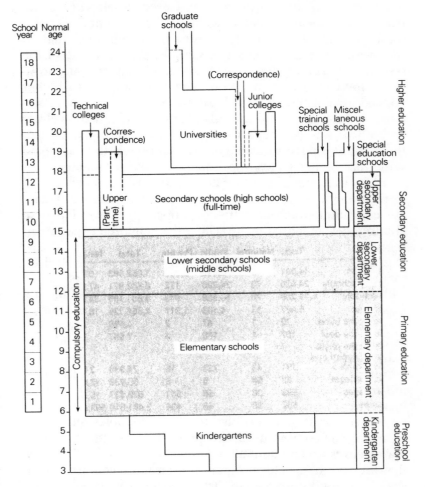

A bottom-heavy educational 'pyramid:' plenty
of kindergartens, not so many graduate schools.

Source: Ministry of Education.
Credit: *Education in Japan*, 1995, p. 15.

with scruffy playing areas and unattractive surroundings. Classrooms are plain at best. There is a definite shortage of teaching and audiovisual aids. Oddly enough, fewer computers are available and these are less integrated in teaching than in other advanced countries.

More seriously, there are proportionately fewer teachers than is common in other advanced (and even developing) countries. The student-teacher ratio in public elementary schools was about 22, a bit better than China but much worse than in the West. For public secondary schools, the backbone of the system, the ratio of 19 for Japan was much higher than the 13 to 16 for China and the West. The same applies to higher education. This means that Japanese teachers have more students to look after, and they also have less adequate facilities and offices, and yet they have to put in many more hours than their counterparts abroad. For this, although they are paid somewhat higher wages, the rewards are rather mediocre.

Inadequate school facilities and overworked teachers could, or so it might seem, be overcome by another aspect of Japanese education which at first sight appears positive. Japanese children devote more time to school than children anywhere in the West (although less than in some Asian rivals like Korea). Despite efforts to reduce the number of classes, the level remains about 32 hours a week during a school year of 220 to 240 days. But that is not the end of it. Japanese school children have a lot of homework, on the average two hours a night. Even during the summer vacation, they are given work to do and must consult with their teachers in the middle.

In addition, the curricula are very rigorous. There is a heavy emphasis on mathematics and hard sciences. This, of course, means relatively less stress on social sciences and the humanities. There is also considerably less time given over to sports or arts and crafts and terribly little that resembles relaxation. Nearly all the courses are strictly prescribed and there are very few electives which might allow students to move in directions that interest them. This program is even more comprehensive than in many European countries and light years away from the United States. Still, or so the 'experts' claim, it guarantees a superior education.

So far everything roughly resembles what is done in other countries, if considerably more demanding. Yet, in one respect, there is an amazing deviation. Elsewhere, and in pure theory, one would assume that the educational expectations would grow stricter the higher a student rises and also that students graduating from each higher level would have achieved that much more. This would naturally derive from exit tests that make it increasingly more difficult to graduate from one level to the next. In Japan, inexplicably, there are stiff exams to get into each higher level, but none to get out.

Thus, not surprisingly, pupils must study assiduously to pass the examinations to get into junior high school, senior high school and college, but once there can coast along if they wish to. For those who want to attend college, the tests are particularly grueling. But, once in college, students can slack off. And most do, for virtually everyone who gets into college can graduate unless they voluntarily drop out or die. There are few tests, and most of them are fairly easy, there are not many term papers, and nearly anything turned in is accepted, and there are no serious examinations to graduate.

Thus, the crucial barrier for young Japanese is the college entrance examination. That is the last real hurdle they will face, and it is a formidable one, for most colleges have the right to design their own examination and there is little uniformity among them. Students must therefore take two, three, four, or even more different examinations. The more, the better. If they fail one, they may pass another and at least get into some college.

While it would seem that there are enough college places to go around, and a large proportion of high school graduates eventually do reach college, there is enormous pressure to get into not just any college but a 'good' college. Since nearly all high school students want to go to the same 'good' colleges, it is even harder to get accepted by the college of one's choice. Just for the record, the 'good' colleges are the older state universities like Tokyo (Todai), Kyoto (Kyodai) and Hitotsubashi and some older private colleges like Keio and Waseda.

It is difficult to conceive just how determined Japanese students are to get into these 'good' colleges, or at least any college. Those who fail the first time around, rather than accept a lesser school, may take the examinations again the next year, and the year after. In fact, at exams, a third and more are *ronin*, students seeking desperately to finally pass, and named after the masterless samurai of yore. They can spend the whole time between exams cramming. And all others who want to go to college, given the tremendous competition, must also cram. Whereas once it was just necessary to prepare for college entrance exams, the competition and pressure are spreading to tests for higher secondary, and lower secondary and, indeed, to get into kindergarten. In fact, there are even courses for pregnant women to teach the fetus such skills as recognizing characters or English words.

Given the overriding importance of one or more examinations, students (and parents) have had to gear up to get through what is called the 'narrow gate.' Students therefore receive private tutoring or attend cram schools (*juku*), with those specializing in college entrance known as *yobiko*.[4] But, if one student can be prepared, so can the others. So there has been a steady escalation in attendance at these cram schools, of which there are now about 40,000. They are attended by more and more students, with the proportion of primary school students attending *juku* rising from 17 per cent in 1985 to 45 per cent in 1990, the rise being 19 per cent to 52 per cent over the same period for secondary school students.[5] And, finally, the number of hours devoted to cramming increases implacably.

It is essential to state at this point that the examinations consist mainly of multiple choice questions which must be answered as rapidly as possible. While they do, to some extent, cover the same ground as the official curricula, there are clear differences in emphasis. Subjects like math, science and history, where questions can be answered simply, are most prominent. For languages, ability to apply them is less important (as harder to test) than petty points of grammar and syntax. There is little, if any, room for more complicated questions involving reasoning or various alternatives. And, as noted, every college can design its own tests. Thus, what the *juku* and *yobiko* do is to have candidates do mock exams similar to those of the schools they want to enter, learning by rote the answers to what have become typical questions and otherwise mastering test-passing techniques.

This parallel 'educational' system, which was not actually foreseen or expected but cannot even be trimmed back, has progressively taken over from the official system. As examination time comes round, and increasingly longer before it arrives, students forget about their regular school work, have no time to do homework and spend untold hours in cram courses. They are soon too tired and nervous to pay much attention to what is going on in school. And teachers, realizing the situation, do not or cannot force them to keep up. Indeed, some of the regular schools have taken to helping their students cram for tests.

Lowering Higher Education

This drive to get through the 'narrow gate' has several other consequences. One is to seek alternative ways of getting into college. This is easiest for children who are not terribly bright, or mediocre test-takers, but whose parents are influential or well-to-do. They can pull strings with the college or high school administration, especially if they are alumni. This happens particularly for medical and dental schools, whose students include an exceptional number of children of doctors and dentists. Otherwise, particularly for schools benefiting from state funds (as many do), politicians can be asked to intercede. They may do this as a favor, or for cash or gifts. Sometimes professors or administrators at the school ease entry or leak examination answers. Many such scandals of 'back door entry' emerge every season. And everyone knows that good connections (*kone*) can compensate for bad marks.

The more common method of enhancing the chances of one's offspring is, in addition to more hours of *juku*, to work back from college entry. For there are 'good' high schools known to be particularly successful in getting their students into 'good' colleges. And there are 'good' primary schools and 'good' kindergartens which have a leg up for the next level. Indeed, in many cases, they are actually feeder or 'escalator' schools which can send a number of students directly to the next level, without having to pass tests. And, of course, there are the 'good' *juku* and *yobiko* known for helping their clients get better test scores. By now, it should be obvious that 'good' has nothing to do with the intrinsic quality of the education as opposed to the ability to facilitate entry to elite schools.

That is, such things should be obvious, if one is willing to see them. If not, it is possible to draw all sorts of different conclusions. For example, according to Ezra Vogel, cramming is not something students dread but something they embrace freely and almost gladly. 'It is unmistakably clear to students that their future depends on meritocratic performance as measured by entrance examinations. Motivation comes from inside,

and the student, mindful of his responsibilities to parents and
school and concerned about his future, wants to learn so that
he may be prepared for the entrance examination.' Moreover,
the outcome is overwhelmingly positive. 'As a result of the
examination system the nation acquires a large reservoir of
well-trained people with a substantial core of common culture,
people who are curious, teachable, disciplined, and sensitive
to humanistic and civic concerns.'[6] How's that for a *tatemae?*
Now for the *honne.*

Finally, after excruciatingly strenuous efforts (plus a little
help from their friends), Japanese students attend higher education. ('Higher,' like 'good,' is used very loosely, as will soon
become obvious.) The Japanese state has been increasing the
number of universities for decades and there are now about a
hundred. But they were insufficient to meet the demand so
private colleges have also been opened, at a faster pace, and
these now account for 75 per cent of all students. Some of the
more recent state universities are rather mediocre. But they
are usually better than the weaker private colleges, some opened
by enlightened social or political leaders, others by businessmen trying to make money. Moreover, some of these are just
junior or two-year colleges which dispense a rather diluted
eduction.

The colleges, state and private, are frequently underfunded,
either because government assistance is inadequate or because
they cannot pack in enough students to cover costs. Thus they
remain quite spartan, often with old and rundown facilities, a
lack of equipment, and professors who teach classes of several
hundred (although the actual turnout is usually much lower).
Professors tend to lecture, making rather dull, unimaginative
presentations that hardly change from year to year. According
to insiders, there is little pressure to do research or publish
and once they achieve tenure, this form of lifetime employment relieves professors of any challenges, as they are promoted regularly and cultivate their own clique. Even the
supposed elite colleges are rather humdrum affairs, with few
widely known scholars and scant research results. In fact, the
University of Tokyo, number one in Japan, is only number 38
worldwide according to United Nations statistics.[7]

All of the colleges come under the Ministry of Education and
are subject to its cumbersome regulations. They must receive

approval for every course and it is extremely hard to launch new or innovative ones. The first two years, no matter what the faculty, are devoted to liberal arts and are for many just a rehash of what they had already learned in high school or cram school. Only, this time, the teaching is even more tedious and the incentive to learn smaller. For there are few tests, and most of them are not hard, those who fail get retakes, and even those who flunk the retakes often pass. The classes are too big to notice who is participating actively, or indeed who is attending regularly, with students responding for one another. Only in the smaller 'seminars' do professors get to know students and vice versa, although this does not necessarily guarantee greater zeal. After all, there are no real barriers to graduation and no exams even faintly equivalent to the entrance exams to make students study.

There are not many graduate schools in Japan, at most enough to take about a tenth of the graduates, although the number of schools and students is growing. Compared to graduate schools abroad, they are pretty mediocre and thus many Japanese prefer getting their advanced training abroad. They find better courses, better professors, better equipment and a chance to mix with foreigners and improve their speaking ability of foreign languages. While graduate school is usually a finishing process and is widely used in Europe and America, where a doctorate may be essential for a successful career, in Japan the doctorate is often seen as a dead-end. It leads only to a job in academia, since companies and bureaucracies seldom recruit from this category. However, they do send some employees off for advanced training and specialization once they have become reliable personnel.

Thus, the educational system, as it appears on paper and was discussed initially, hardly exists. The primary and secondary schools are overshadowed by the cram schools, the curricula are basically ignored for college entrance exams and the teachers become adjuncts of the test-passing machinery. But at least the kids do learn something. That much cannot be said for 'higher' education. Once into college, the professors and courses are hardly relevant for the students. Any rigor is replaced by laxity and more is forgotten than learned. Instead of building on a strong base, the system is truncated and the earlier years of effort are wasted.

If the educational system no longer focuses on education, as opposed to passing tests, then perhaps it should be regarded as something else. And, by most Japanese, it is. It is a way of ranking people on the basis of academic background or credentials (*gakureki*), namely whether they stopped at high school or went on to college, and which high schools and colleges they attended. This is broadly recognized by most Japanese, first and foremost the students who make every effort to get into a 'good' college. As one Kyodai graduate, now a university professor himself, said: '. . . Japanese colleges and universities today are not expected to educate. Their only function in society is to sort and classify students through their entrance exams and, four years later, send them out into the world with the school's brand stamped on them.'[8] Since the schools are better at ranking than teaching, former Minister of Labor Ishida spoke of a 'low academic level – high educational background society.'[9]

Educational Results And Casualties

Although the educational system is not what it seems, and manifestly has serious flaws, these are often overlooked by foreign admirers (if proportionately fewer Japanese). They praise the system because it supposedly delivers results. Some of these results are academic, such as high scores in international comparative examinations and IQ tests as well as widespread literacy. Several renowned 'experts' claimed that Japanese high school students were years ahead of their counterparts in the West.[10] Other supposed benefits are broader, such as cultivated people, a disciplined and adaptable workforce and a democratic citizenry. The *Economist* wrote of an educational system that is 'one of the wonders of the modern world' for inculcating the qualities that make good industrial workers and creating 'a society of astonishing stability.'[11] And so many others concurred that they cannot all be cited.

If you look at the lower levels, primary and secondary school, there is no doubt that the Japanese are given more hours of math and hard sciences and, what with homework and cramming, they do become amazingly proficient in these subjects. They score at the top, or near the top, in many cross-country examinations. However, it should be noted that, while they exceed American students by a large margin, they are not much better than those in parts of Europe and Asia. More worrisome, while they are extremely good at giving standard responses to standard questions, they are markedly less able when it comes to more practical problem-solving.

Still, no country should limit its horizons to math and hard sciences. Pupils should also learn softer sciences and humanities. For these, the Japanese do considerably less well. The most obvious case is English, a compulsory subject which is taught for many years, but which Japanese children have clearly not mastered (aside from rather theoretical intricacies of the language). Nor do they have a second or third foreign language. While they do study history, much of that is quite ancient, since modern politics are glossed over and events during and leading up to the Pacific War are covered up or distorted. Even for Japanese language, the other compulsory subject, the results have been getting steadily worse as concerns the number of Chinese characters (*kanji*) actually learned, the ability to read and especially the ability to write.

While this is somewhat peripheral, there are serious lacks in areas like music, arts and sport. Japanese children are all fairly good at this in primary school but, as they begin preparing for examinations, such skills are neglected. More ominous, social skills are stunted. Pupils see ever less of their friends, meet and play together less. While there is some limited social life at school, there is very little mixing with other children of their age through clubs, sports teams or Scouting. Even personal interests, like playing a musical instrument or collecting stamps, suffer. Leisure consists mainly of watching television, playing video games, reading comics and dozing – most often alone.

So much for the earlier phases. Gradually, as pupils have to prepare for entrance exams at ever higher levels, and especially for college, the social situation degenerates further. After a long day at school and then homework, on evenings, weekends and holidays, for more and more hours a week, they attend *juku*. Often, they simply trudge from normal school to cram school, swallowing a cold snack in the breaks, and otherwise trying to memorize elusive answers to often futile questions. When they return home, they are exhausted but also so nervous that they have trouble sleeping. Contacts with other youngsters, parents and teachers are reduced to a minimum.

They are going through 'examination hell,' and no sober description can adequately portray what happens to the children's lives as they keep cramming week after week, year after year and with increasing intensity as the examinations approach. They spend ever more time studying at home and put in more hours at the *juku*. They bite their lips and dig their nails into their flesh to stay awake and learn more. They recite desperate incantations like 'sleep five hours and fail, sleep four hours and pass' or 'play today, cry tomorrow.'[12] There is no time for fun, relaxation, even sleep – just more and more cramming.

Some students cannot take the pressure, or do not want to compete, while in certain cases parents do not want them put through the wringer. Thus, they withdraw, knowing they will be condemned to a mediocre, second-rate existence. This has resulted in growing absenteeism and dropouts as well as disorder and even violence in the schools. Many of the children, more often those who strive than those who give up, develop serious emotional and psychological ailments. Everybody knows where they come from. Still, for an authoritative opinion, let us quote Professor Toyohisa Murata, an expert on child psychology at Fukuoka University: 'Japanese children are agonizing because of the so-called examination hell phenomenon and intense competition for entering elite educational institutions.'[13]

While the pupils' problems are well-known, and widely commented on within Japan, less is heard of the schools' problems. Teachers and administrators complain that all too many children are only attending school because they want to get into college, or are pushed by their parents, although they cannot keep up. Since they pass almost automatically from one grade to the next, there are many who simply do not understand what is being taught. This is known as the *shichi-go-san* system whereby only 70 per cent of primary school children can follow the lessons, only 50 per cent of junior high school students can do so, and a mere 30 per cent of senior high school students can perform at the expected level.[14] Alas, the hopeless cases (which are a majority by the end of secondary schooling) stick around and get in the way of the others. And, out of kindness, most are allowed to graduate. This obviously debases the value of a high school diploma and makes any claims of Japanese high school students being years ahead of their foreign counterparts plain silly.

By the way, and this is an extremely important distinction, it is this 30, 50 and 70 per cent of the school population who cannot follow the lessons who become Japan's fabled factory workers. More exactly, it is the college graduates who hog all the white-collar jobs and leave the blue-collar ones for their less talented comrades. True, these comrades are reasonably literate, numerate and 'educated,' but far less than those who go on to college in Japan and not much above their counterparts in other countries. Moreover, they are not the intentional result of the Japanese educational system, which is geared toward producing an academic elite, but rather a side-product. What endears them to employers, more than any intellectual attainments, is that the school system has convinced them that they are second-rate and thus they are more docile and obedient and less likely to have exaggerated expectations or demands.

So much for those who flunked the college entrance exams. What about those who passed? What does college hold in store for them? After examination hell, they get as close to heaven as most Japanese ever achieve. College is very relaxed compared to high school, with less insistence on discipline, no dress code to speak of, and not too many rules, at least, not too many rules that anyone obeys. Students tend to pick easier faculties, liberal arts or humanities (and, for some girls, home economics) rather than engineering and science and, within these, they often choose easier courses or professors. Even then, many of them don't bother attending classes, handing in papers or taking tests. They only devote a few hours to studies each day and, according to a recent survey, only spend a quarter as much time on homework as American students.[15] Instead, they engage in club activities, if they are more energetic, or hang out in coffee shops and the like, if they are lethargic. They pass untold hours playing mahjong or reading comic books.

This is no secret to anyone. Student antics are generally known and often commented on, usually negatively, by the media and ordinary folks. Prime Minister Nakasone apparently referred to Japanese colleges as 'leisureland' and a professor at International Christian University, Yasuo Furuya, called them a 'playground.' As he noted, 'Japanese students are less concerned about what they want to study in college than what college they want to enter. Therefore, once admitted into one, they spend more of their time playing mahjong or concentrating on side jobs.' The students agree. When asked what the function of a university was, more of them said it was 'a place to make friends' or 'a place where one can do what one wants' than that it was 'a place to study' or 'a place to acquire special or professional knowledge.'[16] In another survey, this one appearing in the White Paper on Education, only 45 per cent of the students attended 'almost all' their classes and a mere 11 per cent 'understood most' of what went on in class.[17]

The students do not apologize for goofing off. They feel it is their due, a fair return for the exhausting and shattering experience of 'examination hell'. Anyway, according to their professors, many of them are really broken in mind and spirit and too amorphous to absorb much learning. Some professors go easy on them because they are sorry, others do not care that much, and with huge classes they cannot bother with each and every student anyway. The colleges could, of course, intensify the requirements for graduation, at least introducing more tests and term papers and some sort of final examination. But, they are too worried about the reaction of the students, and the parents, who have put time and money respectively into the educational process and expect their reward. More prosaically, many colleges need the tuition fees to survive.

Admittedly, there are differences. Students in the more technical and scientific faculties or professional schools do work harder than their colleagues in liberal arts. The material is more demanding, the testing somewhat stricter and there is apparently a bit more interest in learning the essentials of a trade or career. But, even then, it would be a mistake to assume that a diploma signifies much. And, for the offspring of doctors and dentists, who are guaranteed a remunerative practice, it may mean less. The same lackadaisical approach occurs not only in newer, second- or third-rate colleges but in the top schools as well. Students can also sail through Todai or Kyodai. As a corporate executive pointed out, attending an elite university 'means only that you worked very hard in your third year of high school . . . not that you will actually learn anything useful.'[18]

So, let us return to the question of results. In primary and secondary school, the results are doubtless better than in the United States, itself at the bottom of the pile and hardly a worthy point of comparison. But they are not better than in some Asian countries or much of Europe, assuredly not when the focus is broadened from mathematics and science to humanities and social skills. A college education, on the other hand, is rather perfunctory and a diploma from a Japanese college is barely worth the paper it is written on, let alone being the equal of a diploma from an American or European university. And there is little postgraduate education at all.

This means that, as far as results are concerned, Japan really does not compare well at the end of the educational process, although it may look pretty good earlier on. And it leaves one with some very odd questions. What possible rationale can there be to a system where students work hard in the beginning and goof off at the end? Where high school graduates may actually know more than college graduates? Where it is uncommonly hard to enter schools and breathtakingly easy to graduate?

There also remains the deeper question of just what education is. If it is to amass incredible amounts of facts and figures, and do fancy tricks with numbers and chemical formulas, then Japan has succeeded. If it implies an understanding of the subjects involved, it has not. If it means an ability to respond quickly by rote memory, the Japanese are overachievers. If it requires deeper knowledge, they are underachievers. If the ability to reason, as in the continental mode, or apply common sense of the Anglo-Saxon variety, has something to do with the learning process, then it is even more seriously flawed. Obviously, from this base, there is cause for concern about intangibles like imagination, initiative and creativity.

What about the broader impact of education? The educational system supposedly also created a cultivated population, an ideal workforce and a model citizenry.

True, the vast majority of Japanese are literate, as defined by the Ministry of Education, namely having learned 1,945 Chinese characters (*kanji*). But everyone knows that many more are required to read good literature or even technical manuals. And many adults seem to have forgotten their *kanji* to judge by the increasing need to insert Japanese script (*kana*)

Figure 3.2.   *Number of Book Titles Published by Country, 1990*

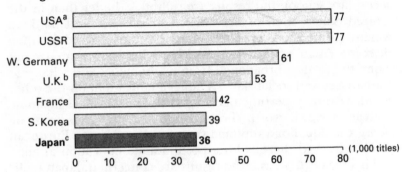

What good is literacy if there are fewer books to read?
Source: UNESCO, *Statistical Yearbook.* (a. 1981, b. 1985, c. 1987)
Credit: *Facts and Figures of Japan*, 1995, p. 101.

to explain things. As for what they read, that is steadily deteriorating as the public switches from real books to comic books and newspapers to picture magazines. Even reading per se is being eclipsed by mediocre television and videos. (Figure 3.2)

There is somewhat more to the claim that the schools are turning out good raw material for Japan's companies. Benjamin Duke writes enthusiastically of schools that produce loyal, literate, competent, diligent workers. We have already seen that this is not always true, but certainly enough to concede that education did contribute to economic progress in the 1950s, 1960s and even 1970s. However, since then, Japan's economy has changed. There is ever less need of workers who can master simple skills and follow orders and ever more need of some who can think on their own, break away from the routine and find new solutions to new problems. There is more demand than ever for imagination, initiative and creativity, the very things the educational system does not encourage.

It is much harder to agree that the schools turn out good citizens. For a good citizen is not like a good worker in many respects, in some he may be the exact opposite. True, a degree of industry and discipline is helpful in running society, but citizens in a democratic system are not supposed to follow orders, they are supposed to give them. They are supposed to decide which policies should be adopted, who should be entrusted with carrying them out, and then participate directly in the process. The Japanese are rather poor at all this, and much of the blame can be placed directly on the schools. As Kenji Ohmae, a management guru turned politician, concluded: 'The Ministry of Education has done a wonderful job of persuading 120 million Japanese that their fate is handed down to them by the government.'[19]

After all, the schools themselves are hardly democratic institutions. There is a very strict hierarchy, not only from administrators and teachers on down to pupils, but from pupils of higher grades down to those below. The youngest batches must speak up to all superiors, of which there are many, and accept whatever formal and informal rules are imposed, whether sensible or not. All the schools are regimented more than in the West, but also more than is really necessary even in Japan, with many imposing uniforms (which have to be worn outside of school as well) and enforcing rules (including nitpicking ones on hair cuts and wearing accessories). Classroom democracy is quite limited and the school does not offer civics among its many courses. Then, suddenly, in college, chaos seems to prevail, perhaps a compensation for the earlier regimentation, but hardly a contribution to a sound understanding of democracy.

More broadly, the whole educational system is strongly elitist and contributes more to hierarchization than equality. First, there is a clear divide between 'good' students, namely those who can reach college and those who drop out earlier. There is the standard distinction between boys and girls, men and women, exacerbated by the fact that while many women do go to college, they study less useful courses. In addition, there is the need to attend a 'good' primary and secondary school and get into a 'good' college, which definitely weeds out lesser elements. And, finally, the fact that colleges are ranked by social rather than academic qualifications. Those who make it to the top certainly feel they are part of an elite, and that is largely accepted by those who failed to rise as high.

But, what sort of elite is this? And what could possibly be the meaning of 'good' schools? This is not an elite selected on the basis of knowledge but rather rote memory and speed of reflexes. There is no evidence that the winners are inherently any smarter than the losers and a truly intelligent person would reject or be crushed by such a system. Nor is there any evidence that the 'good' schools at a lower level provide a better education as opposed to an education geared to taking tests. At the higher level, there is no sign that Todai, Kyodai and the rest offer a better or more rigorous education. They are just older, on the whole, with more alumni holding important positions in the bureaucracy, companies, academia, etc. But their students are often below par because they can goof off and still get by, while those from second- or third-rate colleges have to work much harder to make good. That is the kind of 'elite' Japan is saddled with.

From 'Good' Schools To 'Good' Companies

Normally, the description of an educational system could stop at this point, but not for Japan. It must include the next phase, which is recruitment for a job. While similar connections exist elsewhere, in Japan they are exceptionally strong. For, under the Japanese employment system, new recruits are taken in one batch a year, right after graduation and almost always directly from school. The schools themselves provide placement services to guarantee as much as possible that their graduates get jobs.

This is quite different from the West, and many other places, where students graduate and may or may not get a job right away. Even those who do usually have a break or vacation first, and they can enter at different times. Others will relax, travel, try several jobs to decide what they want to do with their lives. Japanese students cannot afford this. Waiting a year or two to apply would show a lack of seriousness. More to the point, since most companies basically recruit directly from school, most of the jobs, and certainly all of the better jobs, will be gone if they wait. And there is not much of a labor market on which to seek even lesser opportunities later. This means grads must quickly make a decision which is far more momentous than anything in the West, for it is likely to determine their whole career (and life).

This decision, by the way, is quite different in that most Japanese do not take on a 'job,' as it is understood in the West, but rather enter a company. The company will decide which jobs or tasks they should handle and will not hesitate to move them around from one post to another as it sees fit. That much is understood by the school placement offices, which offer not so much a choice of jobs as a choice of companies. And the graduates are equally aware, since they begin looking for a suitable company, one with which they may have to spend a 'lifetime, at an early stage.

While Japan's schools and Japan's companies are quite different from those of most other countries, the passage from one to the other seems to be relatively similar and also fairly rational. Students, all those who want, can apply for entry into any company they want. They line up together and are interviewed and also undergo written tests of their ability. This screening, in theory at least, should determine just who is hired. But Japanese students know that this is one of the biggest *tatemae* that exists.

The *honne* is that in practice most of the fresh recruits will already have been chosen even before the tests and interviews are held. In fact, these are widely regarded as a formality. The actual recruitment takes place in other ways. The most common is for companies to have recent recruits inform them of which younger students, their former colleagues, are promising company members. Those preselected are then screened much more earnestly and compatible ones chosen. It may also happen that company executives suggest possible candidates. To avoid nepotism, some companies will not hire the children of existing staff, so often friends working in two different companies will sponsor one another's offspring. That, of course, applies to public companies; in private companies hiring of children, relatives and assorted friends is rife. This time, connections (*kone*) can be considerably more important than academic results.

In this screening process, as opposed to the formal tests and interviews, there is not too much concern with what applicants may know or even whether they were good students. Far more emphasis is placed on personality. Are they relatively sociable? Can they get along with others? Are they reasonably hardworking? Will they follow orders? Each company has its own idea of what good employee material is like, but few would recruit anyone primarily on the basis of grades or knowledge.

Since so much of the selection is based on personal connections and type of personality, there is a very strong tendency for given companies to recruit from given sources, namely the high schools or colleges their own staff attended. And this is reinforced by the tendency of given schools to pass their graduates along to given companies, which are graded so that some favored firms get the more promising grads. Applicants not from one of these schools will find it very difficult to get into the company concerned.

Even this process could be managed if not for the fact that students want to get into not only any company but a 'good' company. This usually means a large company, because it is more likely to succeed financially and be around long enough to keep them for a 'lifetime' stint. Also, in larger companies, there are more colleagues and a broader range of possible jobs. Even among the 'good' companies, there will be some which are more attractive than others as regards wages, working hours, prospects of promotion, status and so on. Students therefore carefully study the numerous magazines and newspaper articles that compare and grade companies. In so doing, they are inevitably affected by fads which, in earlier years, favored heavy industry, then electronics and 'high tech,' and increasingly the services (as more comfortable) and the bureaucracy (as more secure).

This has created another 'narrow gate' through which students push and shove to get into the best companies. Here again they work backwards. To get into a 'good' company, it is advantageous to graduate from a 'good' high school or college. The colleges which have traditionally been at the top of this pecking order are Todai, Kyodai, Hitotsubashi, Keio and Waseda, the ones whose alumni dominate many companies. In fact, as recently as 1986, these colleges provided 39 per cent of the executives of listed companies, 48 per cent of upper echelon national government officials and 44 per cent of the Diet members.[20] While there is a tendency for their share to decrease, this is a slow process, and they retain a decisive edge.

Not only is there a linkage between 'good' school and 'good' company, there is also a linkage between any college and a successful (actually, more profitable) career. This is reported by the Institute of Labor Administration. According to its surveys, college graduates aged 35 and over clearly outearned high school graduates who had been working longer. By the age of 55, college grads would have earned 17 per cent more than high school grads and 64 per cent more than junior high school grads.[21] They also get larger bonuses, better conditions, more prestige and so on. Moreover, as already noted, college grads become salaried workers for the most part and can be promoted to the top, while high school graduates are largely relegated to factories and attain much lower positions. This, as much as anything else, would explain any supposed 'love' of education.

This is only one way in which the employment system affects the educational system. While it may be regarded as an acceptable tradeoff, that could hardly be said of other aspects of this tight connection.

Most obviously, the recruitment process itself is disruptive. So that fresh recruits may join the company right after graduation, it is necessary to seek them out while they are still at school. To avoid unnecessary disruption, company personnel officers usually agree to wait until July 1st. However, in years when there are not enough graduates to go around, they tend to jump the gun, inviting prospective employees to 'seminars,' often in hotels or resorts, not so much to brief them as to keep them out of reach of their competitors. In years where there are not enough jobs to go around, the students go out and knock on company doors or try to pull strings. Thus, the actual process moves into June, May and even earlier. During that period, students show even less interest in studying than usual.

What is actually more serious is that, since students are recruited before graduation, their final marks simply do not count for much. Worse, their whole college education is of limited value. For they are recruited not on the basis of test results, the impression of their professors or any academic criterion. They are chosen for personality, an easygoing one being preferred to anything such as obsession with studies. They also find it advantageous to join clubs and get to know other students, since *kone* are so important. This all overshadows the educational process and further downgrades the concern for academic achievement.

There is another wrinkle to this which may at first seem odd. While science and technology are essential for Japan's economy, and receive much lip service, students do not tend to take science and technology courses overly much and those they take are often rather general. Nor have high school students been particularly eager to attend the special technical schools. This can be traced to a growing distaste for industrial work which directs more students to liberal arts. But it can also be attributed to the proclivity of even industrial companies to treat scientists and technicians as specialists, who will be relegated to specific chores, while liberal arts graduates and other generalists are placed on a track that is more likely to take them to the top.

Since, partly through their own fault, companies end up with fresh recruits whose education is rather faulty and incomplete, and certainly inadequate for the jobs they will be assigned, they have had to provide supplementary training. This normally consists of two components. First, recruits are taught their jobs, not once but many times during a career, as they shift from one post to another. They are also taught about the company, a form of indoctrination used to turn them into loyal companymen (and sometimes women). This training, it must be mentioned, is not a proper 'education' so most of the lacks and flaws will never be made up. And any college or school education is further devalued in the students' eyes.

The students are not fools. They have been studying all the angles and they realize that being a brilliant scholar will not help. As the personnel manager of a leading bank confided, he looks for students who spent their college days engaging in sports and like activities. 'They needn't have studied hard; most of what they learn in the classroom can't be applied in the real world anyway. We want students with a cheerful and healthy outlook. We believe our employee training program is second to none, and we'll provide all the education the recruits need.'[22] *Kone*, on the other hand, pays off. As a former Todai professor pointed out, 'at university, the human network you develop is much more important than the education you receive.'[23] And joining clubs or hanging out in coffee shops are good ways of making connections. Thus, the students' reactions in college are just as rational (or irrational) as they were in high school, even if they are completely different.

Educational Reform Some Day

There is no area in which the views of the foreign Japanophiles and those of the Japanese people diverge so greatly as for education. Japanese eduction is still highly praised abroad and the United States government, as well as others, have toyed with adopting one aspect or another of it. Until now it has remained a model, although finally some notes of criticism are creeping into the literature. In Japan, already in the 1970s, there was a groundswell of criticism as regards the academic drawbacks and, even more strongly, the degeneration of school life with bullying and suicides. The concerns gradually spread and intensified until it was broadly agreed that education reform must be a top priority.

Indeed, it is becoming harder to find anyone in Japan who openly supports the educational system. Certainly, those subjected to its rigors, namely untold millions of pupils in secondary and gradually primary schools are not happy. They are put under too much pressure to 'learn,' that is, to accumulate facts and pass exams. They have too little time to relax and just live. It is hard to conceive of any worse way of condemning Japanese education than becoming acutely depressed and, in some cases, committing suicide. Those in college, on the other hand, are relatively happy with their carefree existence, a compensation for earlier hard labor. But few of them think college is particularly useful or teaches them much.

Parents, on the whole, are dissatisfied. They are unhappy about the quality of the schools and teachers, the contents of the curricula, the enormous pressure their children are placed under to 'learn,' social abuses that arise from this pressure, and finally costs. This much is common knowledge. And it is reflected by the results of other series of polls. One by the *Yomiuri Shimbun* asked parents what they thought were the most serious problems about raising children in present society. Several answers could be given. Some 64 per cent picked competitive examinations, 41 per cent an educational system in which too much emphasis is placed on cramming, 34 per cent bullying at school, 33 per cent poor quality of teachers and 27 per cent high education costs.[24]

This last point must be elucidated. Primary and lower secondary education are free. Above that, and for private kindergartens, there are fees, and sometimes requests for 'voluntary' contributions. Then come the assorted frills, including school uniforms, materials, meals and so on. But that is minor. The big expense is private tutoring and attendance at cram courses.

They can run as much as ¥30,000 a month for years and years. By the 1990s, the totals had reached incredible levels. According to a Ministry of Education survey costs of tuition, school lunches and supplementary education were averaging ¥195,000 a year for kindergarten, ¥201,000 for primary school, ¥248,000 for middle school and ¥314,000 for high school.[25] And this is nothing compared to the cost of sending someone to a private college. What with tuition, educational material, and often room and board, the total could easily run into several million yen a year. The heaviest burden is for those in the countryside, who have to pay for living expenses in the city where the college is located. By the 1980s, such expenses were clearly too much for families with modest incomes who could not even afford to send their children to free state colleges.

Teachers at the primary and secondary levels are by now thoroughly disgruntled. First, they are upset about their own conditions, being put into classes with too many pupils, more and more of whom are harder to handle. They have to teach too many hours to prepare well and any chance of following individual pupils is out of the question. In addition, the schools are old and rundown, the equipment is limited and, sad to say, the salaries are not all that good given the cost of living. Secondly, they are disturbed by what is happening to their pupils. They do not want them driven into 'examination hell,' which distracts the children from normal classes and creates all sorts of problems from lack of attention to bad discipline. Finally, many teachers are more liberal, and politically further left, than most school administrators. They are also unionized, in one of the more aggressive unions, and the incessant quarrelling adds a further headache.

Increasing numbers of politicians are attuned to the problems and realize there is a genuine crisis. This includes many in the socialist ranks but also among centrists as well, including prominent LDP members. The feeling was sufficiently strong, already in the 1960s, that there was talk of a need for reform and some small steps were taken. Then, in 1984, Prime Minister Yasuhiro Nakasone called for fundamental reform and established a special council to propose measures. This reform was to be as momentous as those of Meiji days and the immediate postwar period, changing not only the structure, schedule and curricula but ending cramming and elitism, promoting patriotism and internationalism, and generating more rounded and creative personalities. Alas, the results were negligible and, when later prime ministers showed less interest or had less time, the movement petered out.[26]

Meanwhile, the business community has become the prime mover. Actually, it had been so earlier. It was a business committee that initially suggested the idea of reform to Nakasone, and businessmen were active in his council and subsequent bodies. Keidanren, Keizai Doyukai and countless business groups have adopted resolutions calling for education reform and stressing Japan's need for more creative workers and mangers better able to face future challenges and act internationally. There are also appeals from important figures in other fields insisting that it is high time for change, including many celebrities and Nobel Prize winners who roundly condemned the existing system.

Who is against reform? While not openly opposed, it is perfectly clear that the Ministry of Education itself is not overly eager for change. This is one of the most conservative, sometimes even reactionary, of the ministries. And it wants to run things as tightly as ever. Its bureaucrats could pass down regulations on nearly everything, from the size of classrooms or teachers' offices to the courses that would be taught and the textbooks that would be used. For material things, it resists change because they cost money which its budget can ill afford. On intellectual matters, many of its officials are narrow-minded or worse, refusing to allow new courses on new subjects and insisting on textbooks that praise Japan and overlook abuses, such as political corruption, treatment of minorities or behavior during the Pacific War. Progress in the colleges, even private ones, is stymied by senior professors, who do not want to learn anything new (or to be replaced by others who do) and control their faculty through patronage and favoritism.

Thus, despite repeated attempts, and a generally agreed need, amazingly little has been accomplished. The school structure was altered somewhat, 'free time' was introduced in small doses and total hours were reduced. But schools were not expanded, equipment was not upgraded, teaching was not improved and cramming actually intensified. The attempt to reduce pressure by introducing a national college entry examination had the opposite effect, merely adding another examination to the many candidates already faced. In short, the general atmosphere, rather than getting better, has taken a turn for the worse.

Why? There are many reasons for this. As always, sheer inertia cannot be overlooked. As in every other sector, it is hard to bring about change in Japan. It is difficult to reach a consensus. It is even harder to put through actual measures. Since the Ministry of Education resists change, and its bureaucrats must implement the measures, they can drag their heels. They are backed by more conservative politicians and businessmen. Moreover, while the business community wants creative and innovative employees, as already noted, it does not really reward this. Thus, until the management system changes, it is unlikely that the schools – so directly geared to providing raw recruits for companies that will train them – will change either.

More broadly, most Japanese are themselves the products of the old system. They are hardworking and disciplined; they are not innovative and creative. And it may just be a *tatemae* when they claim that they want their children to be different from themselves. They have reached their present station in life by plodding. Certainly, they do not want youngsters to suddenly rise and replace them. This is particularly true of those in the 'elite,' for the very reason that this is an elite based on academic credentials it would not want devalued. Moreover, it can only remain an elite by restricting entry through 'narrow gates' similar to those it passed.

Still, this does not explain everything. Surely, most parents do not want their children to suffer needlessly from the educational process. For them it is more than just a *tatemae* when they call for a more relaxed system. But, what can they do as long as that system remains? Children who do not take cram courses, who do not go through 'examination hell,' would fail to pass through the 'narrow gates.' They would thus be condemned to second-rate jobs in second-rate companies and a general second-rate status in society. They do not wish that on their children either. And many children, who would be happier with a more liberal system, are caught in the same dilemma and apparently most agree with their parents. It is better to undergo the necessary hardship now than endure a second-rate existence for the rest of their lives.

So it seems that any chance of reform is extremely remote and the Japanese will have to live many more years with an educational system they increasingly dislike. For, once it has been around long enough, it affects so many people and so many facets of their lives that it is terribly hard to throw off. That might be borne in mind by ordinary foreigners, if not the 'experts' who continue praising Japanese education and urging that it be emulated and copied abroad. It may prove far easier to transplant today than to uproot tomorrow.

4

The State

(Coming Apart At The Seams)

Outsiders who study the Japanese state usually do a rather poor job of understanding it. This is a hard state, of that they are certain. And thus they immediately try to find some figure who 'runs the place,' as in not only the West but most of the developing countries and other parts of Asia. This eventually turns out to be an impossible task, for the politicians, where they first look for the locus of power, don't seem to have much. Only then do they discover that the bureaucrats, and somewhat later, if they are smart, the businessmen are also part of any ruling class. However, the relations between these three components, who does what and who takes the lead, continue to escape most.

That is why, rather than merely assuming that the Japanese state is like the rest, governed by leaders who are either elected by the people or impose themselves, it is better to consider the various groups that actually run Japan, the politicians, bureaucrats and businessmen, known as the 'iron triangle.' During this exercise, again, rather than assume that they do the same things as elsewhere – politicians legislate, bureaucrats implement, businessmen lobby – it is better to examine just what they do do. That exercise is not an easy one and it is very hard to sum up in 40 pages as is done here. Readers might therefore consult an earlier, but still quite useful analysis of 400 pages in *Politics, The Japanese Way*.[1]

Once having figured out who does what, there is still the tricky question of who is on top. Absolute answers are lacking or simply silly. It is far better to do as the Japanese and see how power is shared in various ways between various groups. In defining the power-sharing arrangement, the Japanese often refer to the game of *jan-ken-poh* (scissors, paper, stone) in which the winner constantly varies. This is a game we must play as well. In so doing, we will have to look at one last actor, the Japanese people. While supposedly decisive in any democracy, in Japanese-style democracy the people have been little more than passive onlookers most of the time.

Aside from the question of who runs Japan, there is also the matter of how well they do it. It is assumed by many analysts that the Japanese state is strong, efficient and, on the whole, successful. Certainly, in prewar days, the state was exceptionally strong and quite often ruthlessly efficient, although what it did was not always for the good. The postwar state is considerably looser and weaker, but until recently few would have accused it of being ineffectual. Now that particular illusion is harder to nourish, and it is becoming painfully evident that the state has a lot of difficulty in doing rather ordinary things and sometimes just cannot accomplish anything.

Judged by most objective criteria, this system does not have much to commend itself, certainly not in the eyes of the Japanese. But foreign observers, especially the apologists, found many causes for praise. Indeed, former American ambassador to Tokyo Edwin O. Reischauer and Harvard professor Ezra Vogel regarded Japanese-style democracy as, in some ways, superior to that of the United States. And the ruling Liberal Democratic Party was commended for inducing stability. Now, of course, that the LDP has collapsed and government as such is shaky, these statements sound particularly stale. Still, just to show what critics of Japanese politics were up against, it does not hurt to quote one of the more eminent authorities, Gerald Curtis of Columbia University, in his highly acclaimed if questionable book, *The Japanese Way of Politics*.

> The truth is that Japan, like the United States, has woven the threads of democratic political life – civil liberties, open elections, competitive politics, and responsible government – into the fabric of the nation's social structure to create a stable political system that echoes universal values and behavior while at the same time being utterly unique. And that is what is significant about the Japanese way of politics.[2]

Politicians Without Policies

On few subjects do the views of foreign admirers and those of
ordinary Japanese diverge as much as on the politicians. The
foreigners, who could admire them from a distance, greeted
each new prime minister (and there were many) with words
of praise, Tanaka for his dynamism, Suzuki for his love of harmony, Nakasone for his leadership ability, Miki for his high-
minded approach. Even Takeshita could be welcomed as 'a
consummate backroom politician' and 'prodigious raiser and
dispenser of political funds.'[3] The Liberal Democratic Party
was credited with multiple achievements of domestic and foreign policy, in particular its contribution to Japan's economic
success.

The Japanese, who had the slight disadvantage of actually
living with, or rather under, these politicians and parties often
had strikingly different opinions. They tended to regard politicians in general as relatively untrustworthy, opportunistic and,
sometimes, dishonest. They were lumped with other lowlife and
criminal elements in popular imagery and spoke a language
not far removed from that of the gangsters. When repeated
evidence of corruption mounted, the Japanese felt cheated, all
the more so in that they did not credit the LDP or the other
parties with very great contributions to the national well-being.
Why? A look at how politicians have performed over the past
few decades should provide more than enough explanations.

First, while there have been imposing and enterprising politicians in Japan's history, most of them are long since gone. In
Meiji days, many politicians were pathbreakers and some were
prophets, even if they were often conservative or elitist. But, in
the early 20th century, they were replaced by weaker, more
self-seeking types who were eventually cast aside by the militarists. Again, after the Pacific War, tough and ambitious politicians took over. They were a mixed batch, some reactionary,
remnants of the wartime regime, who were opposed by others
who had suffered under the regime, liberals, socialists and
communists. Thus, during the first postwar decades there were
real politicians, and real parties, with policies and programs
for which they fought, and this meant not only debates in the
Diet but pitched battles in the streets.

But that is all past history. Ever since the Japanese decided that the economy came first, and political quarrels should be toned down so as not to get in the way, politicians have tended not to have policies and parties not to have programs. For several decades already politicians have been exceedingly vague, aside from any ritualistic formulas, as to where they stood on the major issues of the day. All one knew was very roughly where their party was positioned, the Liberal Democrats to the right, Komeito sort of center, the Socialists a bit further left and the Communists on the far end. As they drove about in their loud-speaker vans, candidates simply shouted 'vote for me, my name is. . . .'

As the older politicians, those who had had policies once upon a time, stepped down they were succeeded by others who regarded politics as little more than a trade in most cases. In the conservative camp, this was often the assistants and secretaries of the older politicians, although some elite bureaucrats and the odd businessman were coopted. For the socialists, this was largely trade union officials and, for the communists, party functionaries. But there was soon a large and expanding contingent of *nisei giin* or second (and eventually third) generation Diet members. These included sons, wives or other relatives who inherited the constituency. By the early 1990s, they already accounted for over a third of the LDP members in the lower house and a fifth in the upper house. Exceedingly few outsiders broke into the charmed circle because of ability or achievements, let alone promising policies or challenging goals. Those promoting an ideology or striving for a cause were even rarer.

That does not seem to matter, for the principal occupations of politicians have little or nothing to do with policies. While they have tasks to accomplish at both the central and local level, it is clear that 'village politics' comes first. They have to maintain close, even personal contact, with their constituents, which is done through attendance at weddings, funerals, parties and the like. To consolidate this backing, they have to run a *koenkai* or support organization which also channels aid to the constituents, helping them with petty chores like getting children into college, finding a job, evading fines and penalties or obtaining building licenses and other permits. At a higher level, whenever possible, politicians must bring back government-funded projects, such as schools, highways or social centers.

Pork-barrel politics leave Diet members with little time for politics of a higher order. Indeed, they do not even have time for what is elsewhere the primary task of parliamentarians, drafting and adopting legislation. Nor do they have the expertise. Personally, most have rather limited knowledge of any specialized field and they cannot afford to pay enough advisors to study even whatever legislation they must vote on. Some, who have sufficient seniority, join the so-called 'tribes' (*zoku*) which assume some role in the legislative process, but more to amend and adjust legislation than to draft it. It was claimed by kindly (foreign) academics that by the late 1980s the LDP was really shaping bills and laws, but only at the margin in most instances. Even for such vital items as tax policy, it was the bureaucrats who provided the bulk of the input.[4]

Of course, the politicians are not entirely out of the circuit. Diet members do attend meetings, make speeches and cast votes. Some even call for amendments. But much of this is a charade. The bills are drawn up without them by bureaucrats in the relevant ministries and the ministers are then briefed. Indeed, bureaucrats usually have to answer any questions put to them and explain why amendments are not desirable.[5] Despite the exalted title, ministers have little authority in their respective ministries, which for all practical purposes are run by the bureaucrats who agree upon a vice-minister who is really in charge and keeps the minister at bay. Since most ministers are only in office for one or two years, they could not possibly know what is going on, let alone impose their will.

As for the prime minister, it is hard to determine just what contribution he makes to governing. In most cases, he could not dominate or move the whole bureaucracy any more than his ministers could control their ministries. The mass of legislation is presented to him, not entirely on a take it or leave it basis, but certainly worked out in the smallest details with little need of further input. Thus, most prime ministers simply announced some grand scheme, 'income doubling,' the 'rebuilding of the archipelago,' making Japan a nation of 'quality of life,' and stayed out their normally tumultuous – and short – terms trying to get by from day to day. The only exception was Yasuhiro Nakasone who was prime minister for nearly five years in the early 1980s. He came with a bevy of policies, including major reforms, and sought to leave his stamp on the period. Yet, he proved the rule, for hardly and of his proposals were ever put into effect and then in a very attenuated manner.

Even without legislating, politicians keep busy in normal times. But the demands are infinitely greater during electoral periods. Then it is necessary to rev up the machinery of local contacts. Politicians may have to attend a wedding a week, a funeral a day and several parties every evening to mix with the voters. They must organize dozens of fund raising events and multiply their speaking appearances, at which more is said of what has been given to the constituency and might be gained in the future than irrelevancies like policies and platform. All that matters is that the politician be reelected. For, under the Japanese system, the more often one is returned the more one can pull out of the pork barrel.

Finally, politicians need money. This is called *kaban* after the briefcase used to carry it. It is the third of the three *ban* that are needed to do well in politics. The other two are *jiban* (supporters' networks) and *kanban* (reputation), this latter growing with the length of time served and what that implies in material rewards. The money is required, first, just to service the constituency. For each party, a politician is expected to bring a gift of at least ¥30,000 and ¥50,000 for each wedding and ¥90,000 for each funeral. This alone could add up to ¥200–300 million a year or many times the annual salary. The cost of an election could easily run into half a billion yen or more. And it is estimated that together Japan's parties and politicians rake in ¥300 billion a year.[6]

This endless quest for money, lots of money, placed politicians in serious temptation. Sums this large could not possibly be obtained through normal fund-raising campaigns or contributions from ordinary constituents and other legitimate sources. They had to come from somewhere else. The main source quickly became donations from business circles. Some of it was channeled, legally, given the very loose controls, from business organizations. It was collected more or less anonymously and passed on to the parties which distributed sums among their members. But even larger amounts passed between individual companies and individual politicians, often in return for favors. The overall amounts that changed hands were fantastic. Just how fantastic was realized when the police broke into the office of a leading politician (Shin Kanemaru) and discovered hundreds of pounds of gold and $30–50 million in cash and bonds.[7]

'Money politics' (*kinken-seiji*), namely the need for money, the availability of money, and the proclivity for private arrangements between politicians and businessmen, inevitably resulted in corruption.[8] This could happen anywhere. But, in Japan, it was particularly rife and tended to grow with the years, becoming almost obscene by the early 1990s. There were scandals even in the 1950s and 1960s. A temporary high point came with the rise of Kakuei Tanaka, a politician and businessman, who used his inside knowledge for the benefit of his companies and then accepted huge bribes in the Lockheed affair. There was no end to the scandals. One among many, the Recruit scandal, was fateful because it implicated two other prime ministers, Noboru Takeshita and Kiichi Miyazawa, and cast doubt on a third, Yasuhiro Nakasone. Nakasone and Takeshita, as well as Sousuke Uno, were beneficiaries of largesse in the Sagawa Kyubin scandal. The 'bubble economy' and the bursting of the 'bubble' immersed the country in real estate and financial scandals while during the whole postwar period construction companies kept paying off politicians for access to public works contracts.

These various corruption scandals were notorious for various reasons. First, they involved enormous sums of money channeled by businessmen to specific politicians. Second, and this was even more worrisome, the numbers of politicians implicated could run into the dozens and even over a hundred on occasion. And they included not only the ruling party but all opposition parties aside from the Communists. These were not minor or marginal figures by any means since, as noted, faction heads and prime ministers got caught. Indeed, it often appeared that in certain sectors payoffs to politicians were part of the standard practices while companies wanting special favors had to make special contributions. No wonder politicians were increasingly regarded as corrupt and corruption itself was regarded as part of the political system to the extent that it was called 'institutional.'

If politicians were not what one normally thinks of on hearing that term, the parties – in particular, the long-term ruling Liberal Democratic Party – were not what is normally understood as parties either. Obviously, not having much in the way of policies, they did not consist of politicians and their supporters united to achieve certain clearly, or even loosely, defined goals. Rather, membership covered a very broad spectrum, from outright reactionary to fairly liberal. The only common denominator seemed to be the urge to get elected and share the spoils. Nor did the LDP have what might be regarded as a leader, even admitting that he could be challenged and replaced. Instead, there were a number of factions which waxed and waned but maintained a degree of cohesion because, as part of the ruling party, they could more readily win elections and distribute largesse.

These factions were more coherent units than the party itself, although they too often consisted of sub-factions whose heads tried to dominate the faction. They were bound together not by policy, as they also had a very, if not quite as wide spread of membership, so much as by personal attachment to the faction head. This attachment grew out of mutual support and favors as well as financing. There was no question but that size reflected the ability of the head to collect and distribute money, with Tanaka, Takeshita and Kanemaru (whether as real or 'shadow' prime minister) doing infinitely better than cleaner types like Takeo Miki and Toshiki Kaifu or someone with policies like Nakasone. This was crucial, for most decisions within the LDP were influenced by the size of the factions on each side, whether informally or (more rarely) through an actual vote.

Among other things, it was the factions which decided who should be prime minister. To some extent, this grew out of a more or less orderly wait, in which senior politicians became prime minister before their juniors, until Tanaka grabbed power through the weight of numbers and money. Heads of small factions could only become prime minister if the larger factions could not agree and needed a time-server or a 'clean' figurehead. The choice was usually made solely by the Diet members, although occasionally through votes of the party membership (itself well correlated with faction size). The people, namely the Japanese electorate, had no say in the choice of the LDP candidate, who always won. Moreover, the LDP usually took its decision *after* an election so the people could not even ratify the choice.

This emphasis on the Liberal Democratic Party is justified

because it was the party in power for nearly the whole postwar period. Reference is made to 38 years of rule. But it was really longer, for before the LDP the ruling parties were mainly the Liberal and the Democratic parties which merged to form it in 1955. And, as we shall see, it has not entirely relinquished power even now. Nor should criticism of the LDP be construed as praise of the other parties. They were as much to blame in falling to provide a viable alternative and acquiescing, indeed, sometimes colluding in its continued rule.

Moreover, the opposition parties resembled it in some ways. probably too many. There was a notable lack of policies in Komeito and the Socialists' programs were often so unrealistic as to be meaningless. As for the Communists, they were wedded to dogmas that had lost their appeal long ago. Opposition politicians, just like those in the LDP, were exceedingly eager to be reelected, although they stood no chance of becoming ministers. Perhaps for this reason, they were a bit cleaner. There was no point in bribing them much, although they did obtain some money from big business and the occasional backhander. Even though they were smaller, there was incessant rivalry in Komeito, a split in the Socialists to create the Japan Socialist Party (later renamed the Social Democratic Party of Japan) and the Democratic Socialist Party, and only monolithic control in the Japan Communist Party, which was actually more sinister.

This was the situation in the early 1990s. The LDP was increasingly fragmented and discredited while the other parties, having achieved nothing by opposing its position, gradually aligned theirs to the center. It was felt that the LDP could rule for ever, a prediction made all too often, by joining with Komeito, or the DSP, or some independents. So, there was nothing much the people could do until, unexpectedly, something happened. Within the LDP, there was a quarrel over some of the things that really counted, how elections would be held and how financial contributions would be regulated. This could doubtless have been resolved. But not the question of who should run the party. One of the leading faction heads, Ichiro Ozawa, in order to bring his team to power, broke away and formed a new party that went into opposition against the LDP.

In July 1993, for the first time in decades, the Japanese electorate had a genuine choice. And it voted out the LDP – sort of. For the new government was formed by a collection of ex-LDP members that called itself Kaishin (Japan Renewal Party). But it could just as well have been named LDP-B, since it differed only minimally from the LDP rump, being perhaps more reform-minded. Kaishin could only hold power in a coalition with Komeito, a coalition that proved fragile. When it collapsed, it was replaced in June 1994 by the LDP-A, this time allied with the Socialists under Tomiichi Murayama, an odd combination in general but particularly so since the LDP-A was the more conservative wing and Murayama was a relative leftist. For the first time in half-a-century a Socialist became prime minister, although it was clear that the conservatives dominated the cabinet.

By now it was perfectly obvious that policies meant little and power much in the new order. This disillusioned the Japanese people even more with politics and actually disgusted some politicians. Several LDP stalwarts, including prominent figures, broke away rather than cooperate with the traditional enemy. As the SDPJ jettisoned one postwar plank after the other, the Socialists' ranks also splintered and eventually the party disbanded, leaving behind just another centrist grouping. To increase its following, and boost its finances, the LDP-B joined with Komeito to form Shinshinto (New Frontier Party). Meanwhile, other parties emerged, split or realigned and the politicians were soon back to their old antics.

Then, in 1995, the electorate showed that it was not only tired of the LDP and the other old parties (whether renamed or not), and in local elections systematically voted out many old-line politicians and voted in anyone who could claim to be an outsider and have had nothing to do with politics. This included all sorts of celebrities, including many television personalities, as well as some academics and a number of cranks. Most striking was the choice of a former comedy actor as mayor of Tokyo and a former stand-up comic as mayor of Osaka.

By now, Japan was being governed by shifting coalitions of parties which continued realigning and the old stability was entirely gone. So were many of the erstwhile politicians, replaced by amateurs with little political experience and sometimes little taste for politics. Japan was stuck with a series of governments that could hardly govern and sometimes could not even rubber-stamp needed legislation. Never mind, the Japanapologists and hardened supporters of things Japanese discovered a silver lining. Indeed, it was all for the best to judge by some statements. The *Financial Times*, which should certainly have known better, proudly proclaimed in its lead article:

> A new generation has taken over, without waiting until it has passed what in other countries would be retirement age. A single-party system has been replaced by a multi-party one. From now on politicians and the electorate will both know that the latter can turn the former out of office. Japanese democracy has come of age.[9]

Although it would be lovely for Japan to solve its political problems so easily, it would be hasty to conclude that democracy has come of age, or more exactly, finally reached Japan and that now things will work out for the best, with a two-party system and alternation between parties, as others forecast. In a system known for factionalism, multiple parties are more likely. And it is quite possible that several might devise an arrangement whereby they monopolize power by shifting periodically from one to another, much as the LDP's factions once did. As for the politicians, there is no more reason to believe that the new amateurs will be any better at defining policies and legislating than the old professionals. Nor could any of them get far without the three *ban*, especially money.

Bureaucrats Who Govern

Unlike the politicians, who only retain a limited appeal even for Japanapologists nowadays, the bureaucrats have continued to reap great acclaim from foreign academics and sundry Japan-watchers. They are complimented for covering up the failings of the politicians and running the state whenever necessary. But that is still faint praise. Many feel that the bureaucrats do a vastly superior job and should be allowed to encroach on the politicians' turf. That was expressed most clearly by Ezra Vogel although, without asking them, he put the words in the mouths of the Japanese people.

The public may have no particular respect for the politician who enunciates the conclusion in a policy speech, but it knows that the conclusion has been carefully prepared by the best minds of the country. For most of the public, the outcome appears not as something a narrow group of bureaucrats decided but something 'we Japanese' decided.[10]

Nowhere is this role more highly extolled than in the economic sector, where several ministries and key bureaucrats have been credited with the postwar economic recovery that is often termed a 'miracle.' This view was expressed most assiduously by Chalmers Johnson in his book on MITI, giving the bureaucrats more than their share of the credit for boosting growth.[11] Yet, by the 1970s (well before his book was published), that phase had clearly wound down and growth could best be attributed to dynamic companies and entrepreneurs. Still, showing amazing perseverance, he stuck to his intellectual constructs even when they were being demolished by facts and realities, to produce another book which claimed: 'Japan's economic system is one in which public service is highly evaluated; state bureaucracy attracts the best, young minds; and "economic guidance" by the state is both accepted and ubiquitous.'[12] But Johnson is hardly alone. Similar views have been expressed by other bureaucratophiles (for Japan, not their own country) like the economist Wassily Leontief. 'In contrast to most other countries, Japan possesses an excellent, highly trained and incorruptible civil service that plays a very important – not to say exemplary – role in securing for Japan the position of the most successful capitalist country.'[13]

In order to evaluate the correctness of such claims, it is necessary to look more closely at just what the bureaucrats have accomplished. This can best be done by reviewing some of the key ministries, especially those related to economics. This helps us see how efficient, effective and successful they have been.[14]

Even among the bureaucratophiles, the officials of the Ministry of Finance (MOF) are regarded as the 'elite of the elite.' While they can make mistakes, their track record is supposedly superior not only to their foreign counterparts but also other Japanese ministries. In the early postwar decades, there is no doubt that MOF did stabilize the currency (with the help of the

Occupation authorities), collect taxes and direct substantial funds toward productive investments. Some of this money was channeled through state banks, the rest was generated by private sector banks it supervised. Cheap loans made it far easier for companies to invest in factories and equipment and restore old or launch new industries. Alas, since so much money was channeled toward companies, much less remained for individuals who paid much higher rates (while getting a mediocre return on their savings). The consumers were also short-changed by the insurance companies and stock brokerages which were likewise protected by MOF.

More recently, however, the track record has been less commendable. MOF bureaucrats were initially very proud that Japan had no domestic debt to speak of. But that was mainly due to rapid economic growth and natural increases in tax revenue. By the 1970s, with a new relapse in the 1990s, Japan's indebtedness was larger than many other countries and a huge share of its annual budget, nearly a quarter, went into debt servicing. Inflation was also low, or at least appeared low due to the odd way it was calculated, during most of the period except for the oil crisis of the 1960s. Then, in the late 1980s, there was an extraordinary bloating of assets during what became known as the 'bubble economy,' an aberration the financocrats did more to stimulate than prevent, and which saddled the banks and other financial institutions with huge debts when the 'bubble' burst.[15]

The Ministry of International Trade and Industry (MITI) became world famous for its industrial policy, otherwise known as 'targeting.' It apparently picked one sector after the other, adopted programs to accelerate growth, and created one winner after the other. MITI's biggest backer was Chalmers Johnson, author of *MITI and the Japanese Miracle*. Unfortunately, his book focused mainly on the 1950s and 1960s, when MITI's role was largely positive. It did help promote steelmaking, nonferrous metals, chemicals and petrochemicals, computers, semiconductors and other sectors. Alas, by the 1970s, it was clearly losing its touch. During the 1980s, it had rather few successes and some notable failures such as the Fifth Generation Computer and High Definition TV. And, by the 1990s, its impact was as often negative as positive.[16]

Put in context, even MITI's early successes look less 'miraculous.' For one thing, other ministries promoted other sectors on their own, sharing its glory, such as the Ministry of Transport for shipbuilding and the Ministry of Health for pharmaceuticals. Meanwhile, private companies were also forging their own industries with little help from MITI, such as automobiles, electronics and robotics. More embarrassing, what once looked like successes turned out to be failures. MITI and the others not only promoted; sometimes they overpromoted. The economy was stuck with bloated steel, metals, petrochemicals, shipbuilding and other sectors which had to scrap facilities built at great cost and soon superfluous.

For a while, the Economic Planning Agency (EPA) sported a glowing halo. It could do no wrong. It regularly topped its own ambitious targets. When its first plan forecast 4.9 per cent growth, 8.8 per cent was achieved; when the target was raised to 6.5 per cent, 9.7 per cent was reached; aiming even higher, at 7.8 per cent, it hit 10 per cent growth. Surely this was a MIRACLE. But it was a short-lived one, that ceased in the 1980s. Then, successive economic plans brought in 5.1 per cent instead of the promised 10.6 per cent, 3.5 per cent instead of 9.4 per cent and 4.5 per cent instead of 6 per cent. The only recent cases of exceeding targets were achieved in the late 1980s and were spurious, since this was fake growth due to the economic 'bubble.'

The Ministry of Agriculture (MOA) never shared the enviable reputation of the other economic ministries. True, it did restore the agricultural sector and help farmers modernize. But it was soon spending more than could possibly be justified, targeting crop after crop, even though the soil or climate was not suitable, failing to cut back on rice production even as consumption fell, and maintaining a huge bureaucracy to service a dwindling share of the population. Due to its enormous subsidies it was undermining the budget and, since imports were sold at local prices, the cost of food was exorbitant.

This should certainly raise doubts as to how great a contribution the bureaucrats made to the Japanese economy. In the 1950s and 1960s, they were definitely useful, if not necessarily indispensable. In the 1970s, they could still help out on occasion. By the 1980s, their contribution was marginal at best, and they were constantly getting in the way. By the 1990s, there were endless complaints of red tape and regulations from businessmen who were doing their best to break free of the bureaucracy. In Japan, at least, the bureaucrats had ceased being economic heroes and become economic villains.

More worrying, there is cause to question the success even of the earlier period. For, while creating a vigorous economy, the bureaucrats were also fashioning an extremely high-cost economy. Virtually everything in Japan cost more than abroad: electricity, gasoline, telephone calls, paper, chemicals, steel, wood, even automobiles and electronics. Food was terribly expensive and housing, the largest item in any family budget, cost three or four times more than something much nicer in other advanced countries. This was not an accident, it was due to bureaucratic meddling in the economy. It derived directly from subsidies and support, regulations and red tape, promotion of infant industries and protection of ailing ones. This was a big price to pay for economic 'success.'

More broadly, due to bureaucratic intervention, the economy was distorted in various ways. The bureaucrats gave priority to production over consumption, to heavy industry over light industry and manufacturing over services. There is no doubt that big companies or groups (*keiretsu*) got preference over small ones and old-established companies over young, innovative ones. As for the people, they were exposed to the producers' whims, without proper product liability laws to protect them from injury and malfunction or environmental regulations to protect them from pollution. Consumers were also gouged on price by cartels and collusion among distributors. Internationally, the economy was definitely export-oriented, even after Japan joined GATT and promised to open its market, with imports first blocked by tariffs and then non-tariff barriers. This limited choice and boosted prices while angering Japan's trade partners. The only solution, and certainly not the best, was steady appreciation of the yen which periodically triggered an *endaka* or heavy yen crisis.

True, by the mid-1990s, Japan was the world's richest country with nearly ¥7,000 trillion in assets. But this was meaningless when one considered that virtually all these assets were evaluated at bloated prices, two, five, ten times as high as elsewhere. Its workers were the best paid in the world, with an income of $34,000 a year. But this was equally meaningless when everything they bought with that money cost more than elsewhere. If you add quality of life, aspects like leisure and vacations, cultural and spiritual pursuits, privacy and 'happiness,' they were hardly to be envied. This forced one to question not only the quality of economic management but the quality of the economy itself and wonder how anyone could call Japan 'the most successful capitalist country.'

The other, non-economic ministries never enjoyed the same prestige, nor were they and their projects financed as generously. The school system was unimpressive physically, with shabby schools and facilities, overcrowded classrooms with impossible teacher-pupil ratios and inadequate sports and recreation facilities. The Ministry of Health and Welfare (MOHW) did all right under the first heading, begetting countless hospitals and clinics. But it allowed the doctors to take advantage of their position, becoming rich both on their medical practice and the vast amount of medicine they dispensed, since they tended to overprescribe. The welfare side was short of funds and facilities, and the poor could expect little support while old folks who had worked all their lives were worried about what they would live off. The Environmental Agency, with scant powers and even less ambition, was systematically stymied by MITI and its efforts to temper economic growth with environmental protection were tame.

Whatever complaints can be made in all these areas, they are nothing compared to the harsh criticism directed at the bureaucracy after the terrible Kobe earthquake in January 1995. Some 6,279 people died, many of them unnecessarily because, in their moment of need, help only came slowly and inadequately. Officials were notified late, the defense forces arrived with much delay and poorly equipped, there were not enough medical personnel and yet, at first, foreign assistance was turned back. Despite the knowledge that much of Japan is in a seismic zone, little had been done in preparation. Meanwhile, the earthquake specialists were refining their methods for predicting tremors, an impossible task, rather than working on practical measures to implement *after* an earthquake.

This summary reveals another major drawback of Japan's bureaucracy, namely that it is skewed toward old tasks rather than new challenges and certainly not in a position to face the 21st century. MOF, MITI, EPA and MOA all have huge staffs. Indeed, by now, there are far more personnel than are needed to handle the tasks they have so they are shopping around for new ones. But Japan no longer needs bureaucrats to direct funds, fosters industries and tell everyone what to do and how. These old ministries should rather be shorne of their powers and their staffing cut back. The money and personnel saved could then be directed toward other sectors where the needs have grown, and continue growing, like education, environment and welfare.

But that is unlikely to happen due to shortcomings in the bureaucrats themselves. It was claimed that the Japanese bureaucrats are uncommonly efficient. Observers point to the career officials, who have to pass stiff tests, and many of whom graduate not only from Tokyo University but its law department. However, we have already seen that Japanese universities in general are of rather poor quality, including Todai. And what good is a grounding in law (a superficial one at that, for this is not a true law school) for bureaucrats who will have to deal with finance, economic development, agriculture, health and welfare, or any of the practical fields attributed to their ministries? Moreover, it is only a tiny minority of bureaucrats who are in the 'elite,' the rest are quite ordinary souls.

It is just possible that the elite bureaucrats are high-minded and dedicated, clever and competent, but they are also quite visibly lacking in imagination and innovativeness, two characteristics that are ever more desirable. This was pointed out in a recent exposé written by an insider of the Ministry of Health and Welfare, Masao Miyamoto. The book's title, *Straitjacket Society*, already conveys the message that Japanese bureaucracies are ruled by three great principles: don't be late, don't take time off, and don't initiate anything new. While it is unlikely that an official will get credit for any positive initiatives, it is certain that he will receive demerits for any mistakes, so it is safest to stick to precedent and conform.[17] At least career bureaucrats are fairly capable and diligent. At lower levels, many are just pen-pushers and time-servers, more interested in a secure job and good pension, regular hours and not too much responsibility as long as they do their job.

As for being patriotic, that was probably a *tatemae* even in Meiji days and just after the war. While what they do is supposedly undertaken for the good of the people, the people are never consulted properly and orders are passed down by the authorities almost as in olden days. Meanwhile, the bureaucrats tend to put their ministry's interests ahead of the national interest, the old problem of *shoeki* versus *kokueki*. And they find it hard to cooperate with other ministries and, indeed, sometimes even with other officials in their own ministry. The primary urge is to defend, and if possible extend, their prerogatives, hardly a top priority for Japan today.

Fortunately, most bureaucrats are reasonably honest, at least in the sense of eschewing bribes. But they rarely refuse lavish gifts, sumptuous meals and entertainment, a round of golf or a free trip abroad. And many are overly interested in certain special perks. Admittedly, career bureaucrats do not earn as much as their counterparts in the business world, and they sometimes put in long hours, but they can retire young and take a second job. This is particularly attractive for high officials, who manage to parachute into top jobs in top companies through the practice of *amakudari* or 'descent from heaven.' Little is left to chance, and the bureaucrats know well before retirement where they will end up, MOF-men going to banks, insurances and brokerages, MITI-men to manufacturers, MOHW-men to pharmaceutical firms and so on. There, they are rewarded for services rendered in the past and the strings they can still pull with colleagues in the ministry. This is not corruption, not in the sense of getting money for a specific act, but it is a form of delayed payment that is awfully close to it.

This is already enough to demolish the idea that Japanese bureaucrats are exceptionally capable, efficient or dedicated beings who managed to rebuild the country and economy and can continue leading Japan into the future. But we are left with a lesser argument, almost an excuse, that it is necessary to have bureaucrats fill the gaps left by the politicians. Perhaps they are necessary, but they are not sufficient, for the key function of maintaining contact with the general public is lacking. Japanese bureaucrats tend to regard themselves as an elite, they still feel they are superior not only to ordinary Japanese but even to politicians and businessmen, and they like to order or manipulate others. Some are quite vain or arrogant. Thus, they are still referred to as bureaucrats (*kanryo*) and not civil servants. No wonder they have failed at the tasks that concern ordinary people most at present, like welfare, living conditions and environment.

There is one other problem, although I am almost embarrassed to bring it up since such luminaries as Reischauer, Vogel, Curtis and others pass over it in silence. This is simply not democracy! The bureaucrats are not elected by the people and they cannot be removed by the people. This may just be an old-fashioned quibble of mine, so it can be overlooked by those who know better. But even the finest bureaucrats cannot function on their own. They must be directed and controlled by the people's representatives, namely the politicians, and where possible, directly accountable to the people.

Indeed, whatever the Japanapologists may claim, the Japanese on the whole are not very satisfied with the bureaucracy and the dissatisfaction has been growing over the years. Even before the Kobe earthquake, numerous citizens had gripes and complaints, according to one poll as many as 69 per cent of them.[18] They did not often follow through since, in practice, there was not much an ordinary citizen could do against an official. Even a leading politician like Ichiro Ozawa could complain: 'Our politics does not belong to the political parties, which is to say the people. Rather . . . the bureaucracy . . . is the government.'[19] And Naohiro Amaya, an insightful critic, himself a former MITI bureaucrat, could warn: 'The bureaucracy is now more powerful than the government, with bureaucrats holed up in their ministerial fortresses, drunk on ministerial nationalism and following a course aimed at preserving their power at all costs. These fortresses must be demolished.'[20]

For the various reasons sketched above, and many more, the politicians have repeatedly tried to cut the bureaucracy down to size, or at least contain it. This was done with growing support from business circles and tacit approval of the public at large. After several minor attempts, this developed into a broad movement for 'administrative reform' (*gyosei kaikaku*). A high-level commission was established in 1981 and Prime Minister Suzuki declared that he would 'stake his political life' on its success. But nothing was accomplished by the time he was replaced by Yasuhiro Nakasone, an activist and even more aggressive proponent of administrative reform. Several state companies were, indeed, privatized but little was done to rationalize the bureaucracy per se. All other attempts to the present have been failures.

More recently, the emphasis has shifted to deregulation (*kisei kanwa*). In 1993, Japan had some 1,400 regulations which had to be obeyed by citizens and companies. Some were necessary for health, safety and environmental reasons. Others were just bothersome, like rules making it hard to move a bus stop, sell a used television set or build a house. In some cases, the rules made it more complicated to do business, like those limiting the activities of large supermarkets, or kept prices unnecessarily high, like the restrictions on beer brewing or preventing lower taxi or gasoline prices. Many also inhibited imports, thereby annoying Japan's trade partners as well. But it has been extremely difficult to eliminate much of the red tape and often, after one regulation was removed, it was replaced by another or more subtle (if unwritten) 'administrative guidance.'

If so little could be done under the Liberal Democratic Party, when it was one party and had been in power for decades, when its members at least knew something about running a government and how the ministries worked, there is far less hope now. For governments and ministers replace one another too often, too many inexperienced politicians are expected to cope with problems they know little about, and they cannot even turn to genuine political parties for support. Business circles are more adamant than ever on the need but, without the politicians, there is little they can do. And the ordinary people are not about to turn out the bureaucrats. This makes many Japanese glum. They never particularly liked the bureaucracy although they were willing to tolerate it when it accomplished something of value just after the war. Now they want to cut it down to size, but they just can't.

This obviously makes nonsense of comments by foreign friends, especially academics and journalists, but they seem incapable of grasping the situation. Chalmers Johnson still insists the bureaucrats are brilliant, respected and successful. The *Financial Times* editorialist asks: 'How is it, in a country where the quality of the bureaucracy is unrivalled, that banking supervision can have failed so dismally.' He gives every possible answer (most of them lame excuses) except that, in fact, it is not so great. And Leontief fires off an irate letter to the editor of a Japanese newspaper warning that the 'destruction of the traditional independence of its excellent civil servants would most likely have a negative effect on the long-term performance of the Japanese economy.'[21]

Businessmen Take The Lead

Most political scientists in the West (and elsewhere) assume that Japanese governance results from varying combinations of politicians and bureaucrats, as in most other places. If the business community comes into this, it is largely, as elsewhere, in lobbying for its interests. There is also the unsavory matter of obtaining special favors through bribery. But it eludes them that the businessmen should be full-fledged partners in government, let alone on occasion senior partners.[22] This stems from a faulty reading of the Japanese situation.

Such errors are all the less forgivable when it is so obvious that the Japanese themselves think of business, and in particular big business, as part of the political system, one of the three in the game of *jan-ken-poh*. Indeed, public opinion polls and questioning of ordinary citizens show that they assume that, of the three, it is often the businessmen who are on top.

There are several reasons why the business community (*zaikai*) can intervene in politics more pervasively and effectively than elsewhere. The first relates to its size. The community is an aggregation of big and small companies. The big ones are among the largest in the world individually. Linked together in *keiretsu*, each with a dozen large and countless smaller firms, and a high degree of cohesion and coordination, they have an enormous influence. More, for what it is worth, than General Motors in the United States or Siemens in Germany. The numerous small companies, hundreds of thousands of them, are active defending their interests at lower levels, where it counts.[23]

Their clout is multiplied many times over by the fact that the *zaikai* is so well organized. The small and large companies are members of local chambers of commerce and a central body. Larger companies participate in the work of Keidanren (Federation of Economic Organizations), which looks after general policy. Through Nikkeiren (Japan Federation of Employers Associations) they cooperate on employment and wages. Keizai Doyukai (Japan Committee for Economic Development), a narrower circle, includes more 'enlightened' businessmen who discuss broad issues of national interest.[24]

There is nothing quite like Keidanren anywhere. It has a huge headquarters building in central Tokyo and a vast staff working on innumerable studies and projects. But this staff can be expanded almost ad infinitum by leaning on the research capabilities of member companies. There is every reason to believe that on economic issues, especially those concerning the real economy, Keidanren has access to better information than MITI, MOF and EPA put together and it is more often the bureaucrats who ask it for advice than the other way around. As we know, information is power.

But, especially in Japan's political system, money is even more powerful. And Keidanren has access to incredible amounts thereof through its members. This is not merely left to chance, members are regularly assessed for contributions to the political fund which then distributes carefully calibrated doses to the politicians. This is not left to chance either, and Keidanren's policy has been exceedingly subtle. Obviously, the largest chunk went to the Liberal Democratic Party and now goes to its more direct successors. Still, knowing how the LDP and other parties operate, funds were also distributed to faction leaders. As other parties moved closer to the center, they received some largesse as well.

Money was allocated as a function both of the party or person's receptivity to pro-business policies and relative position. Prime ministers could count on substantial amounts while in office, but considerably more if they favored business. Even out of power, those with good business credentials always did relatively better. And this money, plus business influence, often tipped the balance among faction heads and potential prime ministers. Outside of the LDP, business leaders also rewarded opposition parties for muting their criticism of, or actually endorsing, pro-business policies. Thus, the Democratic Socialist Party was supported to wean it away from the Japan Socialist Party and make it a possible coalition partner for the LDP in case of need.

Normally, during elections, the business community remained on the sidelines. True, it stressed the importance of business for Japan's economy and made it clear that the LDP was the party of business. Still, if it looked as if the LDP would win anyway, it usually did not go much further, although company executives regularly recommended that their employees vote LDP (or DSP). When an election was in doubt, however, they leaped into the fray warning their workers and the general public of the dangers of allowing left-wing parties to come to power. Then they would rally the internal electorate of their companies and strongly urge them to vote correctly.

Under any conditions, the prestige and financial support of the business community in general and Keidanren in particular would have influenced Japan's politics. But in the postwar configuration they were even more decisive, for the LDP was never a popular party. It had very few party members and not many loyal voters. The *koenkai* were not established by voters, like party branches in most advanced countries, they were created and financed by the politicians who did their best to enroll members. In fact, Komeito (supported by Soka Gakkai), the socialist parties (backed by the trade unions) and the Communists (with genuine members), had relatively larger voter pools. This made business help in swaying voters crucial.

Similarly, with its modest popular support, the LDP managed to collect rather little in the way of dues or individual donations, less even than the JSP and DSP. The Communist party, due to sales of its newspaper *Akahata*, often collected more funds than the LDP. Thus, to have the precious money to run and win campaigns, the ruling party was hopelessly dependent on business circles. When even that money was inadequate, the LDP resorted to bank loans (at easy rates) which left it not only morally but financially indebted. That it could possibly turn a deaf ear to business policies was out of the question.

Unfortunately, these were not the only channels for money. Individual companies also passed money along, this time less to political parties than to individual politicians, and this was more often in return for specific services. On the lower level, construction firms were most active in their attempts to win government contracts. But any company that sought subsidies, cheap loans, trade protection or other favors could engage in this, as in the shipbuilding scandal of the 1950s. Those wishing to sell their products, like Lockheed, or win out over an opponent, as in the rivalry between JAL and ANA, could offer huge bribes. Even a businessman seeking to raise his profile, and get some special favors, might distribute funds widely, as in the Recruit scandal. Just how much money was involved was uncertain, as it was often unrecorded, but it was assuredly massive. What share consisted of bribes as opposed to genuine donations was even less certain, but was of uncommonly large dimensions.

The bureaucrats were less beholden to business circles, a point on which they were very proud, and this led them to think that they were more honest and reliable bearers of government responsibilities than the corruptible politicians. Many foreigners, as we saw, actually believed this to be true. But their incorruptibility was only relative. In the early decades, when companies were just getting back on their feet and urgently needed aid and protection, businessmen kowtowed to the bureaucrats. Later on, however, when companies had grown stronger, bureaucrats found it in their interest to maintain good working relations. This helped them avoid unpleasant blames and criticism. They could also count on businessmen for information without which they could not do their work. Then there were the periodic gifts, the entertainment, the golf and trips. And, sadly, also occasional bribes.

But where they caved in most abjectly to the businessmen was in the matter of second jobs. They were desperate for the plums that well-behaved and helpful bureaucrats could obtain on retirement. So they pulled strings for potential employers while in their government posts and then with colleagues later on. *Amakudari* was not regarded as corruption. Money did not change hands directly and the law allowed bureaucrats to accept such jobs (sometimes after a decent delay). Still, it was disliked by the public and even some businessmen, who regarded this as an unwanted business expense. And it was certainly a form of delayed reward which was often more substantial and had a more deleterious effect on bureaucratic practices than an actual kickback.

If the business community had the power to manipulate the politicians and bureaucrats, it also had the will. Initially, after the war, there was almost a class struggle in Japan and even the American occupation was fearful of a communist uprising. The Liberal and Democratic parties were the only hope for a capitalist Japan and businessmen threw their full weight behind them. When the socialists united, and won a first election, business leaders promoted, and almost forced, the merger into the Liberal Democratic Party in 1955. Thereafter, they supported the LDP, urging it to follow policies congenial to business. But, on occasion, they got more deeply involved, favoring one faction leader over another as prime minister and healing rifts between factions that could have split the party. When the LDP actually did break apart in 1993, businessmen were disappointed but did not stop meddling since they could not really trust politicians to run the government or even their own parties.

Meanwhile, the relationship with the bureaucrats had also changed. It was not only that businessmen were no longer as dependent on the bureaucracy but that they were increasingly annoyed by bureaucratic attempts to direct and control business activities. The bureaucrats simply did not know about the real economy and yet they were still targeting industries, protecting irretrievably declining sectors, alienating trade partners by keeping the market closed and hampering the activities of local companies through a myriad of regulations. Moreover, while businessmen were killing themselves at work and had to make profits to survive, bureaucrats had a relatively comfortable and secure career – and after eating at the state's trough they asked to be served at the company's.

These were the more immediate causes for disappointment. But many enlightened businessmen were worried that the politicians and bureaucrats were simply not up to the challenge of bringing Japan into the 21st century. The politicians were too busy squabbling with one another and running for reelection. The bureaucrats were too narrow-minded and could not see beyond their day-to-day tasks and concerns. Japan needed guides who could take a broader view and command more expertise to solve the host of problems on the horizon. These could only come from the business community, or so it was claimed. This was also an old tradition, for businessmen had helped run Japan for centuries, surreptitiously even under the shogun, more openly after the Meiji Restoration, and then blatantly in the early 1900s before the military takeover. Such opinions were frequently repeated during the 1990s, one example being a statement of Ryuzaburo Kaku, Chairman and CEO of Canon and Vice-Chairman of the Japan Association of Corporate Executives.

The conventional wisdom has it that a corporate manager should concentrate on business affairs, even if he passionately believes that Japan needs to become a better country.

Such improvements are seen as the responsibility of politicians and bureaucrats. However, the biggest concern of most politicians these days appears to be their own reelection. Regrettably, few politicians seem genuinely concerned about the future well-being of Japan, much less that of the world. In the present circumstances, a politician who gives priority to global interests and acts accordingly has little chance of remaining in office. . . . Although Japanese bureaucrats are highly capable, they tend to protect the interests of the ministry to which they belong, and move only within the confines of a vertically structured system of administration. Here again, only a small minority of bureaucrats really cares much about Japan, let alone the rest of the world.[25]

So businessmen also had to act, not out of ambition or in their own self-interest, but to fill the glaring gaps in governance left by both the politicians and bureaucrats. And the business community did act, in an amazingly broad range of areas.

Naturally, economic policy was uppermost. Shortly after the war, businessmen did everything they could to extract government assistance. This could take the form of subsidies, cheap credit, long-term loans and other financing. They also sought to keep out foreign competitors, especially the much stronger Americans, and demanded every possible form of protection. This they thought was only right. But industrial policy and targeting never met with much interest, except from companies benefiting directly. Many others preferred going their own way and the youngest and smallest were simply overlooked. Each time MITI tried to expand its powers, business leaders fought back and, by joining with the LDP, avoided further bureaucratic encroachment. Again, the only exceptions were those companies getting aid, now mainly in declining sectors.

By the 1980s and 1990s, the declared goals of most businessmen were almost the opposite. They wanted to rid the economy of unnecessary regulations and, somewhat less convincingly, open the market. They knew that foreign trade partners were tired of the obstructions they faced and could react nastily. And many of the regulations now bound their own companies. Thus, the business community again joined with the LDP to promote administrative reform and deregulation. When pitted against the bureaucrats, they did make some advances, but not many.

The business community was also tired of footing the bill for the national budget. Like businessmen elsewhere, they felt taxes were too high. They were wrong, in the sense that the Japanese paid less taxes than nationals of other advanced countries, but they were certainly right in that some of the taxes were unnecessary. In particular, if the bureaucracy could be reduced through administrative reform, then savings could definitely be made. Still, as the budget rose from year to year, this also seemed to be rough going.

Agricultural reform was a rather special case. Having finally conceded that manufacturers no longer needed subsidies and protection, business leaders urged that they be cut back for farmers as well. This would also be a sop to the foreigners who could export more food to Japan, thereby relieving the pressure to absorb more manufactures to balance trade. Incidentally, cheaper food would reduce the cost of living, saving their own workers money (and perhaps mitigating the need for higher wages). This time the powerful business lobby was pitted against a smaller, but very tightly organized agricultural lobby, which had disproportionate clout among the politicians. Progress was again slow, but it came fitfully.

Showing that they were interested in more than just the economy, it was the business leaders who launched and often directed the debate on educational reform. Here too they had reasons. Companies now expected workers to do more than just follow orders, they had to be creative. And this was most definitely not instilled by the existing system. Here too they were a bit hypocritical, in that they had initially wanted docile and unquestioning workers. But, at least, they realized that times had changed and Japan's educational system was no longer appropriate.

The business community also intervened in foreign affairs. With their network of overseas branches, often located in places where the Foreign Ministry did not have officials, and in closer contact with realities, the major companies had a better idea of what was going on. Through Keidanren, they adopted important statements on foreign policy and often acted before the government had gotten around to a decision, for example, by trading with or investing in former opponents like China,

Vietnam and North Korea. They dispensed largesse on favored countries, inviting their leaders to Japan on private, if very high-profile visits. The companies also engaged in a parallel policy of foreign aid, opening training schools and supporting local projects where they had operations, and bringing promising employees to study at the home office.

In other areas, the contribution was less positive and constructive. Although they had finally come around to paying lip service to environmental protection, businessmen bitterly fought any measures that might limit their leeway or cost them money. They did not want to be hampered by anti-pollution legislation. They were against the product liability law. They circumvented the Fair Trade Commission's efforts to prevent price fixing and control of outlets. Most serious, while cherishing the elderly, they did not want to make retirement too comfortable through adequate pensions and welfare, fearing the onset of the 'English disease.' Aside from any question of principle, companies simply did not want to pay more taxes and nothing could eat up revenue like extensive old age provisions.

There was one other issue that was particularly sensitive, namely corruption. Business leaders saw it not only as a right but a duty to fund suitable political parties. But they were extremely embarrassed when it turned out that some company or other had gone too far and sparked yet another scandal. They tended to blame corruption on greedy politicians, rather than greedy businessmen, although there was no denying that the business community was tarred with the same brush. Thus, they attempted to keep the transfers of money relatively clean by channeling it through formal bodies, and they even accepted certain limitations on amount, but they would go no further.

Obviously, no matter how they presented it, no matter how elaborate the *tatemae*, the *honne* was that many businessmen and the *zaikai* in general were primarily interested in policies that benefited their companies, even if they were also desirable for the whole nation. But many of these policies did meet with support among the population at large. Most people also wanted a more open and deregulated economy. They wanted cheaper domestic products and cheaper imports. Cheaper food was obviously appealing. Most people also wanted to curb a rather bothersome and bloated bureaucracy and pay less taxes (even if they still wanted more old age benefits). The educational system was certainly in need of repair and Japan did have to maintain decent relations with other countries. Since the politicians and bureaucrats did not seem to be doing much to tackle these problems, somebody had to.

People – The Missing Link

Having briefly sketched the roles and activities of the politicians, bureaucrats and businessmen, it is necessary to come back to the question asked in the beginning. Who runs Japan? By now it should be obvious that no one group runs Japan and that the relations between the three groups vary over time. This makes the allusion to the game of *jan-ken-poh* particularly appropriate. There are times when the bureaucrats and politicians cooperate and others when the businessmen back the politicians against the bureaucrats. There are times when the bureaucratic paper covers both the politicians' scissors and the businessmen's stone and others when the politicians' scissors are too dull to cut but the businessmen keep pounding at the bureaucrats (and also the politicians).

In the very first decades, the politicians were much tougher and knew what they wanted. There were repeated confrontations between left and right, as elsewhere in the world, but here the right won out not only partially or temporarily but overwhelmingly and durably. It was not until the focus shifted to economics that the bureaucrats and businessmen came into their own, with the bureaucrats clearly ahead in the 1950s and 1960s, due to masses of regulations and industrial policy. The positions were reversed in the 1970s and 1980s, when the businessmen could get along on their own and had the money to impose on the politicians, who had lost all sense of direction by the 1990s and were soon too disunited to do much. This enabled the bureaucrats to hold onto their old power, although they had no sense of direction either, while the businessmen – who at least knew what they wanted – could not run things on their own.

During the whole period from the 1970s on, it looked as if Japan were just floating with the tide. There were serious problems to solve and challenges to confront. These were even conceded, and plans and reforms broached, but hardly any action ensued. Whether domestically or internationally, the Japanese ship of state seemed rudderless. That led one of the canniest of the Japanwatchers, Karel van Wolferen, to conclude that nobody was running Japan. It was a spider's web without a spider.[26]

While I agree with much of his analysis, and also find Japan uncommonly static, it is hard to agree that Japan is run by nobody. It is simply that the ruling class or elite is much broader, not unusual for a country which places so much emphasis on harmony and consensus. But those in power do wield it, although they have to compromise with one another on occasion, and they tend to pull strings from behind rather than race out ahead as Westerners feel leaders should do. Key decisions are taken by the politicians through the ruling party or parties where faction heads and string-pullers still enjoy considerable strength. The administrative vice-ministers and bureau heads must also bear in mind the interests of the rank-and-file, but the hiearchy allows them to apply pressure. Strong-minded businessmen, especially if backed by business organizations, are always listened to when they talk and also followed if they dangle the right carrots.

In answering the first question, it was necessary to qualify the reply. For the following one, the answer can be more direct. Is this ruling class accountable to the people? While the people are not entirely out of the circuit, it is fairly obvious that the short answer has to be 'no,' or rather 'No.'

Japan is a rather odd phenomenon in that respect. In a dictatorship, the people often cannot vote and those who oppose the ruler too noticeably get into serious trouble. In Japan, people not only can vote, they do vote. But they very rarely impose their will on the government except in rare instances and in fairly amorphous ways. Even on such a key issue as the consumption tax, which the Japanese public overwhelmingly rejected, they had no success. Nor have they obtained what they wanted on education, economic and social policy or even such a vital matter as welfare and old age pensions.

Nonetheless, according to complaisant foreign 'experts,' the LDP was supposedly giving the people pretty much what they wanted without bothering to consult them.[27] Some of the initiatives came from its own members. Others were appropriated from opposition parties or social movements once they showed popular appeal. Yet others were part and parcel of 'modern' policy as demonstrated by Western countries and promoted by the OECD and United Nations bodies. That is true, to some extent, and Japan did adopt a full complement of 'modern' laws and benefits. But it usually did so with considerable delay, frequently less coverage than abroad and, in some cases, just on paper until the funds and personnel could be acquired. Yet, for this, the electorate supposedly mustered enough *tacit* support that the Liberal Democratic Party could remain in power indefinitely.

That could hardly be borne out by reality. LDP prime ministers repeatedly began their terms with reasonable support, but nothing truly impressive, in the 50–60 per cent range. By the time they had been around for a year or two the support rates fell, sometimes quite sharply, dropping to a pitiful 13 per cent for Takeshita and 15 per cent for Miyazawa. Support for the LDP itself was never very high, usually around 50 per cent, but even that fell to 42 per cent by late 1992.[28] More generally, in an annual survey by the Prime Minister's Office, during that period some 70 per cent of the persons polled said that public opinion was not properly reflected in national politics, with negative responses from as many as 81 per cent among those in their early thirties.[29]

The only reason the LDP did as well as it did was that the support levels of the other political parties were even lower. The Communists were generally shunned except by members and ideologues. Many trade union members voted for the Socialists, as they were instructed, but none too happily and over time even the once popular backing slipped. Komeito was supported mainly by Soka Gakkai members with little broader appeal. While their positive attraction weakened, the opposition parties gradually repelled broad ranks of voters who voted not so much for the LDP as against them.[30] Anyway, since there was no hope the other parties could form a government, there was not much point in voting for them. In this sense, the LDP's success was due as much or more to the failure of the opposition to create a credible alternative.

The growing dissatisfaction with not only the LDP but political parties and politicians in general was increasingly evident. It was shown most clearly in the share of unaffiliated voters, those who endorsed no political party. It rose from an already notable 19 per cent in 1953, to a substantial 33 per cent in 1973, and an extraordinary 41 per cent in 1993.[31] But there was nothing the people could do to express the mounting distaste, until July 1993. For the first time in decades, the electorate had a real choice among parties and seized the opportunity to vote the LDP out of office. In subsequent elections, the voters also removed dozens of mainstream politicians of all parties and replaced them with newcomers and outsiders. The parties and politicians finally got their comeuppance.

But what about the people? Were they blameless? To some extent, the Japanese electorate was caught in a difficult position. Voters could only choose between the parties which presented themselves, an increasingly discredited LDP and a fragmented opposition that did not seem capable of running the government and, according to many observers, did not particularly want to try. The politicians they could vote for were largely chosen by the parties, many of them being coopted and an increasing share inheriting the job. Even the prime minister was selected by the LDP, not the electorate. And there were few allusions to policy alternatives by the politicians or even by parties. Intelligent voters, who wanted the government to adopt specific measures, simply did not know who to vote for. No wonder so many became indifferent or alienated from politics.

In addition, politics were widely regarded as dirty. The politicians enjoyed little respect among most people and few thought highly of the calling. Part of this was traditional. Part derived from the way politicians behaved, their promises being less trustworthy and behavior more disreputable than most other trades. With 'money politics' foremost, and endless scandals uncovered across the spectrum of parties, they could hardly be regarded as reliable. For such reasons, many citizens did feel that it was better for the bureaucrats to run the administration and take any decisions and for business leaders to chart new directions.

But the indifference and apathy reached much deeper. Even in school, children had been encouraged (or obliged) to bow to authority. This was further reinforced by every group they joined, not only the company or bureaucracy, even sporting teams and social clubs. One simply did not criticize one's seniors, or superiors, and one did not go against the group consensus. If a person was seriously aggrieved by some action, it was best to keep this a secret and not complain. Resignation, rather than revolt, became the standard, almost inbred reaction. And this sort of conduct was seen by most Japanese as being a good company, or group or national citizen as opposed to standing up for one's rights or, if nothing more, making an effort to determine what is right and wrong.

Thus, most people did not even do what could be done to change the situation. Very few went into politics to improve the situation at the national level or even on the local level – while not easy, this could be done. True, in some communities, mainly during the 1960s and 1970s, grassroots groups were formed to improve the infrastructure or fight pollution and nuclear energy. There was also a period when popular movements resulted in leftist or independent mayors and governors. But this already petered out in the 1980s and the LDP managed to coopt many of the groups, while others just dissolved after having attained their limited goals.

If they had really wanted change, voters could have imposed or encouraged it, if through nothing else than a protest vote against the LDP. But this came rarely enough. And, when a particular prime minister lost favor, he was just replaced by another. This sop was usually enough to overcome criticism and refurbish the party. If they felt so strongly about corruption, then voters could have turned against the corrupt politicians. Alas, they did not. In fact, many thoroughly corrupt politicians ran again, and won. This, they regarded as cleansing them of any misdoing. Meanwhile, fewer people even bothered voting, with the voter turnout dropping from 70 per cent to about 50 per cent over the past decade.

The simple fact of the matter is that all too many Japanese did not care about policies. They did not make the effort to study the economic, social or foreign situation, decide just what they wanted from their leaders and then back politicians who could provide it. If they had insisted on better policies, or indeed any policies, the politicians might have obliged. Worse, all too many of them did vote for politicians on the basis of the services they could render or the quantity of public projects they could wangle. There was an all too clear correlation between the ability to bring back the bacon and political success, as shown by Tanaka, Takeshita, Kanemaru and so many others.

Admittedly, voters cannot be lumped together. There were some who might be regarded as 'traditionalist;' those in small villages and outlying prefectures, especially farmers and shop-keepers as well as small businessmen. They were very keen to receive a concrete return for their votes. The 'moderns' were better educated, often employees in larger firms, some bureau-crats and businessmen in their own right. They tended to have a broader view of things and vote more on policy. And they did tend to vote more often against the LDP. According to Scott C. Flanagan 'less than one-third of the moderns voted for the ruling LDP while over two-thirds of the traditionalists did.'[32]

But they were not quite enough to turn the tide. Moreover, they were not necessarily voting for the good of the nation either, so much as for their own vested interests. These people were mainly urban and happy to reduce agricultural subsidies or open markets to get cheaper imports. They also tended to defend the interests of their companies. But they did little bey-ond just voting. Most of the 'moderns' did not participate in politics by joining a party, helping shape its policies or getting out the vote. More disappointing, unlike the 'traditionalists,' they did not participate very actively in community affairs where they could actually do something. This left most of the urban wards with less grassroots democracy than the old villages.

Thus, if the people could not control the 'leaders,' it was *also* because they did not try. They were more apathetic politic-ally than in most advanced countries and, indeed, many of the developing countries where, although they could do little, people at least tried and, if nothing else, had their own per-sonal views of what should be done. Even public opinion polls asking the Japanese what they wanted, what they did not want, how they might bring about change, collected the vaguest of responses and a large number of uncertain, undecided or sim-ply disinterested ones. Moreover, it was no longer sure just how much change the electorate wanted. In the 1960s, many of the 'moderns' were liberal, even radical, but by the 1980s and 1990s they had turned conservative with little affection for leftist causes. So, when they dumped the LDP, many voted for celebrities and non-politicians rather than opposition parties.

Nor were they encouraged to take a stand by the press. Japanese journalists, unlike their more raucous brethren in the West, were often closer to the side of the government than the governed. True, the major dailies did cover politics and analyze policies. On occasion, they even criticized the ruling party and dug up assorted peccadilloes. But the criticism was more often muted and usually ended up with the formula that, while the LDP was mistaken, it would be hard to expect anything better from the opposition. Although the major scandals were covered, they were rarely discovered by the press and only written up substantially after they had become 'news.' The TV channels were even worse, largely disregarding politics, with few political debates or proper interviews. Only the smaller weeklies and gutter press played up the snafus and sleaze, but they didn't bother much with policies.

Of course, in the Japanese context, it is necessary to do more than just oversee the politicians since the state is run by the threesome of politicians, bureaucrats and business leaders. But the key relationship is with the politicians, because they are the only ones accountable – in theory at least – to the electorate. By electing the right political leaders, and showing that they did enjoy the support of the people, it would be easier for the politicians to win the game of *jan-ken-poh* more often. Indeed, they might even stay on top most of the time as in other real democracies. This would then downgrade the bureaucrats to what they should be, mere civil servants, and the businessmen to no more than advisors whose advice could be weighed against that of other groups or lobbies.

However, once again, the people did not insist on their rights. If anything, most of them kowtowed to the bureaucrats, flattering and playing up to them, giving gifts as necessary. Very few studied the laws and regulations enough to know how they should be applied or bring the case to the appropriate administrative body or court otherwise. In fact, few enough even bothered calling in to special complaint offices, although nearly everyone was disgruntled with the way bureaucrats behaved in general and what had happened to themselves in particular. At the same time, too few even of the 'moderns' realized that they should not necessarily vote as their boss suggested, especially regarding matters where company interests might differ from personal ones, as for consumer and environmental protection, welfare and old age pensions, or legislation on working hours and conditions.

Thus, just as the bureaucrats and businessmen usurped the

powers of the politicians, the three of them made off with the powers that were supposed to reside in the citizenry. Far from being a satisfactory, let alone a superior, democracy, Japanese-style democracy was at the far end of the acceptable range, in some ways more similar to authoritarian governments, and it would look and feel strange to people accustomed to more liberal democracies. As for the Japanese, they must regard 'government of the people, by the people and for the people' as a very appealing sentiment but a hopelessly unrealistic goal.

It would therefore be hasty to assume that Japan has finally resolved its political problems and strengthened democracy. Admittedly, the collapse of the LDP was a momentous event whose importance cannot be overlooked. But this has not gone to the roots of Japan's troubles. In the future, there will still be politicians without policies and parties without programs running governments without power while the bureaucrats tend the shop and churn out legislation. Businessmen will do everything they can to influence that legislation, and the execution thereof, while ordinary citizens are ignored and will probably not do much to impose on their rulers. Rather than claiming that things will never be the same again, as so many supposed 'experts' have done, I would note that *plus ça change, plus ça reste le même.*

Going Nowhere Fast

This brings us back to the last question, namely how well the state accomplishes its tasks. We have already seen that there are such intractable problems within each of the three groups that run the country, the politicians, the bureaucrats and the businessmen, that the so-called 'iron triangle' would seem to have gotten very rusty and brittle. The general public does not make up for any of these lacks, far from it. But what is more alarming in some ways is that it is becoming increasingly difficult for the government, with or without the people, to agree on measures. And, even after measures have been approved, it is almost as hard to get them implemented. Thus, the status quo tends to prevail, which is rarely good in a constantly evolving social context, but can be particularly bad when parts of that status quo are clearly outdated and frequently contested.

Such a political establishment may be treated by ordinary people, including the Japanese, as procrastinating and foot-dragging, and those responsible for leadership as unable to make up their minds, perhaps even gutless. The press, also in Japan, might speak of a do-nothing, know-nothing attitude or hiding one's head in the sand like an ostrich. But the political scientists, endlessly striving to refine their field, have come up with a much more constructive theory of 'immobilist' politics.[33] This was defined by J.A.A. Stockwin, and it seems to apply well to Japan, as 'an inability to do more than accommodate competing pressures and effect a "lowest common denominator" compromise between them.' The opposite is dynamic decision-making, where the decision-makers 'had not simply been constrained by a complex environment, but had succeeded in transcending the limitations provided by the nature of the political system, pressures of competing demands and so on, so as to arrive at policy based on the merits of issues and incorporating structural change where necessary.'[34] That is not common elsewhere, but it does occur.

Before considering what makes Japanese politics, and the state, so immobilist, it is useful to point out that this has not always been the case. Those who ran the state in the early Meiji period and shortly after the Pacific War knew exactly what they wanted and did whatever was necessary to get it. However, in both cases, as the years passed, the leaders were ever less certain of where their interests lay and what might be done to further them. In some instances, rising classes or the general population resisted and little change occurred. In others, there was simply so little energy emanating from the 'authorities' that things just stayed as they were. And ordinary folks, too timid to contest the powers that be and duly imbued with an 'awareness of authority' (*okami-ishiki*), accepted the status quo.

In early postwar Japan, well into the 1960s, there was unceasing conflict between political parties and leaders who knew what they wanted and made every effort to attain it, including not only political debates and agitated election campaigns but external and sometimes violent action.[35] Gradually, over that period, the Liberal Democratic Party created an electoral machine that could not be beaten. With the support of the bureaucracy and business community, it imposed a number of crucial decisions using what was called the 'tyranny of the majority.' They basically set the direction for economic and social policy, defense and foreign policy. As long as the LDP stayed in office it had the strength to maintain the essentials of that line.

Equally significant, those who wanted to change the policies, especially the socialists and communists, gradually weakened and their criticism appeared ever less realistic or relevant. With a move toward the center by all parties, there was an increasing consensus on policy. Yet, even when there was not, there were rarely problems as the opposition was brought into the decision-making process, admittedly as a very junior partner, and could modify policy at the margins. That would seem to be an improvement except that no one appeared capable of modifying any policy more than marginally, even when it was generally agreed that the existing situation was wrong or perilous and reform was needed. We have already seen this sort of immobilism with regard to education reform, equality of women, administrative reform, electoral reform, dergulation, the need to root out corruption and so on.

One of the reasons conflict over political, social, defense and foreign policy issues was muted is that the main focus was on economic policy. It was generally agreed, and this was the widest consensus, that economics came first and everything else should be temporarily downgraded until the goal was achieved. Economic measures were reasonably straightforward, the basic programs and legislation could be discussed rationally and broad decisions reached, with the details to be worked out by the bureaucracy. Since economic growth did resume, that contributed to solving other, more controversial problems since there was more money around. Schools could be built, as well as highways, hospitals and old age homes because revenue was accumulating so quickly. And this could be done often enough without even raising taxes.

That happy state of affairs began souring in the 1970s, and had already ceased by the 1980s. Thus, Japan was now in the more awkward position of having to set priorities, since there was not enough funding for everything. Worse, in order to obtain some things that were regarded as particularly important, it would be necessary to raise taxes on individuals and companies. This was the same bind as in other countries and yet Japan had more trouble than most. Many measures could not be agreed to within the LDP, others could not be agreed to among the political parties in the Diet, and yet others could not gain the support of the politicians, and the bureaucrats, and the businessmen. Some few, mainly tax increases, met with sharp rejection from the people. The outcome was, in short, immobilism.

One underlying cause of immobilism was that the Liberal Democratic Party had remained in power so long, for nearly half a century in practice. All political parties tend to become conservative and arthritic over such long times, even supposedly reformist ones like the Scandinavian socialists, or supposedly revolutionary ones like the Soviet and East European Communist parties, or a centrist group like Italy's Christian Democrats. Some of these parties, just like the LDP, clung to power year after year. To give a more scientific cast to this, certain political scientists came up with the concept of 'one-party-dominant regimes.' Some even spoke of 'single-party democracy'.[36] This at least made it look as if Japan were not unique. But most of the others were voted out or overthrown by the late 1980s and early 1990s. The LDP lastest longest and, as indicated, has not quite been edged out yet.

There are other causes for immobilism in Japanese-style politics. As already noted, parties do not really have clearly delineated policies and programs which they try to impose and thus political debate is incredibly vague and desultory. What is more important is to satisfy the various clienteles, be they organized groups or companies and individuals which have made substantial donations (or bribes). This results in considerable horse-trading. But it becomes even more wishy-washy because of the need to consult with, and please, all sorts of connections and personal relations within each politician's network (*jinmyaku*).

Added to this, Japanese politicians do not like to stick out too much and taking the lead in one legislative debate or another is more likely to create enemies than friends. Even ministers and prime ministers do not take a strong stand since they have to balance the interests of various factions as well as the interests within each faction, including their own. When they do take a decision, they will probably keep it to themselves publicly and only leak it gradually to other members of their own party and then, indirectly, to the people via the press. No wonder, with rare exceptions like Tanaka or Nakasone, Japan has repeatedly appeared leaderless and rudderless.

Then there are the more common aspects of steering legislation through parliament with some quaint Japanese angles. Even within the old LDP, it was hard to get the assorted, sometimes opposing factions to agree on policy, and then bring in enough centrist politicians, who had to be rewarded for this, to obtain a majority. If the opposition was strongly opposed, it had ways of at least delaying action, by making endless speeches or voting with a 'cow walk,' each Diet member waiting until the previous one had returned to his seat before going to the ballot box. Opponents could provoke a crisis by charging ruling party members, even ministers and prime ministers, with incompetence or corruption, never very hard to do given the LDP's proclivities. The old government would fall, a new LDP government would be installed, but this all took time. With new governments formed every year or two, and hectic electioneering occurring almost as frequently, it was hard to concentrate on governing.

With the new political constellation of multi-party democracy things have only gotten more complicated and the immobilism has increased. Now more parties are vying for power and there are more alternative policies, although they are still expressed as infrequently and vaguely as before. Leaders have more trouble gathering their supporters, and figuring out what they all want, before negotiating agreements with some opposition members to get a bill adopted. Even bills of an almost routine nature, and certainly more controversial measures, tend to get sidetracked or forgotten and very few pieces of legislation of any sort are approved. Moreover, after becoming law they may still not be acted upon because the bureaucrats have their own way of leaving things in limbo when the politicians are not looking or are too busy elsewhere.

So, the role of the bureaucracy must also be considered. The bureaucrats could hasten the process, by providing suitable bills, briefing not only the ruling party but opposition members, guiding the bill through debates and then implementing the law quickly and efficiently. If the new measure were less appealing, it could go into reverse. In earlier years, during the economic boom, the bureaucracy was in favor of

almost any legislation for its own reasons: everything gave
the bureaucrats more work, more power and more prestige.
The situation changed dramatically with the economic slowdown, for then it was necessary to reduce budgets, cut back
on recruitment and even eliminate some lesser agencies and
gradually privatize public companies. With the demands for
administrative reform and deregulation, the bureaucrats – especially those in the leading economic ministries – felt they had
come under direct attack and used delaying tactics more than
ever.

This is also standard practice in other countries. The main
difference is the balance of power. In most democratic and
liberal countries, the politicians, backed by the people, have
substantial leverage over the bureaucrats (or civil servants). In
Japan, the bureaucracy is much stronger, the parties are much
weaker, and they are not really supported by the people. Only
the business community can tilt the balance, and it has done
so on occasion. But this is harder when the political parties
themselves are in disarray, an all too frequent occurrence
before, and especially after, the LDP's split.

No matter how unpleasant this may sound, much of the
inefficiency and repeated bungling can be attributed to the
mediocrity of the political class. Politicians have a very limited
understanding of the issues at stake, few have anything that
resembles a platform, and policy is much less important than
wangling goodies for the constituency. All that counts is
getting reelected, by whatever means, fair or foul. For most,
especially the bumper crop of 'second generation' Diet members, this is just a trade, and a lucrative one. Japanese Diet
members and ministers earn considerably more than their
counterparts in the West, with the Japanese prime minister
earning twice as much as the U.S. president, who actually works
for his keep. And then there are the gifts, the perks and the
outright bribes.

Japanese bureaucrats are also paid better than their counterparts in the West, if normally less than Japanese in corresponding business positions. But they have secure jobs and
generous pensions and may finish off a career in politics or
business anyway. It is these perks, not any overpowering patriotism as in earlier days, which move most of the recent generations of bureaucrats. While they are usually more proficient

at what they do than the politicians, it could hardly be said that they are experts on the fine points of increasingly technical issues. For here too the generalists rise to the top and tend to look down on specialists. They also look down on ordinary folks. This makes it harder for them to tailor their legislation and implementation to ordinary needs or be in any great rush to satisfy them.

Equally serious, top politicians and top bureaucrats, the ones with the greatest power, are all quite old. And you cannot get rid of these 'dinosaurs.' Thus, generational change is slow. The average age of Japanese cabinet ministers is in the mid-sixties, that of administrative vice-ministers the mid-fifties. In the Diet, it is only recently that the majority of members was of postwar vintage, but they must still kowtow to a minority of early Showa era (1926–88) and even Taisho era (1912–26) members. Senior bureaucrats step down earlier, but the hiearchy is stricter, so top bureaucrats are in their fifties as well, some with a distinct prewar mentality. Youngsters, those going to school now, may not take control for half-a-century. No wonder those at the summit have so little feeling for what is going on at the base.

So, more often than in most other places, any conflicts and contradictions, even fairly minor ones, lead to impasses and gridlock. And neither the politicians nor the bureaucrats have the ability to get things moving again. Once upon a time, the emperor or his advisors could intervene. Now it is the people who are 'sovereign,' but fail to use the powers they actually possess. Even foreign pressure (*gaiatsu*) does not help much any more. Thus, the Japan of the future will have to continue living with the legislation and regulations of the past. And small problems will grow into big ones and big ones into serious crises that could well have been avoided.

5

The Family
(Splitting Up)

Once the family was the primary building block of society, not only in practice but under very strict rules and regulations laid down by the Tokugawa shogunate, some of them enacted as law after the Meiji Restoration and only lapsing after the Pacific War. Yet, as is becoming increasingly evident to the Japanese, the family is now among the weakest social institutions and ranks after many others in importance. Indeed, the decay of the family is such that its preservation in any normal sense is in danger.

That the family should come under stress and strain is not surprising. There have been far-reaching demographic changes which inevitably dispersed the older extended families and installed the nuclear family as the basic unit. Lacking familiarity with this unit, the Japanese had to reshape relations among family members. In so doing, they were under pressure from various phenomena of modernization and Westernization. Thus, many of the ills and problems the family has been subjected to are blamed on Westernization and Western models, since the Western family is clearly in difficulty as well. Yet the major culprits are not Western but Japanese, namely the Japanese-style company and the Japanese-style school.

However, in order to understand the crisis of the family in Japan, it is necessary to realize that just as companies and schools are different from those in both the advanced and developing countries abroad, the Japanese family is also different no matter how many superficial resemblances there may be. To do that, it is best to define the family members and their relations in order to know what a Japanese family is nowadays. Again, I concede, the description will not be flawless and will doubtlessly overlook certain factors and actors, but it is

114

certainly better than using the term 'Japanese family' so loosely that it is meaningless.

In this section, even more than the others, I will go out of my way to provide as much hard support for my thesis as possible in the form of statistical data, results of polls and surveys, and judicious comments by Japanese. I know that many complacent readers will find it hard to accept that a country known for Confucianism, filial piety and familism could possibly have strayed so far from these sterling precepts. I am further goaded to do this by some very negative reviews which trashed my books every time they uttered a grating *honne* rather than a comforting *tatemae*, like the following, a bit over a decade old but now sounding as if it came from another era.

> The aging population, Woronoff is convinced, will spell trouble in the future for Japan, more so than for its Western competitors which also have aging populations. This dire prognosis ignores the continuing strength of Confucian values in Japanese society. Children still feel very much responsible for their parents to the extent that the eldest offspring will often seek employment in their locality to be close to their parents. This sense of filial duty, from which there is little indication of a decisive deviation, seems likely to ensure that, in this respect at least, Japan will be able to get by on more modest welfare spending than most Western countries. . . .[1]

What Is A Family?

The family has been strongly affected by various demographic trends, in Japan as elsewhere. However, in Japan, most of these trends have been even stronger than in other countries. They have usually taken place more rapidly, accomplishing in half a century what had often taken a century or more in the West. And they have, in some cases, actually gone as far or further than in many Western countries. Some of these trends are natural and/or inevitable, and should be viewed with equanimity. Others, especially when they become extreme, are much more disconcerting.

One major demographic trend is the shift from the extended

family to the nuclear family. The former usually consisted of three generations living together with, on occasion, relatives or adopted children as well. It was a natural outgrowth of life in the countryside and towns where mobility was limited. The shift began in earnest as mobility increased and, especially, younger sons moved from the countryside to towns and cities and formed their own family units. There, due to housing conditions, fewer possibilities existed of three generations living together and, often enough, the older generation was still dwelling in the countryside. Recently, however, aging grandparents have been moving in with the nuclear family or, if it is the grandparents who own the house, allowing the nuclear family to stay with them.

One way or another, there has been a sharp decrease in the share of extended families, representing just about all families in Tokugawa and early Meiji days, but gradually sinking during the modernization of Japan to account for only about 36 per cent just after the war and a mere 14 per cent at present. The share of nuclear families has not ceased growing although, with the advent of the new type of three-generation family, the level has stabilized at about 60 per cent. By the way, some of these nuclear families are 'broken' families, namely divorced women, more rarely men, living with their children.[2]

The remainder is accounted for by a type of 'family' that hardly existed in earlier times, namely the single-member household. Some of these are young men and women who are living on their own or in company housing, although the proportion is much lower than in the West. Others are men, and especially women, who are divorced or separated. The largest and most rapidly growing contingent consists of older people, especially women, whose spouses have died. Already quite high in general, single-member households represent more than a third of all households in Tokyo, and this share is expected to rise steadily in the future. (Figure 5.1)

There is another demographic trend which partly derived from, and partly influenced, the shift from the extended family to the nuclear family. This has been a decrease in the birthrate. Some of this resulted from modernization and a general feeling that a smaller family was more socially acceptable. There was also an element of policy since it was feared that a crowded

Figure 5.1. *Household Structure*

(%)

	1970	1975	1980	1985	1990	1993
Single persons	18.5	18.2	18.1	18.4	21.0	22.3
Nuclear families	57.0	58.7	60.3	61.1	60.0	59.4
Single parent with children	5.1	4.2	4.2	4.6	5.1	5.1
Married couple without children	10.7	11.8	13.1	14.6	16.6	17.7
Married couple with children	41.2	42.7	43.1	41.9	38.2	36.6
Three-generation families	19.2	16.9	16.2	15.2	13.5	12.8
Others	5.3	6.2	5.4	5.3	5.6	5.6

It takes less people than ever to make a household.

Source: Management and Coordination Agency,
Nihon tokei geppo (Monthly Statistics of Japan).
Credit: *Facts and Figures of Japan*, 1995, p. 18.

country like Japan could not accomodate more people and thus birth control was encouraged. But there were other factors as well. The cost of housing was considerable and the housing itself small and cramped, the costs of raising children mounted and the father (and sometimes also the mother) had to work. Although polls indicated that women actually wanted more children the realities of modern Japan convinced them to have less.

For centuries, Japan had been a nation of large families with many children, the average size of normal households being five in prewar days. Since the war, and ever more rapidly of late, the family size has shrunk, with three the norm at present. This drop from five to three, however, means that the average family has only one child as opposed to the earlier three, quite a change in many ways. This resulted partly from the decline in the birthrate (annual births per 1,000 population). Peaking at 36.3 in 1920, it fell steadily to 9.6 at present. This is not only unprecedentedly low for Japan, it is relatively low even compared to other advanced countries.

Meanwhile, the fertility rate (births per woman) has also fallen, slipping below 2.1 by 1974, the minimum rate needed to maintain population size, and hitting a record low of 1.5 in 1992. This means that for two decades already, the Japanese have not been bearing enough children to replenish the population and, if this continues, the total size of the population – now

Figure 5.2.   *Population Forecast for Japan, 1990–2090*

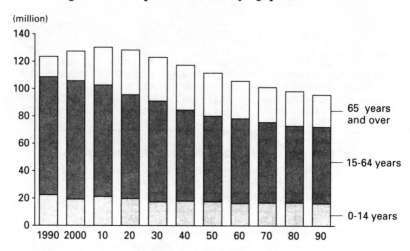

Japan's incredible vanishing population.

Source: Institute of Population Problems, Ministry of Health
and Welfare, *Jinko no doko* (Population Trends).
Credit: *Facts and Figures of Japan*, 1995, p. 15.

some 125 million – should eventually decrease. It takes some
time for these trends to work through but, already by roughly
2010, the population could peak and then gradually dwindle.[3]
According to the Economic Planning Agency it could drop to
70 million by the end of the 21st century. There was no estimate
of when the last of the Japanese might disappear from the face
of the Earth thereby extinguishing the race. (Figure 5.2)

There is a third demographic trend, tying in with the first
two, namely for the population to age. This derives partly from
the fact that there are fewer and fewer children. But the
trend is further accentuated by the fact that Japanese are living ever longer, with a present life expectancy of 76 for men
and 82 for women (up sharply from 50 and 54 in 1947). As
noted, in Japan most trends have been unusually sharp and
far-reaching. It now has one of the lower birthrates coupled
with the longest life expectancy, and this has been achieved
over a very short period of time. Thus, the aging of the population is proceeding faster than anywhere else. By the year
2000, the proportion of people aged 65 and over should reach

Western levels and, by the year 2020, it should be considerably higher than in any other country in the world.

With this, the so-called population 'pyramid' should begin resembling a cylinder, with relatively few youngsters at what used to be a broad base and many more elderly persons at what used to be a slender summit. By 2035 it could turn into a reverse pyramid, with more elderly than young people. By the 21st century, there should be more people aged 65 and older than aged 14 or younger. The more fateful relationship is that the number of elderly persons will continue outgrowing the number of working age (20–64 years) persons. Thus, whereas each elderly person is supported by 5.3 working age persons at present, that ratio could decline to 3.8 by the year 2000 and a mere 2.3 by the year 2035.[4]

It was inevitable that such sweeping demographic changes should cause, and in return be supported by, dramatic social changes. These have also been more extensive and rapid in Japan than most other places.

This is partly due to the fact that Japan had one of the most highly regimented and rigid family structures the world has ever seen during the Tokugawa era. Partly under the influence of Confucianism, partly just to keep society quiescent and controllable, the early shoguns developed an incredibly complete and complex set of regulations determining the relative position of each and every family member and their respective rights and obligations. This was consecrated in the *ie* system.

Under it, the father was the head of the family, of a then broad family which was a kin group belonging to the same official register. His authority was considerable, not only due to custom but legally. He owned the family property and decided how it should be used. The family property was passed down to the oldest son, the younger sons receiving nothing, and owing him deference. Women had no legal status and their main purpose was to bear children and continue the family line. The daughters were subservient to all the males in the family. If there were no sons, one might be adopted into the family, The children of poorer relatives or those in more remote areas might also be taken in, but with no special rights. For all, from the father on down, however, the stress was much more on duties and obligations than rights and the father was held responsible for any transgressions by other family members.

This system was changed and 'modernized' under the more 'enlightened' leaders of the Meiji era (1868–1912). But it was still tightly regulated and fairly rigid under the prewar *ie* code. The wife was still legally dependent on her husband, the children were still heavily dependent on their father, who could intervene in the marriage arrangements for daughters (and sons). The elder son was still the second in command but, with the growth of a modern economy, his position was far less enviable. He inherited the family property, but also the family obligations. Meanwhile, younger sons moved to the towns and cities, got jobs in factories and offices, and often became not only independent but wealthier and more prominent socially. It was not until the end of the Pacific War, and the collapse of the Japanese state, that the old *ie* system was formally abolished and replaced by something more democratic and modern, at the behest of the Americans, and sometimes using American models. The family now consisted of a couple with equal rights for husband and wife and full rights for children once they came of age. The family property could be shared among the members and passed down to sons and daughters equally. The wife and children could keep their own property. The father no longer had to approve of the children's prospective spouses and they could marry whom they wished and move out and found their own households. While the rights of the other family members were enhanced and those of the father reduced, his responsibilities were also sharply curtailed.

Still, it must be remembered that the old *ie* system had prevailed for an exceptionally long time, in its strictest form for nearly three centuries under the Tokugawa shogunate and for another century in more moderate forms up until the end of the Pacific War. Thus, whatever the modern legislation said, many people, especially older people, still thought and acted in more traditional ways and some of the earlier rules were carried down as less stringent customs and habits. While there is legal equality between husband and wife, social inequality and other forms of dependence of an economic or financial nature remain. Although daughters could marry whomever they wanted, it took a very long time for the so-called 'love' marriage to replace arranged marriages.

Nonetheless, the 'modern' family has been proliferating and replacing the traditional family.[5] And it has been shaped by modern forces, economic, social and intellectual. Just how well it copes with them and with other social institutions remains an open question. For the moment, it would seem premature to speak of a successful transition.

Readjusting Family Relations

In the traditional Japanese family, there were manifest differences in role and status. The father, as head of the family, wielded exceptional authority and exerted enormous control over the actions of the other members, for whom he was responsible. The mother had considerably less authority, although she could certainly influence her children as she was largely in charge of their upbringing. But she was definitely not in command, nor could she take essential decisions alone. The father had the last (and sometimes nearly the only) word on what kind of eduction they should have, what profession or trade they should go into and even whom they should marry and when. The children owed obedience to the father and were expected to follow his orders.

There was a lot of rigidity in this relationship and deference had to be expressed formally, in behavior, posture and speech. The father was expected to be strict, and usually was, the mother more caring, if not quite loving. The children had to show signs of respect and filial piety. Still, since they all lived together and saw one another frequently, and also had a vested interest in the success of the family as such, the relations were very close and there was some give and take. Living side-by-side, naturally the parents were the role models for the children, whose learning often consisted more of seeing and doing than formal education.

Of the various family members, the one whose position has changed most over the course of time has been the father. The old Confucian ethic has disappeared: he no longer has any legal authority over his wife, who is now an equal, nor his adult children. Like everyone else, he has to work out new relations with the other family members and fulfill his role in society. In most societies, a man's role is multiple: father, husband, worker, citizen, and so on, and he can balance various aspects. In Japan, all too often the function of worker not only predominates but smothers all others. Nowadays, for some 80 per cent of the labor force, it implies work as a wage-earner in a factory, office, store, bureaucracy or other workplace. Only a minority, mainly farmers, artisans or shopkeepers, still work in or near their home.

As already explained in the section on the company, Japanese employees put in substantially more hours at work than their Western conterparts. They must also commute long distances in many cases. Often enough, even when work is over, they are expected to go for a drink or have dinner with colleagues, superiors, subordinates, suppliers or other contacts. Even on weekends, some of them must engage in social activities with such company-related persons. When they do have some limited free time, most of the men try to catch up on sleep.

This makes it hard to be a father in any normal sense since the father rarely sees his wife or children. He gets up before them, eats quickly and leaves. He comes home too late for dinner often enough. He may not even be around during the weekend or on holidays and vacations. Worried about his career at the company, and entangled in relations with his colleagues and other business associates, he has neither the time nor nervous energy to throw himself into family life as well and becomes a rather distant figure. His primary function is simply to bring home a salary.

This already constrained situation can become even more acute through the Japanese practice of *tanshinfunin* ('transferred alone') which affects about half-a-million men at any given time. Japanese companies, to round out their employees' experience or for purely commercial reasons, such as filling unexpected gaps in staffing or getting rid of deadwood, regularly send employees off to work for a while in overseas subsidiaries or offices in outer prefectures. These transfers can last for two or three years and even four years or more. Although, in theory, they are 'voluntary,' the suggestion would rarely be refused since this would hurt any chances of promotion.

Unfortunately, these transfers very often come in the early years, when many of the men have just gotten married and founded a family, or later on, when many have children attending school. Thus, about a third of the transferees accept to go off alone, without their family, and become *tanshinfunin*.

In return, the companies usually do not even provide allowances to return home with any frequency, so they may be away from home for months, even years on end, and cease being a member of the family concretely. Yet, according to the polls, they see this as a vital contribution to the family since many list as the reason for accepting transfer alone to avoid disrupting family life and especially to avoid disturbing the children's education.

In no country have so many fathers (and husbands) voluntarily abandoned the home to such an extent that one commonly speaks of 'fatherless' families. According to various surveys, only in one third of the families are all members present for dinner every day. Only one working man in 30 does anything resembling housework on weekdays, and even on Sundays they put in less than half-an-hour. More seriously, many school children never talk to their father on weekdays and, even on Sundays, the average working man only spends 12 minutes playing with the children. When asked who should be in charge of the children's discipline, 60 per cent of the parents said it should be the responsibility of both, 32 per cent said it should be the responsibility of the mother and only 8 per cent said the father should be responsible. Many fathers do not even discuss the children's education and upbringing with their wives.[6] Lest it be thought that this is somehow 'Japanese', never in the history of that country have fathers (and husbands) had less to do with the family.

In the absence of the Japanese-style father, the mother has to shoulder a much larger share of the burden of raising a family.[7] One of her primary tasks traditionally, and still today, is to look after the home. But with smaller houses and apartments, fewer family members and more labor-saving devices, this requires ever less time, so she can spend more time looking after the children. This entails normal aspects of raising children, teaching them manners and etiquette, helping them enter broader society and so on. The main responsibility, however, and one that has not ceased growing, is to supervise their education.

With the supreme goal of getting her offspring into a 'good' college still some 20 years off, mothers begin planning early to get them into a good kindergarten, then a good primary school and finally a good secondary school as preparation for the final stage. This implies putting lots of money aside for education and cramming costs. It also involves helping them each step of the way, seeing that they attend school, insisting that they do their homework and then pushing them to cram. This is done to some extent by all mothers. Still, given the overriding importance of educational success, many of them turn into what are called *kyoiku mama* or 'educational mothers' who focus solely on that.

To coax and cajole their children to study ever harder, many mothers become strict disciplinarians most of the time, scolding the children if they watch television, read comics or waste time on some lesser pursuit. They become the frightful *mamagon* or 'mother monster.' Realizing they may be losing their children's love, some then swing in the opposite direction and pamper and spoil them. They offer costly gifts and special treats, sometimes to reward the kids for studying hard, sometimes to 'buy' love. While the relationship remains ambiguous, and some children have strong affection for their mother and others an equally marked distaste, there is no question but that the mother-child link is the strongest in the family. It is equally clear that the Japanese-style mother is under greater pressure than most other mothers.

No matter how important the children's upbringing may be, many women do have to work as well. The husband's salary may not be adequate, given the costs of housing and education. Even if it is just 'part-time,' the number of hours absorbed by work can be considerable. Thus, not only is the father away, so is the mother. This means that in later years for many, already earlier on for others, the children may return to an empty house. And there are ever more 'latch-key' children (*kagikko*) who have to look after themselves after school. While this is unfortunate, it is perhaps less so in certain ways than being hounded to study ever harder.

There is one other task many women have to bear, namely to look after the grandparents. True, there are fewer extended families nowadays, and thus grandparents do not always live in the same house. But families are also smaller and, with only one or two children, the likelihood of having to look after grandparents is greater as is the probability that they will live longer. These grandparents, however, are usually the parents of the husband and not the wife. The chore of looking after them can be particularly unpleasant with respect to the mother-in-law, who almost by tradition is expected to train her daughter-in-law (*yomé*) in how to be a proper housewife, giving her endless advice and scolding her if she does anything wrong. The wife may get some little sympathy from her husband, but he may just as well scold her as well for not doing things right and not getting along with his parents. As people live longer, this increasingly involves actual dressing, feeding and nursing ill and bed-ridden old folks, a time-consuming and unpleasant task, but essential due to the lack or cost of old age homes and nursing facilities.

Present-day children are thus being raised in a very different kind of family. And they are different as well. Obviously, growing up in many cases without a father figure is a drawback, especially as concerns that portion of education that comes from observing a role model. It also deprives them of a source of support or authority, depending on the father's personality. Meanwhile, it leaves them even more under the control of a mother who may alternately be driving them to study harder and smothering them with affection.

But the children, in all too many families, may not have much time to think of that since, at a very early age, they are inserted in an educational system that culminates in 'examination hell.' They too must spend most of the time away from home. They put in long hours at school, attend cram courses and tutoring, and then withdraw to their room (or, more likely, their corner) to do their homework. This absorbs most of the week including Saturday, sometimes the whole weekend, sometimes the holidays and vacations. While success in the exams is important for them, it is also important for the whole family, and consequently the children come under greater pressure to study and sacrifice for the family.

Once the children have grown up, and perhaps left home, it is still inhabited by two persons, a husband and wife. But they may have seen precious little of one another for 20 years and more and their limited relations revolved mainly around the children or, more exactly, the children's education. It is therefore hard for them to form even a pseudo-family. They live in the same house, see one another, but do not communicate much or share common interests and engage in joint activities. They suffer from what is called 'living together loneliness.'

Under these conditions, some of the men apparently develop an aversion to the home, avoiding it as much as they can. Employees, especially in large companies, seek every possible excuse to stay at the office, mix with colleagues or clients and so on to arrive home late. Some actually suffer from what is known as the 'return-home' phobia. When asked if they had ever felt unwilling to go home after work, as many as 31 per cent of the Tokyo salarymen questioned responded affirmatively. The main reasons for not wanting to return were to have some free time away from the family (57%), not to take business-related stress home (41%) and 'to get away from the wife's complaints and grumbling' (25%).[8]

For their part, many of the wives do not want their husbands to come home. They have spent 20 years and more looking after the kids alone, eating meals with the kids and then alone, and living in a home alone. They do not relish the appearance of a husband whom they hardly know, perhaps do not really care for, and who at any rate makes a mess of the place and doesn't clean up, then expects to be fed and looked after. When the husband retires and no longer draws a salary, or the wife is earning enough for her own needs, it is difficult to find even a financial rationale for living together. At this point, many wives take out their accumulated anger on their husbands, referring to them as 'oversized rubbish' or 'cockroaches' and the like, behind their back or even to their face.

These couples, the happy and the unhappy ones, used to live for the most part with their children in an extended family. Now more and more are living alone (39%) or with a married child (39%), since the son is still expected to take care of the aging parents (although most of the actual care is provided by his wife). But an ever larger share is living with an unmarried child (18%), usually the daughter. While many elderly Japanese now prefer living on their own (54%) while they are healthy, most (52%) opt for living with their children in case of ill health. This implies an even larger burden for the poor *yomé* and, perhaps for this reason, is increasingly resisted. Another sign that family ties are weakening is that elderly parents who live separately do not see much of their children. In fact, Western families seem to get together far more often.[9]

To make things worse, this increasingly bizarre assortment of characters out of a Japanese version of Jean-Paul Sartre's

Huis Clos is living in a Japanese house. This means that there is so little space that they are constantly bumping into one another. The rooms are separated by very thin walls, and sometimes just sliding-doors of paper, so they cannot avoid hearing one another. There is no real privacy, no place to let off steam, and no chance to get away from the others except by leaving the house.

The Vanishing Family

These trends naturally generate great stress and strain in the present-day Japanese family, far more than had ever occurred in the traditional Japanese family, and also more than in the old-style family of many developing countries and the 'modern' family of many advanced countries.

The way in which this has led to a breakdown of the family most visibly is through divorce. In 1995, there were some 195,000 divorces, a postwar high, although only representing 1.6 divorces per 1,000 inhabitants, much lower than the American level although not much better than the rates in Europe and worse than those in most of Asia. Along with a tendency for the number of divorces to increase, there is also a trend toward more divorces among middle-aged and older persons. The main causes are a clash of personality, abuse by the husband (for women) and (for men) the spouse's inability to keep on good terms with relatives and in-laws (the *yomé* complex).

But the figures only tell part of the story. Many more Japanese would like to divorce but don't, usually for reasons of face and social relations. The wives do not want to upset their relatives and friends or make things harder for the children. The husbands have similar concerns but most also worry about the effect on their employer, since respectable companies do not like employees to engage in disreputable actions. For the women, there is a further explanation. While they usually receive custody of the children, only about 10–15 per cent get any child support from their ex-husband and the divorce settlement, if any, is normally rather small. Most, quite frankly, could not get by financially.

Still, there is no shortage of reasons for estrangement within the family. The husband and wife have different interests, different schedules, different friends and only a common concern for the children. Even before the children grow up, they may be on indifferent or bad terms. But it is equally hard for Japanese to go their own way, due only partly to social pressure. There are few enough places for middle-aged or older people to make acquaintances, second marriages are still uncommon and the husbands, in most cases, simply cannot look after themselves; they don't know how to cook, do laundry or clean the house. Meanwhile, most women just cannot afford a separation. Thus, many couples continue living together under the same roof, although hardly forming a family. This phenomenon, which is increasingly widespread, is known as 'divorce within the family' (*kateinai rikon*).

While the breakdown of marriage appears more threatening, equally serious problems are arising at the other end of the cycle, in seemingly innocuous trends. First off, people are getting married ever later. For women, the traditional age by which they were supposed to marry was 25, after which they would be literally 'stale goods' (*urenokori*). But the average age has been moving up, reaching 26.1 for women and 28.4 for men, and these trends are expected to continue.

More radically, increasing numbers of women and men are not getting married at all, a once unheard of proposition. After peaking at 10.5 in 1971, Japan's marriage rate (marriages per 1,000 population) declined to about six. Among younger men and women, the number of unmarried persons has been rising rapidly. The rate, according to the Ministry of Health and Welfare, is expected to reach 20 per cent for women in their early thirties, 48 per cent for women in their late twenties, 35 per cent for men in their early thirties and fully 65 per cent for men in their late twenties by the year 2000.[10] Thus the number of couples actually being formed has been declining and can be expected to slip much further.

Why aren't young Japanese getting married? There is no shortage of opinion polls, let alone gossip, on that. Both men and women want to continue associating with their friends, remaining free of the social entanglements of marriage, especially for women who cannot accept the painful chores of raising children or looking after in-laws. Nor do they want to accept the financial burden of buying a house and educating children, which would sharply reduce expenditures on things they like. Women claim they do not want to give up their 'career,' even if that consists of being an eternal OL, nor do they want to stop their many leisure and travel activities or curtail spending on clothing and entertainment. Thus, a survey of singles aged 18 to 34 by the Ministry of Health and Welfare found them more than ambivalent about marriage. While 35 per cent of the men and 71 per cent of the women felt that marriage offered some advantages, 25 per cent of both thought it did not. And 83 per cent of the men and 90 per cent of the women felt there were advantages to not marrying.[11]

Then there are other reasons for not getting married. According to another poll by the Institute of Population Problems of the Ministry of Health and Welfare, again looking into the situation of young singles, about 30 per cent of both males and females said they had no idea how to find a future spouse and 49 per cent of the males and 40 per cent of the females had no 'steady' friends of the opposite sex.[12] Such results would be most unusual elsewhere, but perfectly natural in Japan. While they are in high school, especially as examinations approach, youngsters have no time for leisure, let alone dating. Only in college, for those lucky enough to go, are there many opportunities for men and women to meet. Once recruited into the company, the young men are kept constantly busy, whether at work or socializing with colleagues after work, and only the women have much time to go out. However, with the men busy, the women spend most of their time with female colleagues and friends.

Nonetheless, more and more apparently do manage to find a spouse on their own. Most meet at the workplace, some carry over connections formed in college. But even then many still need the help of friends and relatives to make contacts and, in the company, managers are actually expected to propose potential soulmates. Despite this, there are still about 15 per cent of Japanese couples which have to be formed the old-fashioned way, by getting a go-between (*nakodo*) to make the necessary contacts, work things out with the couple and parents, and then officiate at the wedding. The rise of so-called 'love marriages' (*ren-ai kekkon*) and the decline of arranged marriages (*miai*), however, may well be exaggerated. Announcing a love marriage sounds better, but the parents must still agree, as in the old days, and they carefully vet future in-laws, sometimes by hiring a private detective to check that the family background is good, the person is upstanding and, for men, capable of earning a decent salary.

To call them 'love' marriages is also misleading for another reason. Sometimes they do result from emotions, sentiments and 'love.' More often, there is a cold calculation on both sides. Men still like homebodies, who will not insist on a career, and will cook, clean house and raise children. The women often want a career, but will give it up for a comfortable lifestyle, which again implies that the husband has good earnings potential. It is also common knowledge that women avoid marrying a first son, and increasingly an only son, because that involves looking after the aging parents. In practice, very few female college graduates would stoop to marrying a high school graduate and there are various racial and class differences that inhibit marriage. Not surprisingly, it is hard to find Mr or Miss Right within a small circle of potential mates.

There are other problems relating to the act of marriage. Few Japanese would, or could, get married simply. Rather, they are expected to throw a lavish wedding ceremony and reception, go on an expensive honey-moon and then set up house in style. Despite attempts at cost-cutting, the bill for getting hitched has been bloated, reaching some ¥7.7 million on the average by 1994.[13] Part of this cost is covered by the parents, another part by the reception guests, but over a third of it must be forked out by the young couple. This is a very stiff expenditure, amounting to nearly a year's wages for many men.

Then there is the formality. The young couple, even for love and not arranged marriages, is committing itself before dozens, sometimes hundreds, of guests. These are not just close friends and relatives. There are the families on both sides in full force, school friends and work colleagues and, a Japanese fashion, the employers of both young people and perhaps their parents' employers as well. All of these witnesses expect the marriage to succeed, they are investing in it morally and even financially. Yet, as we know, marriage has become a rather iffy proposition. The whole thing is really very daunting.

That both trends, one toward fewer marriages and the other toward more divorces, are likely to continue was shown by another survey, this one of Tokyo couples by *Nihon Keizai Shimbun.* Although 90 per cent of the respondents claimed they were satisfied with their marriage, 29 per cent of the men and 43 per cent of the women admitted that they had considered divorce and only 38 per cent of the men and 32 per cent of the women said they would marry the same person again if they had another chance. This led an expert on family relations, Professor Yasuhiko Yuzawa of Ochanomizu University, to conclude: 'The "satisfaction" most of the respondents expressed seems akin to a feeling of resignation.'

When asked about the advantages of being married, in the same survey, most of the men referred to being treated like full-fledged members of society or having someone to take care of their needs while 44 per cent of the women mentioned financial stability. As the learned professor noted:

> For many, the benefits lay outside the realm of conjugal love and did not involve the quality of their relationship with their spouse. Indeed, if a way could be found to obtain these advantages through other means, more than half of their reasons for being married would no longer exist. With the growing social acceptance of people remaining single, the proliferation of firms in the service sector that take care of household tasks, and the ability of women to earn their own living, the advantages of marriage continue to dwindle, contributing to the push away from marriage.[14]

There has been a decline in marriages, and the formation of traditional families, in the West as well. But alternatives have also arisen there. It is possible for a man and woman to live together, in their own home, and form relatively stable relations. They may have children out of wedlock which they will bring up quite normally. Indeed, the fact that there was no formal marriage has gradually become irrelevant socially and even legally. In Japan, young people do not so simply move in with one another. Most could not even afford a flat. Instead, like good children, these ever older singles continue living with their parents or, for the men, in company dormitories. If need be, they periodically resort to 'love hotels' or like places.

To many Japanese, these 'Western' alternatives still look reprehensible and, on the whole, Japanese attitudes remain rather conservative. This was shown by a survey on alternative life-styles by the government's Social Policy Council. Just under 50 per cent of the respondents regarded mothers raising children independently after divorce as acceptable and 39 per cent found it acceptable when fathers did the same. The level fell to 10 per cent for unmarried mothers raising children alone. As for couples living together without being legally married, only 11 per cent regarded that as acceptable and a mere 5 per cent accepted the idea of homosexual couples living together.[15] Fortunately, considerably larger percentages were able to toler-ate such practices, for they are no longer 'Western' and are also taking root in Japan. Thus, whether desired or not, it is better for those concerned that they be accommodated and not ostracized.

While it takes two to get married, and two to get divorced, it is rather clear from the statistics that women have a some-what less positive view of marriage and a somewhat more positive view of divorce than men. After all, in Japanese soci-ety, they bear the main burden of raising a family and, if the husband is away too much, also find it easier to live alone. Thus, in a Ministry of Health and Welfare survey, 89 per cent of the women and only 84 per cent of the men saw merit in being single. In another, by the Economic Planning Agency, among those in their twenties and thirties, more than 40 per cent of the women said divorce was better than being in a troublesome marriage while less than 30 per cent of the men felt that way.[16] This mood has been noticed by Japanese com-mentators. According to Shigemi Kono, director general of the Institute of Population Problems, 'It's not a militant thing, but we're seeing a kind of "women's revenge" in this country. Women are showing their disenchantment with what marriage in Japan has become.' And Dr. Yuriko Marumoto, a physician and feminist, saw the low birthrate as a 'silent resistance by women' to a male-dominated system.[17]

Finally, within Japanese families, such as are being founded, the number of children is decreasing. Naturally, since women are getting married later, they have fewer childbearing years before them. Moreover, many couples prefer waiting longer before having children. But more couples do not have any children at all. The reasons for this are numerous, and fairly clear. Most are economic. The cost of housing is exorbitant for a young couple and, without proper housing, it is hard to bring up children. The expense of bringing up children has also mounted, especially with regard to education. Some women do not want to give up their career and, often enough, the family cannot get along without the extra money. Yet Japanese companies provide little in the way of prenatal leave or child-care facilities and, more to the point, often try to squeeze out women once they get married or have children.

There are more egoistic reasons as well. Men and women do not want to give up the relatively easygoing and unconstrained childless life, especially if they have enough earnings to buy a car, nice clothing, meals in plush restaurants, skiing vacations and occasional trips abroad. They do not want all their money to go into raising children. Many women, since the burden will fall on them, do not want to be in charge of the children's education, pushing them to cram and becoming *kyoiku mama* like their mothers. So there is also a growing circle of DINK (double-income-no-kids) couples who would not have it otherwise, no matter what more traditionalist Japanese may think.

Thus, more and more couples are choosing not to have children, something that would have been almost inconceivable not too many decades ago. By 1990, the percentage of childless couples aged 30–34 out of the total number of married households had reached 14 per cent. And the level is expected to rise swiftly, to 23 per cent in 2000 and 29 per cent in 2010, according to a report of the Institute of Population Problems.[18] With this, the one child family and the no child family would have clearly displaced the traditional multi-child family. However, it is hard to tell whether the term 'family' is still appropriate for such units.

This trend toward fewer marriages and fewer children is already an old one, as was mentioned. While initially approved, to avoid overpopulation, it is becoming alarming as the rates fall and depopulation becomes an incipient threat. This has sparked reactions from the powers that be. The Ministry of Health and Welfare has been warning about the problems of a population that cannot renew itself for decades, although in a rather remote and academic way, mainly through White Papers. The government occasionally gets into the act. Back in 1980, Prime Minister Masayoshi Ohira commissioned a study entitled 'Proposals for Enriching the Family Base.' It was long on analysis, but short on solutions, most of them being quite general like cheaper housing, shorter working weeks, more day-care centers and improved medical services.[19] Finally, in 1991, it actually did something, offering an allowance of ¥5,000 for each child of pre-school age and twice as much as of the third child.

The business community was considerably more concerned. It was worried that the sources of young workers would dry up, and the average age of employees would rise, also raising wage costs due to increments for seniority. Equally disquieting, with fewer young workers less money would be going into the social security and welfare kitty, which would have to carry ever more retired and aged persons. Higher social security and similar taxes would be ruinous, or so it was claimed, indicating what had happened to Western countries that took that route. Even Nikkeiren, best known for haggling down the annual wage hikes, called on fathers to speak to their children about the importance of work while the catch phrase 'Brave soldiers at work, good fathers at home' went around in the business world.[20]

Alas, none of this made much difference. Working hours were only reduced slowly and grudgingly, making it almost as hard as before for fathers (and mothers) to spend time with their children, who were actually devoting more time than ever to studying and cramming and thus couldn't benefit anyway. The costs of housing and education continued rising. Companies were slow to introduce child-care allowances or parental leaves. And a mere ¥5,000 a month was at best a marginal reward. Anyhow, these just concerned the material impediments. The social and moral ones remained, and nothing was being done to address them. Thus, precious little could be expected of the nation's leaders. As Dr. Yuriko Marumoto pointed out, 'Our politicians and business leaders only go home late at night. They don't know how kids are raised, or what family life is like. Our political system is controlled by men who know nothing about the kitchen or the home.'[21]

So, these pernicious trends should continue sapping the family as an institution without turning up any valid alternatives. There would then be fewer and fewer families, with fewer and fewer children, more people living alone or under the same roof but with limited personal relations. There would be fewer and fewer young people to do the work of society, to carry the economy, to inject new ideas, enthusiasm and joy. And more and more old people, wondering what had happened to the Japan they once knew and worrying what might happen to them in coming years. In such a context, harking back to Confucian values, filial piety or familism will sound more hollow than ever.

It is not with any relish that I present this even more dire prognosis. It is profoundly sad that the Japanese family has been afflicted by so many ills and has found it so hard to thrive in competition with the school, company and other institutions. All the more so since two of the most promising postwar trends were the emergence of the 'my home' and 'new family' generations. Yet, whatever their hopes and aspirations, they have clearly failed. And this failure, in addition to being sad, is fateful. For the collapse of the family can undermine even apparently stronger institutions upon which broader society is built.

6

The Society
(Destructuring And Restructuring)

Japanese society is obviously affected by the significant trends and sweeping changes that have occurred over the past half-century in the various institutions. Like them, today's society hardly resembles that of any previous era, on the surface at least. Further down there is more continuity than many realize, some of it to the good, some less so. It is therefore necessary to take a closer look at these trends and changes to understand how society functions, who runs it and how these leaders are chosen.

Most noticeable, and uncontroversial, are the broader demographic trends which influence where people live, how long they live, what professions and trades they exercise and what lifestyles they pursue. But other trends have completely reshaped the kind of society they live in, sometimes knowingly and intentionally, sometimes almost accidentally. These trends are less visible and considerably more controversial, for they divide as much as they unite and they have created a situation which not all approve of. It is very different from the society the Japanese originally aspired to and yet they cannot escape it.

In this section, more than others, it is indispensable to look back at earlier eras periodically, not just to judge the distance traveled but its direction. The assumption is that Japan is progressing, not always rapidly, but at least moving forward. Yet, in certain ways, it seems actually to be moving backward toward old conventions which had been regarded as archaic, at best, and reactionary, at worst. This would not matter so much if that is what the Japanese really want. But this movement seems to result more from a state of drift and uncertainty rather than from clearly or rationally formulated intentions.

More serious is that these trends only exacerbate many of

136

the problems and abuses which have been dealt with in earlier sections. And they make it harder to find acceptable solutions, acceptable to the broad range of opinion as opposed to the views and interests of an increasingly powerful minority. This may mute the crisis somewhat and for some time, but only make it harder to actually resolve.

Trends That Transform Society

Just how much the Japanese have changed can already be grasped from some broad demographic and other trends, trends which can be followed through incremental but substantial moves in statistics showing how certain minorities grew to majorities while the old majorities shrank or shriveled. Naturally, beyond the numbers, this entailed far-reaching changes in lifestyles and expectations.

One of the most evident has been the continuing urbanization. When Japan was first 'opened' to the West, in the mid-19th century, the country was almost entirely rural. True, there were some bustling and growing towns, such as Kyoto, Osaka and Edo (Tokyo). But otherwise nearly everybody inhabited tiny villages and hamlets or clusters of farms. Even by the end of the Pacific War, although urban areas had expanded quite rapidly, only 40 per cent of the Japanese were urban, and most lived in towns or cities that were sufficiently small that the countryside could easily and quickly be reached while many areas within the cities were actually still farmland.

During the half-century of the postwar period, the trend toward urbanization has continued. By now, some 90 per cent of the population is concentrated in towns and cities while most of the others live near urban areas. Meanwhile, there has been a definite demographic polarization, for there are now vast stretches of countryside which have become depopulated and whose farms and villages are increasingly deserted. Over against this, certain cities have just not stopped growing, including centers like Osaka, Kyoto and Kobe. But even they have grown less rapidly and, in many ways, are being supplanted by the Tokyo metropolitan area which already embraces 26 per cent of the total population (up from 12 per cent in 1950).

These statistics demonstrate the extent of the shift. But they cannot reflect the depth, which is almost overwhelming. Other countries have also undergone such a transition, and are centered around large capital cities, like Great Britain and France, although there is more decentralization in Germany or the United States. In Japan, Tokyo has not only become the largest city, it has monopolized many urban functions and is the vital center for government, administration, commerce and finance, culture and education. Thus, it will continue attracting more people while every other place loses.

Whereas London and Paris, with a similar position in their respective countries, have at least maintained some rural aspects, Tokyo and other Japanese cities have not. The former have numerous parks and gardens and are only a short drive from the countryside. Japanese cities are densely packed, with houses clumped close to one another and hardly a tree in sight on many streets. The urban sprawl reaches well beyond the city limits, and it can take hours to get out of the city on the rare occasions when the Japanese are lucky enough to have extended holidays or vacations. Youngsters brought up in Tokyo nowadays, and even many of their parents, and some grandparents too, simply do not know what the countryside is like in any real sense.

This rural-urban shift was paralleled by a switch in occupations. When Japan was first opened, nearly the whole population consisted of peasants, aside from limited numbers of merchants, artisans, samurai and nobility. During the Meiji era that was already changing, with the samurai swept away, the share of peasants decreasing proportionately, more merchants and budding entrepreneurs, workers of various sorts and nascent classes of bureaucrats and politicians. Since then, the reversal has been nearly completed, with only 3 per cent of the population consisting of farmers (4 per cent including part-timers). It is now the bulk of the population that engages in other occuapations, with large contingents working in factories, offices and stores, and thriving groups of bureaucrats and politicians.

Again, looking at this more closely, what occurred was not just a change in job categories but a transformation of the jobs themselves. These were no longer merchants but businessmen, from those running ma-and-pa shops to directors of nationwide and worldwide corporations. Some artisans remained, but the vast mass of workers were assigned to assembly lines while more educated ones became technicians and engineers. The salaryman class, just emerging in prewar companies, burgeoned after the war, joined by swarms of office ladies. The bureaucrats lives had become more routine, and there were infinitely more of them. As for the erstwhile peasants, they had become farmers.

This means that it is ridiculous to continue speaking of Japan as if it were still a nation of peasants, subject to the elements, who had to put in endless hours to plant and harvest and could be ruined by natural disasters. Yet, one still common theory of Japanese society is that it is based on rice cultivation, which instills hard work, discipline, community cooperation and so on not only in the farmers but every occupational category. Nowadays, the daily routine is fixed, largely unaffected by the weather, and economic success derives from the use of less, not more manpower. Even the worst recent natural disaster, the Kobe earthquake, only caused a tiny blip economically. As for the farmers, that theory does not even apply to them, since they are all mechanized now and their prosperity depends more on political pull and subsidies than hard work. Anyway, exceedingly few Japanese would take the remaining farmers as a model.

During this past half-century and more, the population's age structure has also changed markedly. This trend was discussed in some detail in the section on the family. But certain aspects also have a strong social impact. Most obviously, Japan used to be a nation with many young people and few old. There are now proportionately many more old people than before. That is due to the rising life expectancy, with men expected to live 76 years and women 82 years. This is much older than in any other country and is, in a certain sense, an achievement. Meanwhile, there are fewer young people proportionately. That is only partly due to the large percentage of those aged 65 and over, which should be higher than in any other country by the year 2020. It is also due to a falling birthrate, initially another achievement but no longer so. For the birthrate has already fallen below the replacement level.

This means that the earlier population pyramid is being turned upside down. There are, and will be, ever fewer young

Figure 6.1. *Japan's Population Pyramid, 1930 and 1993*

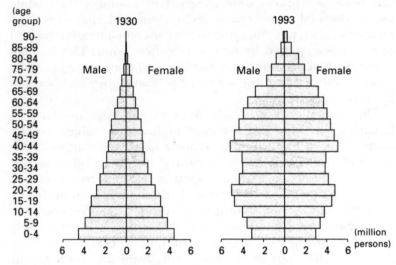

The population pyramid turns into a barrel
and soon an inverted pyramid.

Source: Institute of Population Problems, Ministry of Health
and Welfare, *Jinko no doko* (Population Trends).
Credit: *Facts and Figures of Japan*, 1995, p. 15.

people and ever more old people. The outcome will be, among other things, ever fewer people of working age to engage in the various occupations referred to, and ever more older people who have retired. So, anyone thinking of the average Japanese as reasonably young and energetic had better revise those views. Anyone thinking of Japan as a relatively dynamic and adaptable society should do the same, if for no other than demographic reasons. Other social and economic consequences of this age shift will be dealt with elsewhere. (Figure 6.1)

Fortunately, for all concerned, there has been one other trend, namely for a gradual enrichment of the population. When Japan was first opened, it did have a fairly advanced economy, for an underdeveloped country. There were prosperous merchants and thriving artisans while the upper class proudly displayed signs of affluence. But the vast majority, the peasantry, were dirt poor. Many people lived from hand to mouth and, when there were bad harvests or natural disasters, large numbers starved. Economic growth helped most sectors over the following century, and most people probably improved their financial situation, but the gaps remained large, even larger with regard to the newly rich. It was not really until the postwar period that economic growth accelerated and the circle of those benefiting expanded.

By 1994, the process of catching up had apparently been completed, for Japan had the highest per capita income of any country in the world. The level was a handsome $33,764, according to the OECD. During this time, more and more houses had been put up, many of them owned by their occupants, and these houses had been crammed with every possible consumer durable and household appliance, from color TVs to VCRs, from refrigerators to air-conditioners, from electronic games to pianos. More and more Japanese had cars, with nearly one per family. It would seem that affluence had come to Japan with a vengeance.

However, the situation was not as favorable as it looked. Due to the economic system described in earlier sections, prices were unusually high in Japan for virtually everything, sometimes by a large margin, and they still are. Many food items cost three, four and five times as much as elsewhere. Clothing and durable goods are expensive. Even consumer electronics and cars made in Japan can cost more than the same thing abroad. Gas, electricity, telephone calls, stamps are all more expensive. The biggest item, absorbing the largest share of the household budget, is housing. Here the costs are exorbitant. Japanese can pay twice as much for a home that is not even half as big as the Western equivalent, often also poorly constructed and located a long distance from work.

While most Japanese have managed to acquire individual goods that bear witness to affluence, from Gucci handbags to Rolex watches, they have done less well with regard to communal goods. There are proportionately fewer flush toilets and sewers than in the West and many districts do not even have sidewalks, these being indicated by a line painted on the street. There are not enough normal parking spaces so 'sidewalks' and front yards or gardens are cluttered with cars. And, when they go out for a drive, the roads and highways are densely packed. In the towns and cities, there are not many parks, with 2.5 meters space per person in Tokyo compared to 12 meters

Figure 6.2. *Areas of Lifestyle People Most Want to Enhance*

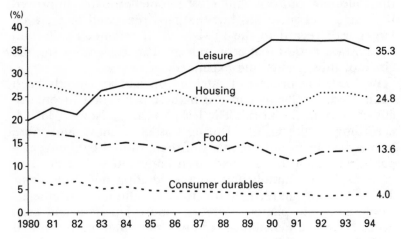

(%)

Leisure — 35.3

Housing — 24.8

Food — 13.6

Consumer durables — 4.0

1980 81 82 83 84 85 86 87 88 89 90 91 92 93 94

For years we have known what the people want.
What a pity that they cannot have it.

Source: Prime Minister's Office, *Kokumin seikatsu ni kansuru yoron chosa* (Public Opinion Survey on the Life of the Nation).
Credit: *Facts and Figures of Japan*, 1995, p. 104.

in Paris and 30 meters in London.[1] Aside from this, there is a shortage of public libraries, cultural centers, sports areas and playgrounds.

Meanwhile, the average Japanese worker still puts in more hours a year, sometimes hundreds more, than workers at a comparable level of affluence in the West. They have to commute an hour or more each way to work. They leave early and return late, and are often too tired on weekends to do much more than sleep or mope around the house. Most Japanese have relatively short vacations and many still remain at home. The reason is that the cost of vacationing in Japan is also very steep, so much so that it is often cheaper to go abroad. This leaves rather mediocre forms of leisure activity for many: practicing golf as opposed to actually playing it, going for a walk in the neighborhood or fishing in an artificial pond. Plus, of course, the old standbys of TV, comics and pachinko. (Figure 6.2)

Thus, Japan's affluence is mainly on paper. People do possess houses, but rather mediocre ones. They do own all sorts of durables, but usually small in size. They can go on a vacation, but not much of one. And they are short of free time. With the highest per capita income in the OECD, they cannot buy as much as inhabitants of countries with a third or a half less. With the longest working hours in the OECD, they cannot aspire to a very relaxed life. Materially, and especially as concerns lifestyle, Japan still lags far behind. Only as compared with the past could one speak of an impressive gain in affluence.

Consequently, in commenting on today's Japanese, it is absolutely necessary to take these four basic trends and others into account. For they are shaping a society that is enormously different from any society Japan has known in the past. While apparently Westernized in many ways, it should be remembered that these trends are not just Western but worldwide by now. And the Japanese have done more than most to adapt them to their traditions, creating not a harmonious blend of old and new but a rough mixture with big lumps of Japaneseness here and there.

Where Are The Virtues Of Yore?

Few countries have ever integrated the individual into society to the extent that Japan has done, repeatedly. The Tokugawa regime was a forerunner of totalitarianism, indeed, far stricter than its uglier, more ruthless later-day successors. It laid down in the finest detail, and with incredible gradations, what the obligations of every person were to society. And, through a hierarchical class structure, it managed to obtain amazingly strict adherence to these rules. Since the system lasted for nearly three centuries, and the Japanese lived in almost total isolation offering no alternative models, many came to assume that this was the only possible social order.

The intrusion of Western powers, with very different mores, naturally upset the previous order which was also being challenged domestically by supporters of the emperor, who wanted to oust the shogun and 'reform' society. This was partially achieved with the Meiji Restoration of 1886, when the old class structure was substantially reworked and all citizens became direct subjects of the emperor. In some ways, this brought an increase in individualism which loosened earlier bonds to the state and also relaxed family ties. Even more important, the trend toward urbanization allowed younger sons to get away both from parental control and into cities which were much more liberal and 'modern.' By the early 19th century, however, some of these trends were being reversed as nationalists took control and demanded ever stricter obedience to the dictates of the emperor (or those who spoke for him) and then more discipline and service to the state. By the time Japan entered the Pacific War, its people were again subjected to an extremely totalitarian regime.

Once again, after the collapse of the Japanese empire, society was extensively reshaped, this time at the behest not of indigenous reformers but of foreigners, the officials of the American occupation. They had Japan adopt a new constitution, with a more democratic and equalitarian bias, which loosened the ties to the state, removed the residual power of the father, dissolved the old ruling class, weakened the *zaibatsu* and put the citizens in charge, on paper at least. Critics never excused the Americans for allowing the emperor to remain on the throne, which kept part of the old system in place. Still, over the years, the emperor's role has been marginal. Other currents and trends were redefining the relations between the citizen and society. Many have already been mentioned: the new educational system, the revamped management system, continuing urbanization and the move toward nuclear and even smaller families, and a ceaseless quest for individualism, sometimes taking the form of 'Americanization' and 'Westernization' but as often merely a variety of 'modernization,' albeit with a special Japanese twist.

At present, the relationship between the people and society, or the state, is not terribly different from the relationship in other advanced countries although, as was indicated in the section on the state, the citizens' input is smaller. Still, on the whole, the Japanese have been content with the changes and even moderately pleased with society per se. In another of those surveys undertaken periodically over the decades, the Japanese were asked the rather vague question: are you satisfied with Japanese society? In the latest edition, 6 per cent were satisfied and 44 per cent were moderately satisfied. This was quite an improvement over 1973, when only 8 per cent were satisfied and 20 per cent moderately satisfied. But the result was hardly brilliant with only half showing some degree of satisfaction while most of the rest were dissatisfied or slightly dissatisfied.[2]

However, any impression of relative satisfaction must be mitigated by the results of more focused polls, both from the Prime Minister's Office. One recently found that 53 per cent of the respondents were uneasy about the direction Japan was taking politically, economically and/or culturally, the highest level ever.[3] The other revealed that 68 per cent of the respondents felt that the government did not reflect the will of the people, again the highest level ever. Equally significant, more and more people wanted to emphasize private affairs and interests over the affairs and interests of state and society, although the latter still had a modest majority.[4]

This was paralleled by indications that there was growing distrust of virtually every institution. Some evidence has already been provided in other sections. But the most startling sign was a comparative study between Japan and the United States, a country not presently known for great confidence in its leaders. Yet, the degree of trust in Japan was far lower in most cases. For example, only 9.6 per cent showed trust in the prime minister, 5.6 per cent in the Diet, 4.4 per cent in the government ministries (that is, the bureaucracy) and 1.5 per cent in large companies, the establishment in short. Nor was there much trust in schools (13.7%), religion in the form of temples, shrines and churches (8.0%) or trade unions (5.0%). Even allowing for national differences, these exceedingly low levels of trust betray an unwholesome degree of alienation from the major social institutions.[5]

There is only one survey which seems to run counter to these trends, namely the professed wish to contribute to society. In annual polls by the Prime Minister's Office, an increasing share have expressed a strong desire to contribute, reaching 60 per cent in 1993, against 36 per cent with little desire.[6] The question, obviously, is whether this is a genuine desire or just a *tatemae*, in the pure sense of a hope or wish or positive sentiment. For it is clear that there has been no parallel upsurge in the numbers of Japanese actually contributing to society in one way or another. We have already seen that ever fewer Japanese are active politically, even to the extent of voting in elections. The situation is not much better as concerns more ordinary social activities.

What is most ominous is that the 'moderns' are apparently less committed than the 'traditionalists.' As noted, Japanese society was extremely tight-knit and close and sustained relations were maintained within the families, villages and broader groupings. The farmers still belong to many organizations, including cooperatives, in which they participate quite actively. Through the cooperative movement, led by the Zenchu federation, they have managed to press their claims for all sorts of agricultural and community improvement projects. The farmers are also very active politically and, what is more, they vote regularly and for what was in the past the ruling party. Supposedly more sophisticated urbanites (workers, salarymen, tradesmen, professionals) have not formed their own, or counterveiling, social and political links and, to a large extent, they have just been floating voters who accepted whatever was dished out to them.

There could hardly be a greater contrast than between Japan's villages and its urban neighborhoods. Down on the farm, although not as much as in the past, people work together for common goals and, indeed, are almost forced to by the exigencies of agriculture. They know one another well, they keep a running balance of who helped whom, and they impose an extra effort on those who would otherwise slack off. In the cities, aside from the shopkeepers and some housewives, most of the inhabitants are away from dawn to dusk and occasionally even on weekends. They live close to one another, yet rarely even know their neighbors, let alone those living a small distance away. There are hardly any local organizations or even local social facilities that might encourage contact. Nobody seems to know, or care, what the others are doing. This may be true of all cities, but it is particularly so of Japan's. The contrast with the past is very conspicuous.

In 'modern' Japan there is not much volunteerism to be seen. Most would cooperate in a natural disaster in their own community, but relatively few if it occurred somewhere else in Japan and even fewer if it occurred abroad. Funds are not collected very widely, nor do they add up to very much, for all sorts of campaigns for good causes, whether to cure a given disease, or prevent an ecological disaster or to aid the Third

World. The movements against pollution, nuclear energy or corruption in Japan have been relatively small and women's lib never even materialized. Organizations with a vast international constituency, like Greenpeace or Amnesty International, have found it rather hard to recruit there. Worse, in some ways, there are not many clubs and activities for youngsters, whether Scouting or Little League baseball. The Japanese are not joiners any more and they leave most charitable activities to the state.

The Japanese do not seem to like society all that much, and certainly do not want to contribute excessively, but they are not opposed to it either. This is significant because it has not always been the case.[7] During the 1950s, young workers and intellectuals fought alongside the socialist parties and trade unions to prevent the 'rollback' of democratic reforms. In the 1960s, partly because of the Vietnam War, they took direct action against the state, including attacks on police, self-defense forces and politicians. The universities, including Todai, became hotbeds of student revolt and groups and bands of various natures proliferated. In the 1970s, countless movements were organized against pollution, discrimination and social abuses.

Then, during the 1980s and 1990s, things quieted down considerably and there were relatively few protest movements of any sort. It seemed that even young people were satisfied with the situation. True, some of them dressed in punk style, and engaged in weird antics in Yoyogi Park or other meeting places. But, on the whole, they seemed uncommonly 'serious.' Yet it was hard to tell to what extent this was approval and to what extent mere acceptance or tolerance of the status quo. For young people still have to worry about residual parental control and stronger action from the schools which could expel them and companies which could dismiss them or reduce their chances of promotion. Much of the calm may have been on the surface while undercurrents were more ambivalent.

For this reason, some Japanese feel that it was a big mistake to repress the earlier movements and create such an indifferent and tame youth. At least, with their predecessors, the public knew that there were problems to be solved and social ills to be cured and the very energy of youth might have been channeled in positive directions. Now, no one really knows what young people want, what they like and dislike, and how they might be integrated constructively into society. Moreover, while they do not express deep-felt grievances, they do not really seem to care what happens and instead look after their own private interests and concerns. They have stopped fighting society, but they do not support it either.

Since Japan's youth is its future, albeit further out than in most other countries, it is important to note that all of the various negative trends referred to initially are most acute among young people. There is less satisfaction with society. There is less trust of social institutions. There is less interest in contributing. Fewer youths join social, let alone political, movements, and now they are even turning away from school, the family and the company. While most Japanese, of all ages, remain law-abiding and well-behaved, especially in public, there are certain adverse factors that tend to be stronger among youngsters and which show that all is not well. True, the situation is nowhere near as bad as in the United States and elsewhere, but it is becoming worse.

Crime is a case in point.[8] Japan has an extremely low crime rate, especially compared to the United States, and even much of Europe. This is attributed to an effective police force and also the remnants of social relationships that discourage crime. Unfortunately, it may also result from underreporting, since most studies show that people have encountered considerably more in their own experience and even the police department concedes that victims are often reluctant to report crimes. It is also low because various widespread occurrences, including some forbidden or regulated by the law, are essentially overlooked, including gambling and prostitution. Although there are few thefts and robberies, there is widespread and endemic extortion which amounts to institutionalized robbery. These are all fields in which Japan's gangsters (*yakuza*), 90,000 strong, are involved.[9]

There are other crimes, which are indeed crimes officially, but seem to be committed almost with impunity. There is a vast amount of white-collar crime, from petty theft to massive embezzlement, which either escapes notice or is hushed up by the company. There is rampant tax evasion, regularly uncovered by the National Tax Administration, but which it has not been able to stamp out. Most noticeable, there is no end to the bribery and corruption occurring in political circles, with huge amounts of money changing hands, sometimes legally, more often beyond the limited amounts, and all too often not for general political purposes but to get specific (and illicit) gains. Yet few of the politicians are ever arrested, even less are prosecuted, and a tiny minority are actually forced to pay fines or are sent to prison. As the Japanese say, the 'law catches flies but not hornets' and 'politicians are above the clouds.'

Thus, at best, Japan can claim a relatively positive record with regard to violent crime, but not other types. And, even then, the trends are not favorable. The share of juvenile criminals, about a quarter of the total, hints that more crime is likely in the future. There is also growing turmoil and violence in the schools. Secretive sects have emerged which the police cannot supervise or even penetrate, and this adds to the worries. For the first time, there are more guns around and available this time not only to *yakuza* but others. Meanwhile, the crime rate, underreporting and all, has been rising and, more alarming, the arrest rate has been slipping. Japan's situation is no longer that much better than many other countries and is worsening. According to one survey, most Japanese had already noticed an increase in crime over recent years and 90 per cent expected crime to increase further over coming years.[10] Thus, in the words of Hiroshi Itakura, a criminal-law professor at Nihon University, 'Japan's law-enforcement system has a reputation as the world's best. Now it is simply a myth.'[11]

Yet, despite the unfavorable trends and the emerging problems, Japan is still treated as number one with regard to law enforcement by foreign admirers. Returning to the scene after an absence of 15 years, David Bayley in *Forces of Order* could wax poetic about a country that was 'heaven for a cop.' Judging by his depiction, it must be so. Japan, according to him, '. . . has a crime rate that is low and declining. Streets are safe and narcotics addiction is infinitesimal. Law enforcement is conducted virtually without stress. Police officers are proud rather than defensive. They perceive the public as supportive, the political environment as benign. The ordinary citizen expects exemplary behavior from police officers and has been given few reasons for believing this unrealistic.'[12] And so on. It would be interesting to see how he explains (away) the sarin gas poisoning, the attack on the chief policeman, outbreaks of

gang warfare in which innocent bystanders are shot and assorted foibles that have occured of late.

If, by some stretch of the imagination, it is possible to blame
certain social abuses on bad foreign examples, others are clearly
home-grown. The sprawling sex industry is one. There are
enormous numbers of prostitutes and dubious bar hostesses,
including Japanese and more exotic girls from Thailand and
the Philippines, most hardened professionals, but apparently
also many free-lancers, from high school and college girls to
housewives eager to make some extra money. Of course, prostitution is prohibited, so the brothels were replaced by 'bath-
ing' establishments ('soaplands' or *sopu*) and the highly popular
'telephone club' (*terakura*) services. There is also considerable
casual, frequently extramarital sex, to judge by the quantities
of 'love hotels.' Although still frowned upon, there is now
more transsexuality and cross-dressing.

Until recently, alcoholism was not regarded as a problem. It
was believed to be mainly social, friends and colleagues drinking together, or bosses going out with subordinates or counterparts in other companies. But more and more Japanese have
taken to drinking, including emerging classes of office ladies
and bored housewives. And the amount of alcohol being con-
sumed is huge and still rising. While most of the drinkers can
handle this, it is evident that there are also many alcoholics
who cannot. Smoking is also a nasty habit which the Japanese
have not been able to throw off.

Both drinking and smoking are excused by society, because
they are not overly disruptive and seem innocuous enough,
and also because it is realized that people need some relief
valves. The same does not apply to drugs. Unlike Westerners,
the Japanese prefer stimulants. But more are turning to narcotics with the official figures for addicts definitely on the low
side given the vast increase in quantities of drugs intercepted.
While most users were initially marginalized persons, often day
laborers or gang members, the share of ordinary citizens
(salarymen, housewives and students) is rising.

The numbers are rising for other social ills as well. There is
a small, but growing contingent of single mothers, many of
them just high school girls. Thousands of teenagers run away
from home each year, some of whom eventually end up as criminals or prostitutes. For years, AIDS was regarded as a 'Western'

disease which did not concern Japan. This despite the hordes of Japanese who go on sex tours abroad or frequent local *sopu*. But that is no longer the case. Japan also has thousands of AIDS patients and HIV-carriers, as officially reported, and perhaps ten times as many including those who keep it secret. For all of these problems, the situation is not very hopeful. The trends are largely negative and yet little is being done to counteract them. Indeed, in some cases, the authorities are doing their best to cover up the phenomena, claiming that they are less serious or quite simply not Japanese. What is needed is, first, a recognition of the problems, second, a policy to solve them, and third, suitable action. For most, the Japanese are still at the first stage, rarely enough the second, and never the third. So, a continuing degradation can be expected.

Beyond specific social problems, it is still necessary to patch Japanese society together. The government is not doing much here. Prime ministers may, on occasion, make uplifting statements about one's duty to society and what the new, future society will hold for the citizens. But this does not have much effect because it is not followed up by actual programs, and so many politicians are known to be corrupt that they can hardly plead for better citizenship and greater sacrifice. Within the huge, sprawling bureaucracy, just the Ministry of Education is doing its bit for morality. But that consists mainly of promoting use of the national flag and anthem, which will hardly turn things around.

Again, only the business leaders seem aware of the implications of certain problems or willing to make concrete efforts. They are increasingly engaging in 'philanthropy,' contributing to good causes of all sorts, educational, cultural, community building, disaster prevention and so on. Some of this is doubtlessly done for the publicity value, the rest because good citizens and good communities are good for business. They are also calling on their employees to contribute more to community projects, to spend more time with their families and so on. They even give them some time off for this. Still, it will take a lot to compensate for the past, when keeping their employees so busy they could not contribute to family or community precipitated the crises.

Unlike other problems, or crises, where the authorities can act whether or not they enjoy broad support, it is quite impossible to forge a satisfactory new social order without the participation of the people. But that is very hard to obtain. For one thing, they are still too busy at school to develop a community sense and at work to do much for community or country, or even family. Moreover, they lack the experience of such action, not having been enrolled in neighborhood activities or youth movements, let alone more active volunteerism. Naturally, many are simply more interested in themselves than others or afraid that they may lose their own hard-won freedom and pleasures. Thus, Japan's predicament is not that it faces problems as serious as those in the West but that, if it does nothing, they could get out of hand.

Creating A New Class Structure

To solve many of its problems, Japan must make a break with the past. But that is becoming ever more difficult because those who benefit from the present dispensation are becoming ever stronger while those who might contest it are becoming weaker. That appears most obvious with the rise of a new social hierarchy that was not planned and not expected but has grown back almost atavistically over the past half-century. It might be mentioned that this is not the first time. The Meiji Restoration and earlier changes of regime just rearranged the social order while the guiding principal of hierarchy was not tampered with.

Back in 1945, Japan's society was more homogeneous than it had ever been. Due to the widespread destruction, most of the former elite had lost its wealth and, for having dragged Japan into a disastrous war, it forfeited any lingering respect. Just in case, so that the old nationalistic Japan would not rise again, the American occupation did what it could to uproot the old class structure and ensure that it would not reemerge. The military was completely reshaped and limited to defensive purposes, the old aristocracy was disbanded aside from the emperor, the wealthy families running the *zaibatsu* were dispossessed and the companies dispersed, many of the old politicians and some bureaucrats were barred from holding office, large landowners lost much of their property which was redistributed through a land reform and workers were supported and encouraged to form trade unions. Another key act was to dismantle the elitist educational system, with Todai at its peak.

These measures, and the guiding equalitarian and democratic principles, were broadly accepted. The losers had little choice but to tolerate them, but they were a minority anyway, and the vast majority of Japanese seemed to prefer the new system to the old. They had had enough of inequality and rule from above, they were tired of bowing and kowtowing to their 'betters,' who held a disproportionately large share of the wealth and property which were then passed down to their children, while it was extremely hard for those below to climb any higher. Equality, democracy, meritocracy were not only enshrined in the new constitution, they supposedly became part of the national fibre.

Yet, over the intervening decades, despite all the lip service to equality and similar virtues, the social structure began to change. Hills arose on the level plains and gradually grew into mountains. Hierarchies emerged in a broad range of sectors and eventually merged. There is already an establishment, and an increasingly hereditary elite, and the gap between those at the top and those further down is widening.

This occurred first in the bureaucracies, where hierarchical penchants are always tenacious, especially so in Japan. There are coteries of career bureaucrats, who rule over the ordinary rank-and-file in the national government, which naturally enjoys a higher position than prefectural or municipal administrations and manipulates them. Within the national bureaucracy, there is a definite pecking order. It starts with the Ministry of Finance, and its related bodies, passes down through the Ministry of International Trade and Industry, lording it over its own subordinates (Economic Planning Agency, Fair Trade Commission, Small-and-Medium Enterprise Agency), some of the other technical ministries, and then to lesser bodies like the Ministry of Education and Ministry of Health. As it happens, the older ministries are often higher than newer ones, except for the military which has indeed been downgraded to a mere Self-Defense Force.

In politics, for nearly half-a-century, the hierarchy was particularly clear and compelling. At the top was the Liberal Democratic Party. It had almost a monopoly of power. Other parties existed, and shared in the charade of government as a loyal opposition, but had little influence. While the structure has changed, and power is spread more widely, it is still concentrated in loose and shifting coalitions of relatively conservative politicians.

But the phenomenon of hierarchy is most visible and widespread in the business world, where it theoretically should not exist since position should be determined by ceaseless competition, and thus constantly altered as companies rise and fall. This does not happen in Japan. There are the big companies, many of them joined together in *keiretsu* (often descendants of the old *zaibatsu*), which easily dominate medium- and small-sized companies. This is sometimes indirect domination, but quite often direct, since they control or manipulate thousands of subsidiaries and subcontractors, suppliers and distributors. Within big business, broader decisions are taken by Keidanren, which also has a pecking order: first the old established companies, then newer ones; first heavy industry, only later electronics and high tech or services.

These are not the only hierarchies: others exist everywhere. In the school system the hierarchy is particularly marked, with Todai again at the top, flanked by some of the older state universites, then the older private colleges, followed by the new state and private colleges, and then by their respective feeder schools at the secondary and even primary level. There are a few national newspapers, each part of a communications empire, which they dominate. Cities are ranked not only by size but by influence, with Tokyo the obvious winner. There are hierarchies, with distinct gradings, in the trade unions and cooperatives, in flower arrangement and martial arts, naturally among the temples and shrines, not to mention the criminal syndicates (*kumi*) and even the Parents-Teachers Associations.

The rise of hierarchies is less of a problem if, within each one, there is enough leeway to allow the ready entrance of newcomers so that the sector can renew itself. But that is increasingly less feasible. The Ministry of Finance controls the budget and thereby remains on top. Yet more stifling, the share of the budget each ministry and agency receives has become relatively fixed, so old ministries have bigger budgets than they need, and the corresponding personnel and prestige, while newer ones cannot expand. The LDP shared all the ministerial posts among its members, usually as a function of faction size, and now more widely with its coalition partners, but again on the basis of political mathematics and not ability or policy. With their alumni placed strategically, Todai, Kyodai, Keio and Waseda can regulate entry to the 'good' companies, which is the essence of being a 'good' university. The *yakuza* control their turf using cruder, more effective means.

The most interesting case remains the business world where, as already indicated, more movement should be expected. In Japan, however, big companies have not only size, they exert control over distribution which means that new companies, with new products, could not even sell them through most of the stores. Should a small (but innovative) company develop an impressive new product, the large companies could easily replicate it and produce it at a lower price and thereby drive the originator out of the market. This has been done repeatedly, most notably by Matsushita (known as *maneshita* or 'copycat'), with regard not only to the bread cooker but the VCR designed by a major affiliate, Victor Company of Japan. Moreover, while large companies have money to spare, small companies lack access to funds and thus find it harder to expand. Recruiting staff for a lesser company is much harder than for an established one, and so on. These and other causes have enabled some companies to dominate certain sectors to the point that there are now oligopolies and monopolies.

Being at the top of a hierarchy brings definite economic advantages. Bureaucracies at the top obtain larger budgets than those further down and can thereby create and control more subordinate bodies. The LDP, and now some partners, have access to ministerial posts and the sources of patronage and campaign funds they command, with the larger factions getting proportionately more. Elite universities, public and private, obtain more government subsidies and/or private contributions. The big newspapers get more advertising revenue. And the larger gangs control larger turfs.

Again, the situation is most striking in the business sector, the one that is most interested in economic benefits. Just after the war, when the economy was being rebuilt and industrial policy reigned supreme, it was the large, often older companies, which actually had the most money and easiest access to private sources, which also received the biggest subsidies and state loans. Now that some industries have gotten into trouble, it is again the larger, more influential companies which are helped the most. Smaller companies, new start-ups, which need finance and assistance more urgently, are in general neglected. Recently, when the economic 'bubble' burst, the government did not hesitate to support the whole banking sector and indirectly the bigger companies, while smaller ones simply went bankrupt.

It is not only the organizations which benefit economically, so do their dependents. The bureaucrats receive bigger pensions than ordinary citizens, they also have access to cushy post-retirement jobs through *amakudari*, with the most lucrative going to ex-MOF and MITI personnel. As already explained, the personnel of larger companies earn more, enjoy better conditions, work fewer hours, receive better retirement benefits, and so on, than those of smaller companies. White-collar staff do better than blue-collar, men better than women, and so on, in keeping with the hierarchical logic of the core system. This time the anomaly is the politicians, especially in the ruling parties, who – despite supposedly crushing expenses – often end up quite rich.

Money is stressed in this context because, without a hereditary aristocracy, money is also a major social divider. But those at the top of these various hierarchies not only obtain relatively greater wealth, they also achieve greater status, in keeping with the ranking system of their organization. They even enjoy more prestige in overall society, being listened to respectfully as they expound on all manner of subjects, some of which they know little about, at high-level conferences, more intimate cocktail parties and banquets, to newspaper reporters or before the television cameras. They are copiously covered by the media which focus on the shakers and movers, Japanese version. Last, and certainly not least, the hierarchs – particularly those in politics, the bureaucracy and business – share the power as outlined in the section on the state.

With the rise of hierarchies and their dependents, with readier access to money, status, prestige and power, it was inevitable that there should be some increase in inequality. Part of that was natural. After the war, everyone was relatively poor, although some worked harder, were smarter or had more luck and got ahead. But it was never expected that certain groups would advance quite as far as they did and that there should be a growing polarization between rich and poor. That went against the whole postwar ethos and seemed to contradict other views, which turned out to be myths.

It is argued, most forcefully by Western management 'experts' and Japanese executives, that pay within a company is fairly even and thus distinctions could not arise. It is pointed out that the boss usually only earns six times as much as a fledgling salaryman. That may be so, but a salaryman earns considerably more than a factory worker in the same company, and men earn more than women. So the gap is not one to six but perhaps one to 16. If you consider that much of the company's work is done by subcontractors, whose earnings are half to two-thirds that of the company's own workers, then the gap can easily rise to one to 30. Moreover, the boss lives in company housing, rides in a company car, eats at the expense of the company and so on. This widens the gap even further: if not quite at American levels, it is not far from those in Europe.

Moreover, this ignores the fact that aside from the one percent of listed companies, most are privately owned. So the whole idea of a wage gap becomes irrelevant. The boss, if he is also the owner, takes a big share of the profits, and these profits can be enormous. In fact, some of Japan's business leaders have become immensely rich and even those in public companies, through some form of participation, also gain disproportionately from the company's success. This can bring the gap even beyond the American level, because there are no shareholders watching over management to keep the financial rewards in line.

It is also claimed that the Japanese are overwhelmingly middle-class and this is supposedly proven by an opinion poll that is frequently cited, but the cards are stacked. Respondents are asked to choose from five alternatives: upper class, upper middle class, middle middle class, lower middle class and lower class. With three of them being middle class, and a generalized dislike of being in an extreme, it is not surprising that about 90 per cent pick some form of middle class. If there were only three alternatives, the result would doubtless be different and the poll might actually have some value.[13]

Equally misleading, this poll measures middle-class consciousness or, more accurately, the feeling of being somewhere near the middle of the Japanese class structure. It does not consider the wealth of the respondents, namely whether they are upper, middle or lower-class in financial terms. When actual assets are measured, the class structure is much more skewed. There are many middle-class households, but there are also some pretty rich families and considerably more that are terribly poor. Over the years, the rich have shown a definite tendency to become richer and the poor to become poorer as society is increasingly polarized.[14]

While income, which is most often referred to, remains fairly even, if less so than before, assets are what really express wealth and they have been rising much faster than income, itself roughly paralleling the inflation rate. The two main assets are real estate (land and property) and financial assets (stocks, bonds, and so on). These two categories have appreciated enormously over the whole postwar period, admittedly with many ups and downs, but nonetheless two, three, four and more fold over a decade. For smart players, with good connections and access to leverage, this could just as easily be five-, ten- or twenty-fold. Asset appreciation has generated far more yen billionaires than normal business ever could.

Amazingly, as early as the 1980s, Japan had more dollar millionaires and even billionaires proportionately than any other country although it had only five decades to create them as opposed to centuries in the West. Also in the 1980s, people who were rich did not hesitate to make this known, buying expensive cars, second and third homes, jewelry and old master paintings. Those less wealthy, especially the young ladies, aped them and decked themselves out in fancy clothing and accessories. In the early 1990s, the 'bubble' burst and some of the rich got hurt. But the smart money pulled out on time and will be able to boost these fortunes yet further. Indeed, by mid-decade the number of taxpayers in the highest brackets was rising again.

At this point, it is necessary to add that there are not only extremes of wealth but also extremes of poverty. Many farming areas, with particularly bad soils or climate, are backward and impoverished although, in a sense, less of a problem as they are now becoming depopulated. Once-prosperous towns, which depended too heavily on ailing industries like coal mining, textiles, or shipbuilding, or where the one factory has closed down, are also stricken. In larger cities, especially Tokyo and Osaka, there are neighborhoods inhabited by day laborers, often recruited by *yakuza*, who cannot make ends meet and live in flop houses and on skid rows. Even in the center of Tokyo, in and around subway stations and parks, bag ladies and bums congregate and spend the night. Millions of Japanese pass by but somehow they manage not to see them.

The emergence of a monied elite would be less worrisome if there were other ways of rising in society. The main alternative was education, with a system that was supposedly equalitarian and meritocratic. Everyone could study for exams, and whoever passed them could enter the better schools, and then move into the better jobs, and thereby climb above the others no matter how humble the starting point. This process did, indeed, work in the first few postwar decades. However, at the present time, educational success has also become a function of money.

To pass the exams, it is essential to cram, and cram courses and tutoring cost a lot of money. To enhance the chances of getting into any college, it is best to take more tests, and that also costs money. Anyone who fails the exams can come back again as a *ronin*, but it costs money to continue cramming and get by without a job. Aside from that, with money it is possible to get into one of the feeder schools or buy into a private college. And richer, higher-status people can more readily pull strings. Thus, over the years, wealthier families have been sending their kids to college while poorer ones often cannot. Quite naturally, at the next level, 'good' families could help their offspring enter 'good' companies.

This general phenomenon was accentuated by the so-called *nisei buumu* or 'second-generation boom.' It was already customary for children to succeed their parents in *kabuki* and traditional arts, farming and small businesses. Increasingly, the children of monks and abbots inherit the temple or shrine and the offspring of doctors, dentists and lawyers inherit their practice. Similar things are now occurring in large companies, many of them private such as construction and retailing firms, but in public ones as well, including big names like Canon, Toyota or Tokyo Gas. Most noticeable, and notorious, are the second (and sometimes third or fourth) generation politicians, mainly in the LDP and its offshoots. There are hundreds of them in the Diet and thousands in prefectural and municipal assemblies. Among the more famous heirs are Shinzo Abe, Kazao Aichi, Yohei Kono, Tsutomu Hata, Ichiro Ozawa, Makiko Tanaka. The Hatoyamas are already in the fourth generation. Nepotism seems to be replacing meritocracy as the key social mechanism for upward mobility.

This already makes elite membership increasingly self-perpetuating, with the children of richer parents tending to earn more and become upper-class, and those of poorer families tending to earn less and stay poor, while the rest remain in the middle. It is further reinforced by the accumulation of wealth, which could be handed down to children. The size of inheritances, and the number of large estates, has not stopped growing. True, there are heavy inheritance taxes, but there are countless ways of getting around them. And, even if all the money is not passed down, enough is handed on so that many young people are starting life much richer than the rest. The wealth, and the related attributes, are becoming hereditary.

The final stage is for individual elite families to merge through marriage of their offspring. The trend is not at all surprising in a society which places so much stress on status and where many marriages are still arranged. Even for those which are supposedly based on 'love,' there is a definite tendency for the children of the rich to mix and mingle and get to know one another. After all, they go to the same expensive private schools, attend the same elite colleges, work in the same large companies, eat in the same exclusive restaurants, and so on. Their parents may well know one another through the many links mentioned above and can promote such a match. This kind of marriage is already quite widespread. An interesting example is Ryoei Sato, best known for his collection of French Impressionists, but also the head of Daishowa Paper, whose brother was governor of Shizuoka prefecture and is married to a Toyoda (of Toyota) and whose son is an LDP politician.

Thus, in only half-a-century, the initial postwar configuration has been radically altered and Japan is looking ever more like its prewar – and supposedly repudiated – self. People are being sorted into classes, sometimes related to professions, with prominent politicians, bureaucrats and businessmen at the summit. Even within the same company, the distinctions between white-collar and blue-collar are reappearing. Farmers, while privileged, are a dwindling category. Meanwhile, there is some danger that an unemployed, transient underclass could emerge. The elite, once arising almost spontaneously, is increasingly fixed with financial assets, status and power passed down within the family. If this is an achievement, it is hardly one Japan should be proud of, and it could result in social sclerosis and class consciousness.

Rise Of The Follower-Leader

As noted, not all the social trends have been moving in the same direction. There has been an increase in social stratification and hierarchization that should induce greater rigidity and, at the same time, various trends toward greater individualism. It might thus be thought that the two would counteract and a new, possibly more flexible, social arrangement be reached. However, it must be stressed that the former trends affect mainly those at the top while the latter influence especially younger folks at the base. Since Japan is manifestly ruled from the top, the tendencies toward stability and stagnation won out.

This proclivity is further reinforced by Japan's style of leadership and the process of becoming a 'leader,' if that term can be used.

It must be remembered that traditionally Japan's leaders were supposed to be quite different creatures from leaders elsewhere. They were not expected to stand out as much and had to consult with, and refer back to, their closest supporters, who might then do the same with the next echelon down, and so on until there was far-reaching agreement right down the line. The widest possible consensus was sought. This was not actually democracy, in the sense that the views of those above nearly always prevailed. But they had to consult, keep their followers informed and show a degree of humility. This meant that any decisions were likely to be rather broad, generally palatable, hedged in all possible directions and, on occasion, simply unclear and ambiguous. They could also take a long time to be reached.

This does not mean that Japan's leaders could not lead. They could. Consensus or not, they were the ones who formulated the basic issues, who had the greatest experience and controlled the sources of information. They could manipulate and intrigue to get their way. In some cases they could use naked force. But, on the whole, they did have to follow the forms of decision-making even if the realities were very different. There have also been strong leaders in Japanese history, usually at times of rapid social change and renewal, as for some of the earlier warlords and shoguns, the *genro* (advisors) and founders of *zaibatsu* in Meiji days and some of the politicians, bureaucrats and especially businessmen after the Pacific War.

Also worthy of note, it was not always the formal leader who led, due to another time-honored tradition for someone who is not officially in charge to pull strings from behind, acting as a 'shadow shogun' or kingmaker. It was often such a person who selected the formal leader, advised on policy and encouraged those at different subordinate levels to agree, meanwhile working out any necessary compromises and providing compensation to those who had to make sacrifices. As is widely known, it was not the emperor who ruled Japan but the shogun, then the *genro* and ultimately the militarists. This tradition has not died out. Within the LDP, it was not always the prime minister who was decisive but someone in the shadows, a Sato, Tanaka, Takeshita, Kanemaru, Ogawa or others. This makes leadership even more nebulous, and sometimes splintered.

Yet, whoever is in charge, the LDP or the opposition, the politicians, or the bureaucrats, or the businessmen, there are factors which make it hard for them to lead even when they want to. One is the basic decision-making process. This involves endless discussions, ceaseless give-and-take until all concerned (but not necessarily everybody) is brought in and a consensus can be reached. This is known by the Japanese expression of *nemawashi* or 'root-binding' and it can take longer than public debate or private jawboning elsewhere. More seriously, consensus implies that virtually all concerned agree, which is a much more stringent demand than a mere majority, or even two-thirds majority, vote.

Another problem is the general respect for precedent. There are societies which, perhaps wrongly, like change and assume that anything new must be better than anything old. Japan is the opposite. Precedent is almost sacrosanct and anyone suggesting change, no matter how justified, no matter how desirable, must expect resistance for no other reason than that it was not done that way in the past. Businessmen, who have to adjust to changing conditions constantly, are less bound by precedent, which may explain their more active role. But the politicians have greater respect, especially when it is a precedent they laid down some time ago or even one that was laid down by a respected elder several decades before. There are no greater sticklers for precedent than the bureaucrats. While they could waive this when it was in their interest, now that more of the change is likely to hurt them, they become protectors of the good old ways.

With leadership so low-profile and entangled, it would be exceedingly difficult for anyone to lead, from the front or from behind, if not for the fact that traditionally the Japanese have also placed incredible stress on followership. Youngsters are taught to obey orders, show discipline and in general keep their heads down and their views to themselves. One of the most popular phrases is that 'a nail that sticks out gets hammered in,' and it is clear that a Japanese at any level who stands out is taking an unnecessary risk. What is done for youth vis-a-vis elders and especially leaders is also done for women against men, and those of lower social status with regard to their betters.

This relationship is not only a social tradition with an intriguing historical flavor as in many places, it still prevails in practice due to another old tradition that one would have expected to disappear long ago. That is seniority. In nearly every society, respect for the elders was inculcated. In some, especially in Asia, it was built into the social order. But only in Japan has seniority remained as potent a factor. In nearly all social institutions, seniors – not necessarily the oldest but those who have been around longest – are in positions of authority.

Seniority has already been encountered in the study of the more significant institutions. In all of the political parties, it makes a very big difference whether one is a junior or a senior member of the Diet, prefectural assembly or town council. In the LDP, which earlier on allocated ministerial portfolios, it was necessary to be returned seven times to get such a post. And, on the whole, seniority was also considered when selecting the prime minister, until Tanaka jumped the queue. In companies, due to the career escalator, company employees rise gradually from year to year, and the status and authority are adjusted carefully to the number of years with the company. In government service, obviously, there are fine gradations of rank and power of each and every type of bureaucrat from entry until exit. Something like this applies for school administrators, university professors, trade union officials, even journalists or gangsters.

The emergence of rule by the seniors, a variation on gerontocracy or rule by the elders, has had many effects on society. The most obvious is that, quite simply, by the time people finally reach a position of leadership they are pretty old. Already after the war, leaders were fairly old, but not so much as before and not uniformly so because many of the earlier ones had died or been dropped due to democratization and exclusions. However, with each passing generation the average age of higher-ups has mounted, and this was further exaggerated by the increasing life expectancy. By now the average age of a prime minister or minister is in the late sixties. Company presidents are often as old or older. Those who win Japan's Cultural Merit Prize usually have to wait until they are eighty. Only in the bureaucracy is the age lower, with most career bureaucrats retiring by 55 (but soon reappearing in key posts in business and politics).

This means that Japan's leaders, who are considerably older than the mass of the population, are frequently out of tune with the times. It has taken until now to have cabinets consisting largely of Showa era ministers, namely those born just before or during the war, while previous cabinets consisted of Taisho era ministers, of definite prewar stock, although the majority of the Japanese were born after the war. Thus, leaders are truly of a different epoch than the rest. Having spent most of their career working their way up the hierarchy, and mixing with other potential leaders, they are out of touch with normal everyday life. This certainly affects their leadership style, and also their chances of success, very markedly.

But nothing shapes them more than the fact that, for 20, 30 or 40 years, they have been followers. In most social institutions, it is not until a person has been a member for well over a decade that the first crack at leadership comes, as a middle-manager, junior official or committee member. And, even then, the possibilities of exerting influence are limited, as opposed to the need to carry out the orders of those higher up. It takes another decade to start giving orders, while still fulfilling the will of the top. Finally, for some at least, there comes a taste of genuine leadership toward the end of a very long career.

While long sought after, and sometimes largely anticipated, it is a redoubtable challenge. For, during most of the previous period, every effort has been made to follow orders properly as opposed to giving them, to implement policies instead of formulating them, to absorb the surrounding ideas and mood rather than shaping them, to keep carefully in the background and never step into the limelight. Now the complete opposite is required. Some highly adaptable individuals can undertake the transition successfully. Most others find it exceedingly difficult or impossible. Decades of followership are hardly the best preparation for ultimate leadership.

Of course, other factors are also at play in the choice of leaders. The most obvious is family ties. In private companies, and even many public ones, the owners' children are slated for managerial positions. The offspring of politicians often know they will eventually inherit a Diet seat. Children of monks will one day run the family temple. Since this is known well in advance, these heirs can at least be trained and prepared. But there is no reason to assume that they possess the essential qualities, and an easy life is not the best way of bringing these out. Where the children are manifestly incompetent, they may be replaced by other relatives, in-laws or adopted children. Yet, even then, the chances that the best leaders will be found in such restricted circles are extremely limited.

While leadership usually comes slowly and predictably, and cannot be hastened much by the individual, there are ways in which sufficiently ambitious persons can get ahead. In some cases, this can involve coming up with good ideas, working harder than the rest, showing an ability to lead. But these are rare cases as, in Japan, they are more likely to worry one's colleagues and superiors than otherwise. It is much safer to act cautiously and quietly, gradually establishing close and amicable relations with colleagues and especially superiors. It is possible to do favors for one or another and, in keeping with tradition, demand return favors later on. It is advantageous to join a faction, help it become the most influential, and then reap the benefits this brings. It is at the higher levels that personal relations and favoritism make the biggest difference in coming out on top.

With most of Japan's leaders ascending to that position through 'followership' and some hastening the rise through family ties or intrigues, future generations of leaders could be even worse than the already mediocre present generation. They could consist even more of time-servers, spoiled offspring and flunkies. It is hardly to be expected that such leaders will introduce new and daring policies to solve the festering problems or that they will inspire their fellow citizens to greater efforts. Rather, they are more likely to stick to the beaten paths, cover their rear with larger doses of consensus and manipulation and adopt policies that are particularly amorphous.

Actually, this process has already begun. Recent cohorts of politicians have been far less dynamic and determined than earlier ones and the last prime minister who even tried to take charge was Nakasone, back in the early 1980s. Since then, prime ministers have been happy to just hold on to the job for a while. With the fall of the LDP, and shifting coalitions, future prime ministers are even less likely to lead. This lack could be made up by the bureaucrats, but they have also become noticeably less energetic and dedicated than their predecessors. This leaves the businessmen.

Alas, the biggest change has doubtless occurred within the business community. After the war, the old *zaibatsu* had been swept away and it was possible for entrepreneurs to form their own companies and expand rapidly. Some moved into new and innovative fields. Many had to become competitive abroad. Facing such daunting tasks, it is clear that in this one sector there was a genuine need for leadership. And leaders did arise, including such figures as Konosuke Matsushita, Akio Morita, Shoiichiro Honda and many, many more. But the founders are now retiring and some have passed away. It is already evident that their successors are often not equal to the challenge of holding the companies together, let alone leading them in new directions. These troubles will also leave them less time to participate in the triumvirate ruling Japan and, when they do speak, it will certainly be with less assurance and authority than the old spokesmen.

So, where are new leaders to come from? Certainly not from an increasingly bureaucratized bureaucracy. Probably not from ever more institutionalized companies but, just conceivably, from the political class. The collapse of the LDP left room for newcomers and some were elected. But most were celebrities, and it is uncertain what can be expected of newscasters, let alone sitcom stars or stand-up comedians. More broadly, it was hoped that the new parties would generate new ideas and that a two-party system would result in which different programs would contend. Alas, so far, the parties have all rehashed the same old policies, the only new thing being their names, and the chances of any of these policies ever being implemented remain low.

Can leaders come from other sectors? Perhaps, but it is hard to see where. The intellectuals are a possible source. Some academics are very knowledgeable, but they are even more remote than elsewhere, living in more forbidding ivory towers. The so-called 'critics' look more promising, and they do publicize new ideas, but they tend to exploit these ideas commercially, selling articles and books, and then move on to yet trendier ideas without caring whether any ever become a reality. The media also participate in the debate, elucidating and evaluating policies. But they rarely take a strong stand or risk alienating those in power or those who advertise. Foreigners have periodically injected 'alien' but useable concepts and practices, but Japan is more closed than before.

In today's Japan, there does not seem to be any potential source of new leaders who could replace or even interact with the old leaders or their followers and chosen successors. There does not seem to be any untapped source of new ideas which could help the leaders strike out in more promising directions. This has the makings of an intractable leadership crisis. It would be silly to go further and say that never before has Japan faced such a crisis because, sadly enough, it has done so repeatedly in the past. The same mixture of the need for broad consensus and dislike of 'leadership' per se, expanding use of nepotism and favoritism to pick leaders who, on the whole, are just followers become leaders, and the aging and inbreeding of the whole elite have periodically led not only to crisis but to collapse. Now that the process has been going on for half-a-century, it is not at all surprising that there is another crisis nor is it clear how further decay and collapse might be avoided.

7

The Nation
(Ties That Don't Bind)

Like any nation, to be a success Japan must represent more than just a combination of social institutions or a collection of individuals living on the same territory. Its people must be joined by higher principles, common aims, a web of social links, a feeling of belonging together and a willingness to cooperate in their mutual interest. If this is lacking, the nation would be badly flawed and fatally weakened.

To many observers, it would seem self-evident that Japan possesses this in overabundance. That would be the view of those who distrust Japan as a monolithic mass, marching in lockstep toward sometimes unavowable goals laid down by a domineering leadership. It would be shared, for completely different reasons, by those who are influenced by the Japanapologists who portray the Japanese as a people who form a tight-knit race, with common roots and goals, and who naturally strive for the common good in a society that treasures harmony.

However, when you start looking, it is not so easy to detect any higher principles or common aims which unite the Japanese and there are fewer links than one expects. Religion is one place to seek any spiritual bonds, all the more so since religion and state have been so closely connected in the past. But that is no longer the case. Indeed, with a continuing proliferation of sects, there can be more divisions than links. Anyway, religion is a less modern source of unity: that is now found more often in some overarching ideology or philosophy. But Japan has also absorbed a multitude of ideologies, only one of which – the most sterile, namely materialism – is widely adopted. Many of the others create as many barriers as bridges. Still, there is a definite recrudescence of nationalism in as yet ill-defined and fortunately relatively innocuous forms.

168

This does not mean that the Japanese do not agree they belong together, or must cooperate with one another, but there can be less positive causes for that as well. For the Japanese can sense that they are Japanese not only for what unites them but for what makes them different from others. And differences from other countries and peoples are legion. Actually, today's internal unity may be increasingly just a reflection of the widening gap between the Japanese and outsiders.

If you ask the Japanese themselves, or monitor their behavior, there is little sign of patriotism. When asked by yet another public opinion survey, this one on society and state, only 16 per cent of the respondents felt a strong attachment to Japan, and another 36 per cent rather strong, accounting for just over half. But this patriotism amounted to rather little: love of country and nature, maintaining law and order, hard work and so on. No one was being asked to risk his life or material well-being. When asked if they wished to be of any service to society, just over half said yes. When asked if they attached more importance to national interest or personal benefit, the respondents were divided. However, on the crucial question of what they should do for their country versus what it should do for them, 42 per cent wanted to receive some benefit from the state while only 15 per cent wanted to help the state, the rest being undecided. If patriotism is weak now, it could become much weaker in the future, because young Japanese are far less patriotic, a mere 2 per cent showing a strong attachment to Japan in the 20–24 age category.[1]

A Plethora Of Religions

Many countries are held together by a common religious culture and numerous fanciers of things Japanese have referred to a strong religious streak. My favorite commentary is that, whether true believers or not, 'the Japanese are strongly imbued with what has been called "irreligious religiosity," an abiding concern with what transcends daily life.'[2] More dogmatically, despite abundant evidence to the contrary, Ian Reader asserts that 'religion is not now (nor ever has been) out of date or step with contemporary society in Japan.'[3] This would seem to be borne out by the existence of multitudes of temples, shrines and even churches in every town, village and urban neighbor-hood, even at offices and factories. Many homes have both a Shinto altar and a Buddha image clearly on display. Indeed, for those who believe statistics, Japan may be the most religi-ous country in the world. According to the *Religious Almanac*, there are some 220 million followers of the various religions in a population of only 125 million, some having opted for two and even three religions.[4]

Yet, things are not so simple, for there are many religions, and they have had periods of rise and decline, none more notably than the original folk religion, Shinto. This grew out of worship of local deities (*kami*) residing in striking natural phenomena and gradually emerged as a broader communion with specific precepts and rites. After Buddhism was introduced in the middle of the 6th century, Shinto was gradually driven back and replaced by or mingled with this newcomer. It seemed to be disappearing, or at any rate fading rapidly, under the Tokugawa shogunate. But it made a striking comeback after the Meiji Restoration, when it became the state religion and served as a source of legitimacy for emperor worship. Gradu-ally it merged into the rising tide of nationalism. With defeat in the Pacific War, it was disestablished and measures were taken to avoid its reappearance in pernicious forms. At present, Shinto is followed by some 117 million Japanese.[5]

Buddhism, with which Shinto sometimes clashed, sometimes blended, had an equally uneven trajectory. When first intro-duced, it was rejected by the people who remained loyal to the local gods. But it was promoted as a higher, more advanced religion, and imposed as the state religion in 594, when a clan which had embraced it won out over its rivals. This was followed by a massive spread of Buddhism, however, in many different forms, some of them borrowed from various parts of China and Korea, others springing up under indigenous preachers. Under the Tokugawa, everybody was expected to be Buddhist, although many still retained or admixed Shinto. Then, nearly 13 centuries after it was formally adopted, Buddh-ism was disestablished in 1868. Nonetheless, it had strong roots and continued to flourish, given a further boost as a 'peaceful' religion after the war. Buddhism, according to the official figures, now has 90 million followers.[6]

Christianity was introduced in the 16th century, a latecomer, but a religion that proved popular among numerous persons in lower classes or outlying regions who no longer found solace in Shinto and considered the Buddhist monks too worldly and remote. Although there were rather few missionaries, and the religion was officially disapproved of, it spread rapidly claiming devoted converts who were willing even to face death for their faith. This made it a potential threat and the early Tokugawa shoguns took measures first to suppress and then to eradicate it. Missionaries were expelled, local leaders and followers tortured and forced to abjure, while the more recalcitrant were killed. By the end of the century, Christianity had disappeared although, in 1873, when the ban was lifted, many crypto-Christians came out of hiding. Thereafter, more missionaries arrived and Christianity was revived, although it never grew to more than about 1 per cent of the population. But its impact has been far greater than numbers would indicate due to the broad influence of Christian schools and the Christian content of Western television, movies and other media.

These three religions have all survived in relatively pure, traditional forms. But they are now being rivaled, and gradually overshadowed, by literally tens of thousands of so-called 'new religions.'[7] There have been three waves of such 'new religions.' The first came after the Meiji Restoration, at the end of the 19th century, some related to Buddhism, many others to Shinto. Tenrikyo is one of the largest and most famous of these. The second wave came in the 1930s and 1940s, during the period of nationalism, and then again just after the war, this time more often related to Buddhism. Soka Gakkai, another major religious group, was part of this wave.[8] The third wave, consisting of the 'new new religions,' is spreading at present, abetted by the current drift, lack of goals and also economic problems.

The 'new religions' differ widely, some tracing more of their ancestry to one of the basic religions than the others, although the number of religious communities in each of the three basic groups roughly parallels the membership figures already given. Some of the latest batch, however, mix precepts, practices, doctrines and gods or prophets to an incredible extent. Thus, for example, Happy Science has within its pantheon, among others, Buddha, Zeus, Jesus Christ, Abraham Lincoln and a space-travelling giant called El Ranty. Aum Shinrikyo, about which more later, mixes Buddha (and peacefulness) with Shiva (Hindu god of destruction). Indeed, nearly all the *new* 'new religions' are exceedingly eclectic. The number thereof cannot be estimated with any accuracy, but there are clearly thousands of them, with over a hundred new groups formed each year.

The older 'new religions' sought members or converts among the lower classes, those who had not benefited as much economically, and those who felt alienated from society. But the newer ones seem to be focusing more on young people, educated or not, from all sorts of social backgrounds. Their methods of prosyletism are often sophisticated, including sales of magazines, books and videos and the holding of media events. Many are publicized by celebrities who have become members. But the main drawing card, in many cases, is a living founder or guru. Many of these arose from quite ordinary backgrounds, yet they possess or have created some sort of charisma. This may derive from spiritual experiences, much exaggerated in the retelling, or blessings they provide through faith healing or good fortune in business or personal matters. Again, the latest techniques are employed to stage extraordinary religious ceremonies, replete with exotic costumes and music, often held in showplace houses of worship.

It is not at all surprising that many Japanese, especially younger ones, should be attracted to the new 'new religions.' They have very little familiarity with, let alone attachment to, the older religions and sects, most of which appear exceedingly old-fashioned and inaccessible. If they join, they feel lost amidst a multitude of believers, many with a longer association and thus greater seniority. The 'new religions' are smaller, more personal, more open. Many are still growing. It is possible to join them and rise in the hierarchy. The fact that their precepts and rites are extremely eclectic, borrowing from a broad range of predecessors, is not that confusing and seems to demonstrate an openness and universality. The possibility of a personal association with the founder or guru, and close social relations with other members, satisfies deep-felt needs in many loners, and the religious fervor fills the emptiness of boredom and sloth.

There are thus many different strands to Japan's supposed 'religiosity,' clearly of unequal strength, but all with some influence on the population. On the whole, the people make a mixed use of them, turning to one for some things, to another for others. It is commonly remarked that the Japanese are blessed as children by a Shinto priest, have a Shinto, or Christian, or both, wedding ceremony, and finally are buried with Buddhist rites. They apparently turn to the 'new religions' for fellowship and mutual support. Due to the syncretism, the tendency of so many people to 'belong' to more than one religion, and the ability of diversified religions and sects to cater to all possible types of needs, religion is in some ways a uniting element.

However, it can also be divisive, for the various groups, and especially their hierarchies, are obviously competing with one another for members and money, and in some cases on doctrine as well. Just how splintered the ranks can be is shown by the existence of about 184,000 religious groupings according to the *Religious Almanac*. Of these, 47 per cent are Shinto, 42 per cent Buddhist, 2 per cent Christian and 9 per cent 'others,' many of these being 'new new religions'. Some are quite large, with millions of members according to their own estimates, such as the older Soka Gakkai, Rissho Koseikai, Reiyukai and Tenrikyo or the newer Happy Science. And more are springing up all the time.

There is a second, more significant divide which is appearing between the three basic religions and their more mainline affiliates, including most of the first two waves of 'new religions,' and the latest wave. Most of the former, even the recent ones, are reasonably stable in membership, have an established hierarchy and a fairly conservative doctrine. But they are now losing members, or having trouble attracting new members, because of competition from the third wave of 'new religions'. Some of these latter engage in very hard-nosed proselytism which is not short on invidious comparisons to the older groups.

More than divisive, some of the 'new new religions' in particular have become disruptive of society. For they have the characteristics of sects as narrowly defined, forming groups that look inward and are secretive or separatist. They make extensive demands on their members with regard to time, energy and money. Sometimes the rites and rituals are so absorbing and exhausting that participants retain little ability to behave as normal members of other bodies. And the leader or guru may demand complete attachment and total obedience. Children are often torn away from their families and, equally seriously for Japan, salarymen have trouble keeping up with the company's demands.

Increasingly, the religious groupings are intervening in politics, commanding support from politicians to whom they offer votes and financial contributions in return for favors. These are usually narrowly focused, with some more reactionary Shinto groups insisting on greater respect for the emperor and war dead, and all religions, whatever their convictions, defending their tax privileges not only as concerns donations but even in respect of commercial profits. More specifically, Soka Gakkai has already formed its own political party, Komeito, with which it always maintains fairly close relations despite any squabbles. Other religions became influential backers of the LDP and the new centrist parties. This gave them more than enough clout to block measures for strict financial control or supervision of religious groups.

While most religious groups policed their own members and insisted that they behave correctly, some engaged in anti-social actions including kidnapping and sequestering members who wished to leave. There were also doubts as to their financial dealings, both as regards donations from members and commercial activities, most of them supposedly making little or no profits. Some few did not hesitate to use pressure or force as necessary. But none broke the bounds like Aum Shinrikyo, whose guru set up a parallel government and warned that the end of the world would come in 1997. To precipitate events, it committed crimes on a massive scale, including sarin poison gas attacks which left a dozen dead and 5,000 injured. Meanwhile, enough weapons and poison gas were hoarded to wipe out tens of thousands of people.

However, there is another even more glaring gap between theory and reality. For, despite the supposed religiosity of its people, when asked whether they have any religious faiths or beliefs only a minority of the Japanese respond affirmatively. The Institute of Statistical Mathematics has been carrying out the same survey every five years, recording a high point of 35 per cent 'believers' in 1958 and a low point of 25 per cent in 1973. At present, only 30 per cent of the population actually claim to be religious. More seriously, only 10 per cent appear to engage in any regular religious activity, meaning that 90 per cent do not.[9] This, admittedly, does not disturb those who cling to the ideal of Japanese religiosity or who point out that traditionally actual attendance at services or practice of specific rites has not been essential.

Still, the degree of religiosity would seem to be rather shallow for most. They are nominally Shinto and/or Buddhist on the whole, but they rarely go to a shrine or temple and many do not even know the basic precepts and doctrines. True, they may be blessed by a Shinto priest, married by a Christian pastor and buried by a Buddhist monk. During important holy days, especially for New Year, they may pay another visit, perhaps pray or make an offering. And the odds are high that they will buy good luck tokens. But religion is very secondary and superficial for masses of Japanese, and they admit it. Under these conditions, the term that applies best is irreligious or secular and, on occasion, superstitious.

Even More Philosophies And Ideologies

In addition to the various religions, assorted philosophies and ideologies have contributed to today's stock of ideas and values. It has often been claimed that the wise (and wily) Japanese managed to borrow the best aspects of each and turn them into a wondrous blend which harmonized with traditional Japanese precepts. As will soon become evident, that was not the case and much of the borrowing was helter skelter, as for the religions. Also, again, the blend turned out to be very different for different generations and also different persons in each generation. Thus, while it does provide many common bonds there are also many barriers and sources of controversy or conflict.

The strongest and most lasting philosophical influence came from Confucianism. K'ung-fu-tzu, who lived around 557–479 BC, developed concepts which were passed down by his disciples, many of them relating to political and social ethics. In some ways, he supported the status quo by insisting that men play their allotted roles correctly, be they rulers or subjects, fathers or sons. The lower were to obey the higher and nobles should be allowed to run the state. He praised virtues like integrity, loyalty and righteousness and stressed ritual and moderation, the middle path. On the other hand, he insisted that the rulers should adopt proper conduct and set a good example. If this were not done, people would find it hard to accept them. To keep them on the right track, men of superior learning should advise the rulers.

If it had remained just a philosophy, this code of ethics would have been a mere footnote. Instead, it was adopted by Chinese emperors, who attempted to rule suitably and created a bureaucracy to aid them. It was also adopted in Japan, initially by Prince Shotoku in 604. He created Japan's first central government, under a supreme ruler (himself) and with a bureaucracy. Ranks were introduced at court and were made hereditary and common folks were supposed to behave like proper subjects. This basic schema was adapted by successive rulers, and worked out in even greater detail during the Nara period and after the capital was moved to Kyoto. Over the centuries, the country expanded and provinces were created, each with its own hierarchy, theoretically subject to the emperor but in practice controlled by military leaders with various titles until the Tokugawa shoguns of the late 16th century.

This time the system of political control was refined in exceptional detail. The shogun, who spoke for the emperor, dominated the various lords (*daimyo*) and their respective domains (*han*) not only through sworn allegiance and strict rules but by counterbalancing alliances, with the 'inner' *daimyo* traditionally loyal to him watching the 'outer' *daimyo*, the nobles, samurai, peasants, artisans, merchants and outcastes bound to their duties and lorded over by the first two, village heads responsible for the acts of the villagers and fathers for those of their household. The role of each group and its respective members, what they could do and not do, how they should behave and even dress, were carefully prescribed. To make the state more effective, the samurai – who had once been warriors – were turned into a hereditary bureaucracy. To make the system more palatable, it was claimed that this was the proper moral order based on hierarchy, loyalty, filial piety and other good Confucian virtues. During this period, Confucian scholarship proliferated and any 'educated' person was expected to know the classics, usually learning them by rote, and to perform the appropriate rituals.

Alas, later shoguns were weaker, the samurai became lazy and arrogant, some merchants and artisans grew rich and actually financed the rulers, all very un-Confucian practices. Worse, it was realized that the emperor was not playing his proper role, which was to rule, and this point was stressed by the 'outer' *daimyo*, tired of being subservient to the 'inner' *daimyo*. The intrusion of Europeans and Americans in the mid-19th century contributed to the collapse of the Tokugawa regime and the restoration of the emperor in 1868. This brought one setback after another for Confucianism, or so it seemed.

The old social order, based on Confucian ethics, was replaced by more modern, Western models. But the Meji regime maintained the family system (*ie*), albeit somewhat looser than before. The samurai were abolished, but a new class of nobles was invented. The samurai schools, which taught the Confucian classics, were replaced by new-fangled schools, but the stress on education was greatly reinforced. And one primary purpose thereof was to train bureaucrats. Despite any lip service to democracy and equality, the new nobility and bureaucrats were firmly at the top of the hierarchy and ordinary citizens, and subjects, were well below.

Confucianism still served as a source of virtues for the new nation: respect for the emperor, acceptance of hierarchy, continuing filial piety and subordination of women, and a taste for ritual and role playing. But its influence was fading fast. It was unable to suppress the popular support of more equalitarian principles or the growing power of political parties, which raised high the banner of democracy. In a looser society, more enterprising individuals could rise, mocking the ideas of fixed hierarchies and classes with immutable roles. Confucianism soon appeared stodgy, at best, compared to the breathtaking variety of Western philosophies and ideologies arriving all the time. Its last gasp, again seemingly, was as one of several props for nationalism, Shinto being far more important. It could, however, hardly be implicated in the militarism that exacerbated this nationalism and brought the country into the Pacific War, for soldiers were not recommended as advisors by Confucius.

It would take forever to go through the multitude of philosophies and ideologies imported by Japan during the century-and-a-half since it was opened by the West. Some were popular at one time, some at another, and all still have some adepts or at least persons who absorbed them knowingly or unknowingly. There was individualism and the cult of the self-made man in Meji days, capitalism and socialism by the early 20th century, and then communism and Marxism and, more recently, free enterprise and free trade. Kant and Hegel were passing fancies, as were Darwin and Freud. To this must be added nationalism and colonialism, now formally banned. But there were many, many more. So many, indeed, that the Japanese were confused about just what each one signified, how they should be used and what any disadvantages might be.

It should be noted that this hodgepodge of ideas and concepts, like the hodgepodge of religions, tends in many different directions. There is democracy and dictatorship, individualism and communalism, regulated and liberal economies, and so on. Again, this means that the philosophies and ideologies were also not necessarily a source of unity. Quite to the contrary, very acrimonious and sometimes bloody disputes arose over which was the proper path for Japan in prewar and early postwar days. The only reason there is more unity now is that some lost out abroad, and were thus discredited in Japan, and others just withered. Japanese Marxism, for example, was preached so much like a religion that it had little practical use and Japan's Communists and Socialists steadfastly refused to update or accomodate new forces and just lost relevance.

The only '-ism' which seems to unite the Japanese and has again in recent years become an overpowering urge is materialism. It is not as if this did not also have deep and honorable roots. Despite any otherworldliness, Buddhist temples engaged in gaudy displays of wealth and the monks often led idle and lascivious lives, requiring great sums of money. The upper classes spent vast amounts on palaces, garments and gifts and the merchants, while forbidden public displays of ostentation, secretly hoarded their wealth. Today, as in the past, people often visit temples and shrines for material reasons like passing exams, finding a suitable husband or blessing cars and houses.

The Japanese, bitterly poor after the war, were obviously fascinated by the wealth of their victors, the Americans, and they launched into a mad dash to catch up economically. While not quite getting there in real terms, they began accumulating all sorts of material tokens of progress which they glimpsed in TV shows. They also competed with one another to see who had the finest clothing or fanciest cars. Keeping up with the Joneses, traditionally known as *hitonami* consciousness, became a very earnest matter. It was always strong but, during the 1980s, it broke out in all sorts of garish forms, with young ladies wearing the latest Paris fashions (or equivalents thereof) and flaunting their accessories and jewelry. Men also improved their wardrobes and sometimes bought sports cars which could hardly be used on Japan's roads.

Materialism may have been a normal reaction, given the poverty of the early postwar years and the temptations that existed. But at least the older generation knew that there was something else, and that one had to work hard for affluence. Since then many generations have grown up, each in increasingly comfortable circumstances, and they have not known – or even been told about – the alternatives. For them, materialism is the only way they know. While they do not quite worship material goods, they find it ever harder to do without them. Now, when young women think of marriage, the wealth of the prospective husband becomes an essential factor. And, in a survey of junior high school students in Tokyo, almost half thought that money is the most important thing in life. One-third of them already had a cash card and many wanted a credit card.[10]

There are signs that this materialism is abating. From year to year, the Japanese have been asked by a government poll which is more important – material affluence or spiritual health. Up until the mid-1970s material affluence won out; since then spiritual health has not ceased rising. By 1994, 57 per cent of the respondents chose spiritual health and only 30 per cent material affluence.[11] The trend is perfectly clear, but the interpretation is still uncertain. There may be a genuine urge for spiritual uplift, or most people may simply have accomplished their main material goals and be looking for something else. Also, spiritual uplift may just be fashionable.

Concrete examples point in both directions. What some people are thinking of is less work and more leisure. Others want greater attention paid to enhanced medical and welfare facilities, more attractive housing and better amenities. These are more communal, less self-centered goals. But they are nontheless material, requiring money to be fulfilled. Meanwhile, there has been an increase in young adults turning to religion, especially 'new religions.' That seems to point in the direction of spiritual progression. Yet, all too many 'new religions' not only stress material rewards, they are fund-raising operations collecting vast amounts of money from their members and also commercial enterprises running all sorts of businesses.

Despite the ultimate priority on materialism, expressed through a single-minded urge for growth in which GNP (gross national product) assumed almost mythical significance, Japanese materialism has been a rather unsatisfactory affair. The Japanese already have the world's largest national assets and the world's highest annual income. But, given prevailing costs, they do not buy as much as elsewhere and the purely material standard of living remains below many Western countries. When one includes aspects related to quality of life, like housing, amenities and leisure, Japan remains fairly low in the listing. This means it has not really caught up and will have to strive even harder to do so, given the increasingly adverse circumstances.

As bone fide materialists, the people do not have much to show for it. They live harried lives, with long commutes on crowded trains to and from work, where they put in more hours and days than their counterparts in advanced countries. Their homes, on the whole, are rather small and rickety. They are packed to the brim with material goods, from rice cookers to refrigerators, from TVs to VCRs, so that there is hardly room to move about. Yet this generates a rather mediocre lifestyle with which the Japanese are no longer satisfied.

Considering that they have been busy building for half-a-century, it would be thought that at least Japan's major cities would be cosmopolitan wonders. Admittedly, here and there, clusters of skyscrapers create a modern skyline, but they tower over undistinguished commercial districts, decorated with flashing lights and plastic cherry blossoms, and showing little class. The nondescript residential neighborhoods that stretch endlessly in all directions are scruffy, to be generous, and hardly what one would expect as the abode of the affluent. Tokyo and Osaka thus compare rather poorly with New York, London or Paris and do not even offer the charm of Nara or Kyoto in their heyday. Visitors from another planet overflying Japan would wonder how this could possibly be one of the Earth's most advanced civilizations.

In return for this second-, third- or fourth-rate materialism, the Japanese have had to give up a lot. These things are not expressed in material terms, and do not add to GNP, so they often go unnoticed, but they are precious. What is more, before the mad dash for growth and prosperity, many Japanese had them almost free of charge.

One such is a culture that satisfied the yearnings of the people, whether through music or painting, religious ceremonies or village festivals, Noh or Kabuki. They were even highly admired by foreigners of quite alien cultures. Yet, nowadays, alongside the shortage of roads and sewers, there is also a scarcity of theaters, concert halls and even cinemas. The cultural amenities of Japan pale in comparison to those of Western countries and that is not likely to change as long as the state's cultural budget remains pitifully small. No wonder when visiting musicians and singers arrive the tickets are quickly sold out.

Related to this is a once deep aesthetic sense, expressed not only through the cultural aspects mentioned above, but the ordinary person's way of life. Temples were elegant and uplifting, houses had appealing proportions and forms, clothing varied from simple but graceful to ornate yet elegant. Arts and crafts were pursued and beautiful objects produced. Many individuals knew how to sing, dance or play instruments. Now housing is so shabby most Japanese are ashamed to receive visitors. While some temples became tourist attractions and others were turned into parking lots, many of the newfashioned places of worship are almost grotesque. What passes for class, especially for the bachelor aristocrats, is any fashion article with the designer's name or initials clearly emblazoned on it.

Traditionally, nature was part of everybody's life. It was not only that most Japanese, like most other people, once upon a time, lived closer to nature. For the Japanese, their early religion Shinto was in part nature worship. Even when they moved to towns and cities, the first generations preserved a love of nature and at least cultivated *bonsai* trees. Yet now millions of Japanese live quite contentedly in neighborhoods without parks and gardens and almost barren of trees and flowers. They no longer make the long pilgrimage to the countryside, preferring to spend their vacations in other cities. And even smaller towns and villages, which are physically closer to nature, have become petty, ugly replicas of Tokyo, complete with identikit stores, bars and night clubs, ubiquitous vending machines and pachinko parlors.

Finally, the hustle and bustle of modern living has destroyed the inner life for most. It is hard to believe that Buddhism, and particularly Zen, placed emphasis on silence and meditation. For it is almost impossible to escape the clamor in the cities and, even when going to more remote places, so many citified Japanese come along that the silence is destroyed anyway. Maybe silence and meditation are no longer fashionable, to judge by the small number of Japanese and large number of foreigners inhabiting the *zendo* nowadays. But at least people could turn off the television and read a book or engage in a civilized conversation without the adjunction of alcohol.

Whatever the Japanese may list as their future goals, it is apparent that presently the broadest common denominator is materialism. And, since it is such a rudimentary form of materialism, it will probably remain the primary thrust for many more decades until at least a decent material living standard is achieved. Alas, by then, it may be impossible to seek spiritual health or restore the precious legacies of the past. Moreover, whatever desires this materialism may fulfil, it cannot really bring the Japanese together.

A Strange Blend Of Precepts And Principles

From these various religions, philosophies and ideologies the Japanese have distilled a body of precepts, principles, ideals, goals, practices, and so on, that they follow to a greater or lesser extent. The extent depends on the exposure of each person to one source or another and other circumstances of his or her life. There are also definite generational differences, with older generations more imbued with Shinto, Buddhist and Confucian feelings while younger ones are more familiar with Western and Christian sentiments, on occasion, than traditional Japanese ones.

Also, as elsewhere, some of the precepts and principles contradict one another. The clash between those of Shinto and Buddhism and those of Christianity is fairly obvious. But there are also Shinto practices that counter or nullify Buddhist ones and, quite often, Western philosophies and ideologies that point in very different directions from one another. Thus, rather than some magic blend, in which the Japanese – we are told – take the best from each, it is more likely to be a mixed batch, some good, some bad. This is not said to criticize the Japanese, such things exist elsewhere. Only, having borrowed so much, from so many places, there is bound to be a lack of homogeneity.

In presenting these precepts and principles, obviously it is not possible to include all. Certain features, which I regard as particularly important for understanding Japanese society, were selected. They may not always be the right ones. Nor will they always be correctly expressed. This is just another attempt at figuring out what makes Japan tick. And, in another 15 years, I may have refined it further. But it is essential to have something to go by now or the social crisis will make no sense.

Hierarchy is certainly one of the most fundamental characteristics. The concept, and practice, were adopted largely from Confucianism, although other religions and ideologies also stress it in one way or another. Hierarchy, as was indicated, can be found in virtually every Japanese social institution. But what concerns us most here is that there are various types related to various factors for ranking.

Traditionally, and in many other societies, age has been a critical factor and, what with the principle of respecting one's elders, this was always notable in Japan. Unlike most other societies, however, this principle has not faded because so many present-day bodies still rank members by something related to age, namely seniority. Company employees rise on the 'career escalator' from year to year. Junior Diet members rise each time they are reelected. In school, the move up from freshman, to sophomore, to junior, to senior is more meaningful than elsewhere. Gradually, as one ages, one progresses toward the top of this pecking order.

In the past, this could create a gerontocracy in which the aged, foolishly also deemed the wisest, might rule. But that is not exactly the present situation. Seniority prevails, which means that even a younger person, who joins earlier, comes ahead of an older person, who joins later. This enhances the advantages of getting in quickly, whether it be for a company, club or religion.

At the other end, old age no longer carries much weight once one has retired from the organization. Retirees are just old folks, not seniors, unless they can still pull strings through their acolytes.

Naturally, the ranking by age has to compete with other rankings, the most significant being ranking by position or authority. As noted, while most newcomers rise year by year, some manage to push ahead, whether because of birth, ability or intrigue. If they achieve higher positions, whatever the age ranking, they can give orders and must receive respect. Despite any talk of 'the company belongs to its employees,' ranking in companies is as strict as ranking in the military, with certain grades clearly signified by titles while those beneath are classified by year of entry. Even in the West, where bosses are supposed to reign supreme, young employees are not graded by how many years they worked for the company. And this is nothing compared to the ranking and grading in the bureaucracy.

Ranking by age and authority is especially potent in Japan because of the language. As already intimated, it provides for precise distinctions which cannot be avoided. A younger person must talk up to an older one, and a senior must talk down to a junior, on formal occasions at least. Within companies, the bureaucracy, the military and other bodies, superiors must talk down to inferiors and inferiors must talk up to superiors. Since, in many social situations, men also talk down to women, and women talk up to men, there is also a ranking by sex, although in certain settings that can be overruled by the age or authority ranking.

Given the emphasis placed on education, another hangover from Confucianism, there is also a ranking by education. And it remains true to its Confucian roots, since it is based on success at passing a rather small number of rather meaningless tests. This ranking is fairly thoroughgoing as well, with a first basic division between those who graduate from high school and those who make it through college (but not graduate school). This is further graded by the type of school and then the school itself, with Todai at the apex. This is more than theoretical, given the impact on the ranking by authority, and differences are often expressed in language and demeanor.

The last ranking stems from materialism. It is the latest to appear, but it seems to be making rapid progress. There is no doubt that those with money are being shown more respect than in the past, all the more so if they also possess authority, which often happens, and sometimes greater age. In various ways, money is also affecting the other forms of ranking, since money makes it easier to get into 'good schools' and then 'good companies.' And it helps those who want to marry into 'good families.' Unlike other attributes, there is no age limit, a rich retiree is still rich.

The result of hierarchy has been the 'vertical society,' a concept introduced by Chie Nakane and broadly accepted.[12] Unlike most other societies, he explains, Japanese society is based primarily on vertical links between a parent/father figure (*oyabun*) and others assimilated to children (*kobun*). These links are not left to chance but carefully cultivated so as to resist weakening due to other factors. Tradition, practical arrangements, authority ranking as affected by seniority and so on have preserved this structure more than elsewhere. Still, the vertical links are not as resilient as they used to be. Over recent decades they have been weakened whenever undermined, rather than reinforced, by ranking according to authority, education, wealth and even sex. Equally important, the horizontal links have been consolidating. There is more rapport among persons of the same entry year in companies, schools, and so on, if for no other reason than to resist the pressure from above (and impose a bit of respect on those below). This also has its traditions, since young Japanese were also customarily organized by age groups and it is easier to get along with such relative equals since one can speak more freely and openly.

Hierarchy is also under more direct attack from countervailing Western principles like democracy and equality. These were written into the constitution, and then incorporated in the laws of the land, and have brought about far-reaching changes in relations between parents and children, men and women, younger and older, proper Japanese and members of various minorities, and so on. While they cannot affect the hierarchy within political parties, or indeed the selection of the prime minister on many occasions, they can determine whether specific politicians will be elected and thereby continue to rise in the hierarchy. They are of less use within the company and most other hierarchies, especially the bureaucracy. But, because they remain ideals, democracy and equality have been undermining the role of hierarchy ever since Meiji days and, with renewed vigor, since the time of MacArthur.

Their effectiveness would have been greater if the Japanese had not given a special turn to these principles by fusing them in the concept of meritocracy, which was to prevail. Of course, everybody would be given an equal chance to succeed and success would be measured by the results on specific examinations, examinations which everyone could take on an equal footing. This would prove the person's 'merit,' or lack thereof. However, once merit had been ascertained, once and for all, hierarchy would take over through the ranking by education, which then affected the other rankings as those with merit entered the 'good' companies and so on. Alas, as was shown, merit has had ever less to do with success while money has played an increasing part.

A second major principle is communalism or groupism as expressed by the constant calls for unity and the insistence on reaching consensus. This also has its Confucian and religious roots with the strong appeal for harmony (*wa*). These have been reinforced by social practices that prevail today. Every social institution is tightly structured, so that there are sharp distinctions between insiders and outsiders. This idea of *uchi* and *soto*, as practiced in traditional villages, finds its counterpart not only in religions or arts associations but in schools (with their uniforms) and companies (with their uniforms and badges). There it is most refined, through what I call the core system, since the corps of regular workers and those of peripheral workers are separated with exceptional rigor.

Yet, despite all the stress on unity and harmony, the Japanese are continually at odds with one another. Throughout Japan, village competes with village, school with school, company with company, political party with political party and so on. There is also incredible competition among families to get ahead and for children to pass the stiffest exams. This competition can be exceedingly bitter, with no quarter given or asked, and the devil take the hindmost. Losing out can be painful, or worse, as for students who cannot get into college or companies which go bankrupt.

This is hardly in keeping with Buddhism or Confucianism and may come from Shinto and even more primeval memories. But it also derives directly from the principle of communalism.

Units are so tightly organized, so cohesive internally, and so unconcerned about what happens to outsiders, that there are fewer bounds on village, school or company animosity or rivalry between persons and families. In the companies, moreover, there are unusual business practices that push them to be ruthless, none more decisive than the struggle for market share. If they sought profits, it would not matter all that much what the competitors were doing, since all could prosper (or not) in a given field through their own efforts. However, market share is limited, by definition, to 100 per cent. If one company's market share rises, that of another *must* fall. And, if it falls enough, that company is out of business.

This rivalry and the barriers between insiders and outsiders make even ordinary cooperation such as occurs in the West quite difficult. There are so few people who have militated within one party and then another, worked at one company and moved on to another, even taught in one school and given a few courses at another that it is hard to find anyone who is accepted by two competing units. For them to cooperate, for them to even communicate, requires special middlemen or go-betweens, not so different from the *nakodo* at a marriage, who can establish relations and help them negotiate. While some of this is done by respectable persons, many are just fixers or deal makers who manipulate and pursue their own agendas as well.

While competition and rivalry between different groups might be expected, division within the groups would appear misplaced. Yet there is no end to that either, due to factionalism. It also seems to have ancient precedents, to judge by the tales of treachery and betrayal from feudal times, only slightly more gory than what happens today. There are all sorts of factions (*batsu*), many of them being personal, forming around a more charismatic or dynamic person, who adopts the role of *oyabun*. Others link graduates of the same school (*gakubatsu*) or people coming from the same town or prefecture (*kyodobatsu*). They exist within bureaucracies (*kambatsu*) and political parties (*habatsu*), most noticeably the old and the new Liberal Democratic Party but others as well, school administrations, university faculties or criminal syndicates. More surprisingly, they are widespread even within the company 'family,' be it the company as a whole or specific divisions. A survey by Dai-Tokyo

Fire and Marine Insurance found that factions and cliques existed in as many as 62 per cent of the companies and roughly 53 per cent of the Tokyo salarymen polled belonged to such groups.[13]

Factionalism can be traced, among other things, to the vertical society for the very reason that horizontal links are so weak. Basic, elongated units are formed by an *oyabun*, who recruits one or more *kobun*, who then recruit other *kobun* in a pyramidal configuration. When the 'father' dies, or steps down, if there are two or more juniors with equal seniority (and authority), they may quarrel over the inheritance and split the group. Even before that, a particularly charismatic or clever junior, if he is a bit of an intriguer to boot, may find that he has enough followers to break away and form his own faction instead of waiting for the venerable master to fade away. Thus, as long as hierarchical links remain strong, factionalism will remain a threat to every hierarchy in every human community.

While communalism can be undermined by competition and factionalism, the worst danger is that it will not be weakened enough. For groups tend toward excess, and there are ample precedents for this as well, including the Pacific War. They take one decision, which imposes another, and another, and they find it extremely hard to stop. They take one step, and then another, and another, and keep going in the same direction. Even if that was the right direction at first, somewhere along the line it is necessary to turn in order to adjust to changing circumstances or to avoid running into a brick wall. Instead, rather than retreat, or even veer to the side, they move ahead. The outcome could be the destruction of the community itself.

There is no derivation for this in Buddhism, with its appeal for a middle way, or in other traditional sources, let alone Western influences. But the proclivity for excess may grow out of communalism itself, since all insiders – when facing competitors – pull together and attack. Since all decisions are taken by insiders, they are not open to outside views which might argue for other policies, and thus they tend to pursue whatever policy was initially adopted (even if under other circumstances). And, should some insiders realize that to continue in the old direction would be disastrous, aside from any accusations of failure to abide by precedent or even treason, they still have to convince each and every other member due to the rule of consensus.

The only visible corrective to communalism seems to be individualism. This characteristic will be discussed more at length in the section on the individual. Suffice it to say, for the moment, that it is both alien and poorly understood by the Japanese, often equated to egoism, and it has also given rise to excesses. Still, if the individual's egoism can mitigate the group's egoism and the individual's excesses can temper the group's excesses, it could make a precious contribution.

One last series of principles, more formal than fundamental, must be considered. They are the urge for rite and ceremony, for ritual and role playing, which pervades Japanese society. This probably derives from Confucianism, with its insistence on a rectification of names, where a son should behave like a son and a father like a father. But, if this does not come naturally to the son, or the father, or the boss, or whoever, then it will only result in going through the motions. If no one can afford to lose face, another venerable tradition, then the play acting must go yet further. The final result can be two conceptual levels, those of *tatemae* and *honne*, which have been so often encountered.

How much longer this play acting can continue is uncertain. Young people, and women, and lower classes, and those who in general have the more demeaning role to play and who have to swallow the *tatemae* of others are becoming tired of this. But they do not yet have the power to do much about it, so they avoid such ambivalent situations as much as possible. And they go their own way. Of course, in doing so, they make believe that they are model children, wives, employees and so on, since that is the easy way out. Hypocrisy must therefore be added to the social practices.

While many things have been absorbed from native and imported sources, others appear to have been overlooked or failed to take. Most surprising is benevolence and philanthropy, so much a part of Buddhist and Confucian teaching, or charity, coming from Christianity. The Japanese do not seem to love one another particularly, and certainly not outsiders. Unlike the Chinese, individuals do not endow schools and hospitals very much and the companies have come late to philanthropy. There has not been much kindness shown to the poor, sick and aged, pollution victims or China orphans (who are Japanese), and even less to comfort women and refugees (who are foreigners). The only ones who help them are their direct relatives or group members or, failing that, and certainly not generously, the state.

Even more serious is the inability to fashion a generally acceptable code of ethics or even enforce respect for the rule of law. This is odd, since the primary concern of Confucianism was to impose a strict system of ethics and Buddhism is replete with moral precepts. There are also the moral values and legal rules imported from the West, drawn from religions and secular sources, and sometimes enshrined in the constitution or basic legislation. Yet, while they do pay voluble lip service, the Japanese do not abide by such absolutes. Rather, they devote their attention to 'human relations' with one another and especially with other members of their group. If the others are doing something, whatever its moral or legal value, it must be acceptable. This creates a morality that is particularistic and situational and inevitably flaunts general principles and laws.

Unfortunately, this saps one of the most essential foundations for any society. The same code of ethics, and certainly the same laws, must apply equally for all if everyone is to feel part of the same broader community. And what goes for ordinary citizens should go double for those in authority. Yet, politicians do not hesitate to accept bribes, excusing themselves because this was done for the party. Or they wangle public works and other benefits for their constituency, not to get reelected mind you, but for the good of the people, 'their' people. There are even more cases of bribery and white-collar crime which, if done for the good of the company and not personal gain, are supposedly all right. In this way, 'absolute justice has become secondary to insiders' justice, and public ethics has taken a back seat to the internal ethics of the organization.'[14]

As expected, some of the precepts and principles are relatively positive, others relatively negative. The trends are also mixed, with some signs of improvement, some indications of regression, and assorted aspects that are not changing much. Actually, on the whole, there is probably more good than bad in this picture, and yet there is no reason for hope. Much of the improvement and progress is occurring among younger people, with a more modern outlook and attitudes more in keeping with present circumstances. But the country is not run by younger people so the prevailing order will be that imposed by older generations with older ideas.

Aside from any question of 'good' or 'bad' trends, which is unavoidably subjective, there is the somewhat more objective matter of whether Japan's panoply of precepts and principles is uniting or dividing society. While hierarchy unites some people, it obviously separates them from others, and this is exacerbated by the strict distinctions between insiders and outsiders. Tightly-knit groups do integrate their members, but they often engage in competition and rivalry that divides. Such divisions can even seep into the groups, through factionalism and cliques. Other distinctions reinforce generation, gender and religious or racial gaps. So, it is hardly here that one can seek whatever cement holds the Japanese together.

Nationalism, Not Quite Forgotten

Among the philosophies and ideologies, one was not mentioned that should presumably go to the top of the list, namely nationalism. True, the Japanese are comparatively nationalistic and the feeling of being part of a nation is very strong when dealing with foreigners. However, that nationalism is often not expressed verbally because people are so impregnated with a national consciousness that it is not necessary. They feel part of the group, the broadest group, namely the nation, and growing up within a society that is exceptionally conformist they tend to behave pretty much alike. This can create an optical illusion that they are marching together to the same drummer when, in fact, they are not.

In practice, as we saw, the goals have often been different for different groups and different ages and there can be incredible contrasts and conflicts. Thus, it is often at times of maximum disunity that it seems necessary to create an overt feeling of cohesiveness to stifle the centripetal forces that could tear Japan apart. That is particularly important when, in addition, Japan is under attack from outsiders.

One such time came after the Meiji Restoration, when the threat of foreign intervention and influence was particularly acute as Western powers carved out colony after colony in Asia and Japan could have suffered a similar fate. Respect for the emperor was raised to a higher duty and the Japanese were warned that Western influences could corrupt them. To maintain order, the hierarchies were reinforced and control over the subjects was tightened, while myths such as the divine origin of the emperor and the emergence of the Japanese people from the sun goddess Amaterasu were refurbished.

Due to colonialism and imperialism, soon practiced by Japan as well as by Western powers, there were more than enough causes for drumming up nationalism. Japan remained on a fairly even keel for awhile. It was frequently run by liberal parties whose economic and social concerns prevailed. There was also a growing opposition of trade unionists, socialists and Marxists who rejected nationalistic pleas. This was again a period of discord, individualism and egoism, to say nothing of corruption, which antagonized groups that preferred the old order and wanted to instill greater patriotism. They would probably not have achieved much if not for the military, especially younger officers, who sought to expand Japan's budding empire. Through force and terror, the trade unions and leftist parties were suppressed, then the liberal parties were undermined, and the military took over. Respect for the emperor was pushed to an extreme, school children were assiduously indoctrinated and sacrifice for the nation became the supreme goal.[15]

True, this was not Nazi Germany. There was no true all-embracing party (aside from a simulacre of a united front) which could impose its ideology on those who accepted while sending the rest to concentration camps. There were considerable divisions even within the ranks of the patriotic associations and the military. And the national leader, General Hideki Tojo, had infinitely less power than Hitler. But the Japanese were probably already imbued with a deeper sense of being one nation, one nation in conflict with the rest, before the process began. And the devotion to the emperor and the will to sacrifice had already been cultivated for decades, in some senses, even for centuries. In addition, those who dared to protest openly were relatively few (courageous, but few), and the jails sufficed for them. Quite simply, the essential props were already in place, it was just necessary to apply a thin gloss of nationalist ideals and slogans except that, just to be sure, the authorities laid it on extra thick.

Japan's once pervasive and virulent nationalism seemed to crumble after defeat in the Pacific War. Having been told so often that they could not lose, and being reassured that the Japanese spirit must prevail, most people realized that they had been lied to and awoke, as if from a bad dream. They were willing to accept the instructions and advice of the American victors, only partly because there was not much choice. Nationalism in general was regarded as an evil and those who had led the country into war were arrested or barred from holding office. This included members of the patriotic parties, the top military brass, managers of the economic combines and *zaibatsu* and part of the elite. The only exception was the emperor who, having renounced his divinity, was seen as a possible constructive element. Meanwhile, a whole new slate of principles, ideals and goals was adopted that should prevent nationalism from ever emerging again: these included democracy, equality, fair play and the rest. They were to be supported by small farmers with their own land, workers who could organize in trade unions, small businessmen and entrepreneurs and new generations of children taught by 'enlightened' teachers.

Unfortunately, at least for those who wanted a new and different Japan, many of these plans were aborted when the Americans decided that world communism was a greater present threat than the old ideology of a defeated Japan. For there was more talk of collectivization, socialism and communism than could be tolerated and subversive movements were forming. Thus, a reverse course was initiated in the late 1940s. During this 'rollback,' as a first step, all leftist groups, whether political parties or trade unions, were contained. Meanwhile, former nationalists, many of them unrepentant, returned to public life. They often surfaced in the 'liberal' and 'democratic' parties and play a significant role in the Liberal Democratic Party down to the present day, with many becoming cabinet ministers. Rehabilitated, if still unconverted, bureaucrats who had run the war economy and helped colonize Asia reappeared in the ministries, including MITI, where they introduced 'industrial policy,' among other things. The ministry in which they were most active was a key one, the Ministry of Education.

Thus, the purge of fascism and nationalism in Japan was decidedly less thorough than in Germany, partly because the victor had no time. In addition, the victor was very easily fooled by the new leaders, who preached whatever seemed to be appropriate but did not let that interfere overly with practice. Unlike Germany, where most new leaders were genuine democrats, who had suffered during the Nazi period, and where former Nazis were arrested and tracked down and Nazi principles and paraphernalia were legally banned, Japan did its best just to forget the past. This meant, among other things, not bothering or even criticizing, let alone jailing, those who had misled the country. But it also involved a massive cover-up in which the Ministry of Education was crucial. Rather than produce textbooks which were critical of Japanese wartime actions, or at least fairly objective, it purged all the critical material even on such obvious abuses as the conquest of China and the Nanking massacre. Even more effective, the history of the embarrassing prewar and wartime periods was simply not taught, stress being placed mainly on earlier centuries or the new, peacetime Japan.

Some Japanese even took the offensive in rectifying the past in such a way that, rather than be a perpetrator of evils, Japan was somehow the victim.[16] This effort joined together rightists and leftists, the LDP and the trade unions, unreformed militarists and convinced pacifists. This was done through an antinuclear movement emphasizing that Japan was the *only* country on which the atomic bomb fell, not only once but twice. No other country had suffered this unique fate. That the bombing might have shortened the war and thereby saved lives was not mentioned. That other bomb attacks, in other places, had been equally devastating was not considered. Far worse, that the American decision was the result of Japanese provocation and that Japan's own actions were in many ways infinitely crueler and less justified, was simply glossed over. The emerging message was that all nations go to war, Japan being one, but only Japan was punished in this horrible manner. Thus the Japanese were absolved from 'war guilt,' to the extent the concept even existed, and was one of the victims, the biggest lie (not just a *tatemae*) ever.

Still, what an active and conscientious policy might have accomplished in a shorter period has been achieved by the passage of time. Today's Japanese are not rabid nationalists or proponents of Japan first. The wartime slogans mean nothing to them. They look askance at the small radical groups which drive around town, dressed in old uniforms and displaying old flags and other symbols, blasting wartime songs from their loudspeakers and haranguing the passers-by. On the other hand, they do not know what hardship and misery was sown by the war, why their parents and/or grandparents allowed themselves to be enrolled in fascist organizations and then marched off to conquer other countries. Above all, they ignore the suffering of those other countries. Thus, they could be sucked into such a movement with less resistance should it ever emerge again. They do love 'peace' and all that is good, but rather shallowly, not knowing the contrary.

This is not just theory. There have been recent trends toward a glorification of the past that are far more subtle and effective than the crude efforts of the old-school nationalists or right-wing extremists.[17] Books and movies are appearing which put Japan in a better light. It went to war, not out of mean or egoistical motives, but to free the rest of Asia from the yoke of Western colonialism. Its military, leaders and soldiers, were considerably more civilized and dashing than their opponents and behaved quite humanely, given the circumstances. If anyone is to be criticized, then it is the Western powers which refused to give Japan its place in the sun and then drove it into a corner. Even an unprecedentedly benign occupation is turned upside down. Gone is the image of the American GI who distributed candy bars to children, replaced by the bully who beat up local people and seduced and/or raped the women.

Over the years, at a more fundamental level, writers and popularizers have been busily concocting a strange new philosophy. And they have been very active. They have already generated thousands of books and articles, some of them even best-sellers, which are analyzed by the press, discussed on talk shows and presented on TV. Its pretentions are high for, rather than being just a philosophy, it passes for a science, the science of who the Japanese are or *Nihonjinron*. Due to its demands for belief, either explicitly by the authors or implicitly because the ideas cannot be grasped without a leap of faith, some regard this as almost an Ersatz religion.[18]

One aspect is that the Japanese are one race. This notion was not only discredited after the war, it denies the uncertainties over the origin of the Japanese people, who probably came from both Southeast Asia and East Asia and, more significantly, the fact that the Ainu inhabited much of the Japanese isles until pushed back, and largely decimated, by the 'Japanese.' At various times, Koreans and Chinese migrated to Japan, sometimes as leaders. These first admixtures could be absorbed over the centuries, not so the later ones. For there are still hundreds of thousands of Koreans and Chinese, brought to Japan for forced labor during the war, and their offspring. There are also distinct social categories, especially the *burakumin* or *eta*, descendants of the former outcastes.[19] This made the remarks of former Prime Minister Nakasone on the 'homogeneity' of the race particularly embarrassing abroad. At home, however, such comments would meet with considerable acceptance.

Secondly, according to *Nihonjinron*, this race is in many ways unique.[20] In fact, uniqueness is a sustained leitmotiv in countless works written about the Japanese by Japanese (and also foreigners). Just how unique sometimes stretches one's credibility. They are, of course, more community conscious, more disciplined, more industrious, more loyal, more harmonious, than others. They live in a 'vertical society' as expounded by Chie Nakane.[21] Their psyche is different, as theorized by Takeo Doi.[22] Thus Japanese psychology and psychiatry must be different, almost turned inside out, treating patients for being too independent rather than insufficiently so. But this is just the beginning. One author has explained that the Japanese brain functions differently from the Western brain. Another found differences even between the behavior of Japanese and Western honey bees.

Attempts are now being made to relate the present generations to past generations, despite the obvious contrasts. Although rice is grown – and eaten – ever less in Japan and only a tiny minority of Japanese actually grow rice, there is a sustained current of writing describing all and sundry behavior as a reflection of a rice-growing culture.[23] This explains why the Japanese work so hard, why they are so cooperative, why communities are so cohesive and so on. Meanwhile, there is constant fascination with the past, the cult of the samurai film being more widespread and prolific than that of the cowboy movie in America. For the more serious, NHK produces epics on historical figures that go on for months and months and are followed devotedly by numerous viewers. Fortunately, there has been little attempt to restore emperor worship, although there are still many who call for far more respect than at present, with the imperial family part of the society column for some and an anachronism for others.

Inevitably, the idea that the Japanese are separate, and special, leads to the next extrapolation, namely that they are superior. Here, it is not just a matter for the adherents of *Nihonjinron*. Everybody pitches in. Japanese bosses, with their concern for the workers, are better than Western bosses who hire and fire. Japanese 'human capitalism' is better than the cruder everything-has-a-price capitalism in the West. Japanese families are more united, Japanese school children study harder and learn more. Japan does not have broken families, single mothers, drug addicts, AIDS carriers – or, at least, not as many. In most cases, an enticing *tatemae* portrays Japan while some distasteful *honne* is applied for the others. This is done in everyday conversation by ordinary people. But equally distorted views appear in proper newspapers and, much more so, improper magazines and scandal sheets. Even major television channels have programs that grossly belittle everything non-Japanese.

This sort of portrayal naturally distances insiders from outsiders, all the Japanese being *uchi* in this instance, and all the foreigners being *soto*. It also ties up with earlier nationalistic views of the Japanese as a distinctive people and culture (*kokuminshugi*). But there is another aspect to this division, which is even more insidious. It is claimed that only the Japanese can understand Japan and its behavior and that foreigners, no matter how hard they try, will never grasp its essence. It would therefore be just as well they do not try. And thus, since foreigners cannot understand, their comments and criticisms are not very useful. This opinion is only confirmed by foreign 'experts,' those who pretend they have uncommon insight into Japan and have created their own genre of *Nihonjinron* in which they explain, and extol, the Japanese. Their books are also translated and read in Japan, leaving the Japanese yet more convinced of their distinctiveness and superiority.

The question here is not so much whether *Nihonjinron* and Japanapologetics are right or wrong. It is awfully easy to disprove their facts and refute their conclusions. More important is what happens to people who believe that they are separate, special and superior. The first thing, obviously, is to become even more separate and special, stressing their uniqueness and what distinguishes them from others rather than what they have in common. Over the years, they become homogenized and stereotyped, in some ways almost to the extent of becoming caricatural or weird. Considering themselves superior is even more dangerous, for then they fail to notice minor flaws and weaknesses which can grow into major abuses and threats. And, not deigning to listen to outsiders, who cannot understand anyway, there is less notice of excesses and fewer notions for improvement.

This is where one would have had to stop during the late 1980s as Japan became ever more sure of itself and its once humble voice became raucous and arrogant. For the first time, the Japanese insisted they were not getting the respect they deserved and wanted to impose the Japanese model on the world. The most blatant claims were made by the LDP Dietman Shintaro Ishihara in *The Japan That Can Say No, Why Japan Will Be First Among Equals*. Alas, the 1990s showed most Japanese that their society was, if still special, certainly not yet superior. They still have a lot of problems to solve and the solutions will not be easy to find. But that has not precluded the rise of a defensive nationalism of sorts, in its sillier moments fed by the *Nihonjinron* cranks or obsequious foreigners. Indeed, it cannot be stopped until the Japanese cease even wanting to be separate, special and superior, which may take a long time.

Obviously, this petty nationalism is nothing compared to what materialized during the early 20th century. It is much tamer and has weaker roots. More significant, there is no military that could manipulate it, the Self-Defense Force being not only a negligible factor at present, it is not even popular among the Japanese. So, it is much too early to speak of a threat and cry 'wolf.' But it is rather sad that the only thing that can unite the Japanese is this web of fiction and anecdotes, wishful thinking and xenophobia. And it would be even sadder if it should cut them off from the outside world again.

Internationalism, Not Yet Achieved

While nationalism, whether of the now fading prewar type or the emerging *Nihonjinron* variety, remains a prominent feature of Japan, it has long competed with another current which nowadays would be termed 'internationalism.' This too has waxed and waned, depending on the period, domestic and external circumstances and what the Japanese regarded as the higher goal. It has also tended on occasion toward excess.

The Japanese islands, located at a considerable distance from the continent, long maintained a remarkable degree of isolation from events elsewhere in Asia and developed an insular character. This was only exacerbated by friction and warfare among those who inhabited the islands, and had enough to contend with there. Still, as one kingdom succeeded another, and the portion that ultimately became 'Japan' grew, there were periodic openings. Moreover, during much of the early period until the 9th century, there were substantial migrations from Korea, including aristocrats, scholars and artisans who made a disproportionately large impact on contemporary ideas. Among many other things, they introduced the alien religion Buddhism, which was quickly assimilated.

This was built upon by the massive, and largely official quest for contacts and knowledge (nowadays 'knowhow') that began with the embassy sent by Prince Shotoku in 607. For decades these missions continued, gradually being bypassed by private ventures, often of a commercial nature, this time directed mainly to China but also other parts of Asia. They introduced countless alien ideas, which were again adapted and absorbed, including more Buddhism, Confucianism and other philosophies, Chinese characters and literature, architecture and town planning, and more. The Japanese court was reshaped into a replica of the Chinese court, with its emperor and aristocrats, form of government, bureaucracy, rituals and ceremonials. The Japanese turned out to be excellent copiers (and adapters) and went to excess in their craze for Chinese learning. This phase petered out with the Mongol conquest of China in 1279 and the threat to Japan (only averted by the *kamikaze* or 'divine wind').

Although relations did not cease, with China and Korea in

disarray, and Japanese kingdoms evolving, there was less to borrow and contacts were limited to commerce and piracy. But there was one last thrust outwards. Having conquered more of the Japanese islands, and expanded his empire, Hideyoshi sent a military expedition to invade Korea in 1592. It was a dismal failure, due to the Korean navy and Chinese aid, and ultimately had to be withdrawn. But it was a national disaster for Korea and left exceedingly bad memories.

As of the mid-16th century, Western traders began visiting Japan, first the Portuguese, then also Spanish, English and Dutch. They were mainly of interest for their weaponry and, had they stuck to trade, might have remained welcome. But they brought Christianity with them, which caught on and spread, much to the annoyance of the Buddhist and Shinto establishments. It was not so much the religion as the possibility that it could weaken their power, and give the Europeans a foothold, that worried the secular authorities. So they turned against the foreigners, finally deciding to chase them out aside from a tiny community of Dutch and Chinese in Nagasaki. To further prevent foreign influences, this time not only European, Japanese were forbidden from traveling abroad and thousands of Japanese living abroad were not allowed to return. Meanwhile, domestic Christians were repressed and Western learning suppressed. This 'closed country' policy imposed an isolation such as Japan, and few other nations before or after, had never experienced.

It allowed the Tokugawa to rule in peace and to impose favored philosophies and religions more effectively. Subsequently, in many areas, especially economic development and science, Japan fell way behind. When the door was prized open again, in the mid-19th century, and especially with the Meiji Restoration, the country was overrun with foreign products and ideas. Thus commenced one of the most active, and fruitful, periods of international intercourse. Admittedly, the Japanese rulers tried to channel this, gladly accepting material imports like manufactured goods and weaponry but eschewing Western concepts that might contaminate the people. The slogan was, as earlier with the Chinese, 'Japanese spirit, Western techniques' (*wakon yosai*). But it was easier said than done.

By the early 20th century, Japanese traditionalists and nationalists feared that foreign influences were growing too vigorously and crushing native ways and ideas. They were increasingly supported by the military, for their own reasons. Again, internationalism was suppressed, ever more sharply as Japan prepared for and entered the war. This attempt at banning things foreign often went to extremes, including prohibitions of foreign books, games and songs. Obviously, in this context, foreign meant basically Western (with a muted tolerance of Germany) but it also embraced Asia whose cultures were regarded as inferior to Japan's. Meanwhile, everything Japanese – genuinely so or artificially created – was exalted. Japan was once more a closed country.

It was reopened, this time more forcefully, by the Americans whose influence and attraction were infinitely greater this time. Soon Japan was wallowing in foreign imports again. These included products, with American-made goods better than those Japan churned out just after the war and every new-fangled gadget catching on almost immediately. But there were also intellectual imports, new concepts and philosophies, new songs and dances, new fashions and lifestyles. This sort of internationalism has been going on for five decades and, during this period, the Japanese have borrowed (and adapted) an incredible amount. Finally, they are beginning to run out of new acquisitions. And they are developing more discernment, realizing that not everything foreign is good. More notably, as indicated before, they increasingly feel that the Japanese have their own practices and ideas which should be preserved, all the more so when they are superior to foreign ones. This rather tame nationalism, supported by a rather shallow ideology of Japaneseness, is now alas rejecting not only negative acquisitions but some potentially positive ones because they are 'foreign.'

However, on the official level, the Japanese government and business community are busily promoting *kokusaika* or 'internationalization.' They realize that it is essential for Japan to cooperate more fully with other countries, individually and through international organizations, including the United Nations. It is even more crucial that the world trade system, from which Japan has benefited immensely, remain strong and open. For trade has become Japan's most important form of international relations and the country could not prosper, perhaps not even survive as a 'modern' country, without it.

Kokusaika is thus constantly played up in speeches by politicians and businessmen, newspaper editorials and television commentaries. Becoming good *kokusaijin* or 'international citizens' is praised more highly than being patriotic. Yet, so much is said, and so little is accomplished, that this is beginning to look like another *tatemae*.

One reason why Japan is not showing much progress toward this goal is that, as noted, nationalism is making a comeback. In rather few cases are there hardline nationalists, whether from the older generation of diehards or right-wing extremists. Instead, on the whole, younger Japanese are increasingly peering inward rather than outward, finding pleasure or satisfaction in their own backyard, with its many material gimmicks and pastimes. True, more Japanese than ever travel abroad, millions of them, but they usually travel in groups and mix very little with foreigners. There are also more foreigners than ever in Japan, not only tourists, but hundreds of thousands of students or businesspersons, who spend longer periods of time. Yet, they are still treated largely as foreigners (*gaijin*) and few manage to fit into both worlds, although some become unhinged by trying to be more Japanese than the Japanese. Even on the eve of the 21st century, outsiders remain outsiders and insiders remain insiders.

There is one group that has been singled out to span the cultures and build bridges, namely the Japanese stationed and living abroad.[24] There is not much hope for the parents, with the father entirely absorbed by company business and the mother often too timid and living in a Japanese ghetto. But the children should spawn a new generation of *kokusaijin*. Alas, more and more of them are now going to Japanese schools abroad or, if attending foreign ones, have to spend too much time cramming. Moreover, it is a bit much for anyone to combine the very different mental sets of Japanese and Americans, or Europeans or other Asians. Still, this exposure to the outside world could help Japan if it were tapped suitably. This means more than putting the 'returnees' in mixed schools with normal Japanese or recruiting them in companies for the international or PR department. It means making them part of mainstream Japan and eventually inducting some into the leadership, few signs of which appear at present.

In the future, as at present, 'true' Japanese will remain the leaders and have to play Japan's role in the world. Unfortunately, they are among the worst qualified for this task. They work their way up slowly through their own hierarchies, mixing relatively little with others in Japan, let alone foreigners. Many do not speak any foreign language. When they are in a position to become 'internationalists,' they are awkward and ill prepared. They have little familiarity with the international bodies and, in fact, little knowledge of the subjects under debate. And there is no one to brief them suitably since Japanese ambassadors are mainly reconverted bureaucrats who, like those in the Ministry of Foreign Affairs, are mainly concerned with pleasing their clientele. It is not surprising then that Japanese representatives are better known for smiling than talking and accepting the initiatives of others rather than making their own proposals. The only Japanese prime minister in 50 years to aspire to a more dynamic role was Nakasone, and that got him nowhere.

There are also cultural ticks that the Japanese will have to shed in order to behave normally in the international community. One is the continuing preference for hierarchy over equality. Certainly, the notion embodied in international organizations that all states are equal is a rather threadbare *tatemae*. The truth is that big differences exist. But only the Japanese seem to be so preoccupied with ranking who is higher and who is lower, who is stronger and who is weaker, who is richer and who is poorer. Having developed its economy so rapidly, and generating high levels of production and income, Japan again slots itself in with the higher, at least economically. And it takes great pride in belonging to the OECD, the Group of Seven and smaller, more elite circles. Having chosen economic success as the touchstone of success in general, it overlooks or forgets its political, diplomatic and military weakness.

This urge for hierarchy is particularly burdensome now that Japan is haughtily determining who else is on the top. It feels that it has passed most of Europe, with lower production and income and, especially, exports that cannot compete with its own. It also spies many signs of decay and decadence in Europe, from the 'English disease' to 'Europessimism.' There is no doubt that the developing countries are much further down. This applies not only to rather backward ones in Africa, or quarrelsome ones in Latin America, but even those which have been advancing nicely in nearby East and Southeast Asia. They are still dependent on Japanese loans and technology. The only superior, for many decades, was the United States. This was Japan's 'big brother,' an expression that would never occur to Europeans in the same position, as well as its primary ally and backer on all sorts of matters. But the signs of decline and degradation in America are even more glaring and, worst of all, the American economy has become distressingly weak and could easily be overrun by Japanese exporters and investors. Japan does not feel it is ready for the pinnacle of the hierarchy, but it does not really see who else might go there.

Another problem is competition. This appears endlessly in the field of trade, the most important one for Japan, where it feels it must succeed. And, to succeed, it deploys every effort and uses every trick to get ahead. It continues blocking entry in the domestic market and allows its companies to export massively abroad, no matter what the impact on the importing countries. If local industries are crushed, they were probably doomed to disappear anyway, and what happens is not really Japan's concern. This contrasts with the easier-going, more relaxed and more businesslike attitude of most other countries, especially when they practice free trade and free enterprise. For them, trade is not a proxy for war or self-assertion, they just want to sell goods. And they accept Japan's more ruthless approach as long as they can, although with rising trade deficits that cannot be for ever. By repeatedly pushing the United States and much of Europe to the wall, the Japanese may be 'winning' the economic war but they are alienating their closest trade partners who, in addition, are allies and supporters.

Japan might replace this opening to the West with another toward Asia, a card that has often been talked about but rarely played. For, as noted, Asian countries remain in the camp of the inferiors which Japan can talk down to and 'help,' but not yet treat as equals, which they insist on. Moreover, relations are still overshadowed by the events of the Pacific War. For half-a-century, Japan has steadfastly refused to 'apologize' for the war. Indeed, it took decades for the emperor and political leaders to concede that it was a 'regrettable' incident. This is partly, or so it is said, not to aggrieve the families of the war dead or, it is also claimed, because this was supposedly a war to save Asia from the colonial depredations of the West even if what Japan then did was considerably crueller and bloodier. But it is due more to Japan's refusal to lose face by apologizing to its lessers. Still, until Japan makes appropriate amends for the past, as Germany has long since done, it cannot really become part of a new Asia.[25]

Finally, Japan has to put some heart and soul into its relations. Most of them are purely mechanical, the exchange of ambassadors, official visits, attendance at conferences, adoption of resolutions and, most important, provision of funds. When it is necessary to help people, by looking after refugees, or participating in person-to-person campaigns, or sending in troops, the Japanese adopt a very low profile. Only when it comes time to pay, and sometimes only after making a ludicrously low initial offer, can the Japanese be talked into contributing more money. By now, Japan has become the world's largest aid donor and a major financier of the United Nations and other bodies. But footing the bill, while giving it greater respect, does not really win it friends.

Thus, Japan remains an economic giant and a political midget on the outer periphery rather than among the core leaders. This is most assuredly not the fault of the other countries, despite some grumbling that everybody else is jealous of Japan. To the contrary, most other countries would like Japan to assume a more active role. But that is very difficult for an elite which is so busy handling domestic concerns that it has little time to familiarize itself with international issues while many ordinary Japanese, at all levels, still feel uncomfortable when dealing with foreigners. Thus, the best that could be hoped is that Japan should at least become a 'normal nation,' as urged by Ichiro Ozawa, if not necessarily a leader.[26] Until then it will be an unreliable ally and a feckless friend.

Summing up, Japan is badly fragmented as concerns internal relations and even divided with regard to external relations. These realities, which are painfully obvious to the Japanese, however, are rarely noticed by foreigners who appear almost compulsively attached to the notion of solidarity and unity. We are constantly bombarded by clichés which convey such ideas, one of the most charming coming from a neophyte 'expert,' Michael Dobbs-Higginson. His deep understanding derives from two years spent as a monk in a Buddhist temple and then a stint with Merrill Lynch. As he sees it:

> ... while the rest of the world (the West and East included) is largely populated by troupes of bickering individualistic monkeys doing their own thing and often paying no more than lip service to the concept of good of the community or nationhood, Japan is a gigantic, rich, and frighteningly efficient ant colony.[27]

8

The Individual
(Still The Weak Link)

As noted in the introduction, the chapter on the individual more logically comes after chapters on the various social institutions of which individuals may be members – in Japan, at least. Traditionally, that is how they were seen. From time immemorial, and particularly in the Tokugawa era, people were assigned to some station or class, namely nobility, samurai, peasants, artisans, merchants and outcastes in that order. They were expected to behave according to rules laid down for each category and to show due deference to any category above them and also, be it mentioned, appropriate contempt or disdain for those in any category below them. The shogunate left little flexibility, spelling out in incredible detail what were the obligations and rights of each category, what were their tasks and duties, how they were to go about accomplishing many of them and even how they were to dress and what material goods they might possess.

People were also members of families, extended families at the time, and they had to adopt suitable behavior for whoever they might be, father, mother, first son, other sons, daughter and so on. The rules in Tokugawa days, strongly imbued with the Confucian ethic, were uncommonly strict and being a good son or daughter was not enough. It was necessary to use the appropriate words, strike the appropriate poses and, once again, show deference or disdain in keeping with one's position. The rules were 'modernized' and relaxed somewhat under the Meiji *ie* system, but even then they were stricter than in many other countries, not only Western but Oriental. This has been dealt with in the section on the family.

It was only after the Meiji Restoration that the Japanese began experimenting with the concept of 'individual,' conceding that a person was something more than a member of a class and family and could have personal attributes and interests that, by definition, were not fixed within any existing system but had to be worked out in practice. For decades, individualism was only approved of by a minority, those who wanted faster change, while the majority regarded it as akin to egoism and saw it as disruptive of established society. The swing toward individualism, which was gaining strength during the early 20th century, was sharply repressed by the nationalists who deemed it Western and decadent. But it has come into its own over the past half-century, sometimes in ways that appear strange to foreigners but make greater sense in the Japanese context.

To see what changes have come about, it is useful to consider some of the broader trends which affected society as a whole, with both positive and negative moves over the years as one generation succeeded another. It is also necessary to look at different groups: youth, men, women and the aged. They are not the only possible categories and there is obviously some overlapping and gaps in the study, but even this subdivision is a vast improvement on any futile effort at defining a general all-purpose Japanese. Like all others, the Japanese are very different depending on whether they are men or women, young or old, and part of one generation or another.

What is most interesting here is that while some of the changes were specifically sought or urged by the government or people, many of them resulted from unexpected pressures arising in the basic social institutions. The Japanese have become more individualistic, but the individuals they have become were frequently not the individuals they wanted to be and bore characteristics imposed on them willy-nilly. They were shaped by the Japanese company and family, by the educational and socio-political systems, which created Japanese-style individuals rarely seen in other habitats.

Gaping Generation Gaps

It is pointless to refer to the 'Japanese' as if they are homogenous, all thinking and acting alike. And it is equally absurd to assume that what the 'Japanese' think or do in the 1990s is the same as it was in the 1950s or 1850s. The 'Japanese,' to the extent this term has any meaning, are constantly changing and it is helpful to follow some of those changes, while conceding that none of these observations are generally valid for all. One of the better ways of doing this is to trace the expressions the Japanese used to describe themselves or one another in different periods.

Given the postwar ethos, and a traditional emphasis on the male, the first terms were clearly sexist. During the initial phase, as was already mentioned, there was much talk of the *moretsu-gata* or hardworking company man (*kaisha ningen*). They gave their all for the company and found fulfillment in its achievements. They had little time or energy, or perhaps even interest, in their family and broader society. Such men still exist, often referred to now as 'workaholics,' a considerably less complimentary expression. But most have already retired or are nearing retirement age. Little was said of their wives, who apparently counted for less.

By the 1960s, younger classes emerged which were often referred to as the 'my home' or *mai homu* generation, which had a much more balanced view, willing to work hard for the company but wanting time to develop a home life. They could get along with the *moretsu-gata*, if not quite keep pace with them, but they did not agree that the company always came first. Their juniors, in what was known as the 'new family' or *nyu famirii* generation, were even more insistent on keeping their career and family life separate and in reserving more time for the latter. They became more numerous during the 1970s and probably account for the bulk of the middle-aged workers by now.

By the 1980s, there were generations of workers who, unlike their elders, had grown up entirely in the affluence of the postwar period and knew nothing of the poverty and suffering of the war and therefore found it harder to accept the old discipline. They were often referred to as the *shirake sedai* or 'reactionless' generation. And this applied not only to work. More broadly, they were regarded as lacking certain characteristics which older generations deemed both essential and 'Japanese.' These were the 'five absent qualities' (*gomu-shugi*), namely the absence of spirit, interest, emotion, sense of responsibility and manners.

But the youngsters in this generation, coming of age in the

1980s very roughly, had their own ways of referring to established society and called themselves the *shin jinrui* or 'new human race.' There were many passing fads during that period and, in the earlier part, men and women were felt to belong to a 'crystal' generation, with an emphasis on material satisfaction and otherwise little interest and general aimlessness. Even younger Japanese were soon talking of a *shin shin jinrui* or 'new, new human race' which had its own behavioral patterns and interests. What all this involved is not clearly defined, but it was perfectly obvious that it was meant in contradistinction to their elders, who formed the *kyu jinrui* or 'old human race.'

Admittedly, these generations consist of millions of individuals, all different from one another, and who would sum up their views differently. But it does give more flavor than surveys and statistics to quote some of them. One of the *moretsu-gata* explained his behavior, so different from that of his younger subordinates, as follows: 'We firmly believed that the only way to self-fulfillment in life was total organizational commitment, since most of the lifetime would be spent on the job, except for sleep. We thought that was self-evident. As fellow workers, we always worked overtime together, drank together and, on Sundays, played golf together.'[1] A younger worker, referring to the older generation, commented: 'My friends all say we should not be like our parents, who are still healthy and have time and money but do virtually nothing for fun.'[2]

Each one of these generations evolved characteristics that differed somewhat from its predecessors. And, over the decades, the cumulative change has been substantial. Several of these social trends can be summed up briefly here, since they are referred to time and again in other sections. Yet, even from the briefest summary, it must be evident that over the past half-century even some supposedly 'typical' Japanese features were transformed beyond all recognition. Quite obviously, what was meaningful and even sacred to older generations counted for rather little among younger generations, while what young people sought was beyond the ken of traditionalists.

One of the best known surveys is the periodic one on the 'National Characteristics of the Japanese' by the Institute of Statistical Mathematics. It reveals that the overall approach to life has been changing dramatically, with a definite shift from more 'serious' and 'communal' to more 'frivolous' and 'self-centered' attitudes. Once, the most popular lifestyle was to lead an honest and straightforward life with the wish to work hard and get rich and the desire to devote one's life to the good of society also making a reasonable showing. In the meanwhile, these responses have receded, making way for a desire to lead a life shaped to one's own tastes, which is now by far the favorite, followed closely by the wish to lead a carefree and comfortable life.[3]

Given this turnabout, it is obvious that the work ethic has suffered, as indicated in the section on the company. The Japanese, or so it was assumed, enjoyed work or at least found fulfillment in work and also worked very hard. This was never the absolute truth but it was certainly closer to the truth 50 years ago than today. Indeed, to show just how much the work ethic has declined, a revealing poll by the Chiba Productivity Center found that 11 per cent of the Japanese respondents did not like or want to work compared to only 4 per cent in the United States and 8 per cent in Britain. And 22 per cent of them added that they take it easy at work while 42 per cent put priority on enjoying life.[4] As for job satisfaction, 53 per cent of the people polled in the United States said they were very or fairly satisfied while only 15 per cent of the Japanese gave those responses.[5]

Closely related to this is the idea of perseverance. While in school, this is preached endlessly and cries of *gambare!* (persevere!) can be heard frequently. But perseverance no longer ranks very high in young people's lists of virtues. In one poll after the other, they state that their preference is for a comfortable, easygoing lifestyle. When regimented by the school, company or some other institution, they will make believe they are plugging away at their work. More often, they are carefully gauging how little they can get away with and not arouse suspicion among their superiors. Thus, in an NHK survey, whereas many older people listed 'effort' as their favorite word, those in their teens or twenties chose 'freedom.'[6]

The Japanese have long been reputed to be frugal and thrifty. Frugality and thrift were inculcated as indispensable virtues during centuries of poverty, when they could scarcely be avoided, and decades of sacrifice to develop the economy and reconstruct after the war. However, now that the economy has advanced and most youngsters were born into an affluent society, such virtues make less sense. The youngsters would rather spend money and enjoy themselves. Indeed, many are spending money faster than they earn it, borrowing from friends and relatives or using credit cards. Meanwhile, the savings rate is decreasing and the number of personal bankruptcies is rising.

Affluence has had a much broader effect, as noted in the section on religion, turning younger Japanese into hard core materialists. Nearly all their activities are related in one way or another to money. They choose their professions and companies as a function of what they can earn, their spouses are expected to contribute to a yuppie lifestyle, and they try to gain status through worldly possessions. This is an approach which not only could not have been sustained before the war, it would have gone against all the precepts of what is Japanese and doubtless been eschewed by most. That thought is not only lost on young Japanese, it would not even occur to them.

The following quotations from the Japanese writer Seiko Tanabe give a more palpable feel for the extent of the change, not only as regards the attitude towards money but also the relationship between parents and children. Thinking back to her own childhood in the 1930s, she noted:

> The customary New Year's cash gifts from parents, relatives, and family friends were nothing compared with what children expect nowadays. Even so, my parents kept careful tabs on how much I had accumulated and made sure I never held on to it for long. 'Children shouldn't have money. The police will come around and investigate if a child has too much money,' my mother and grandmother would say as they relieved me of my New Year's haul. I never did get my money back.

However, nowadays:

> People seem unable to limit the amount of money they spend on their progency. In the late fifties, parents complained that their children were extravagant in their demands. By the late sixties, they considered it their purpose in life to satisfy each of these demands. These pampered children are now parents, and it is hardly surprising that they indulge

their own offspring, especially since they generally have only one or two children on whom to lavish their love and devotion.[7]

There have also been fads in materialism so it did not take the same form for every generation or both men and women. During the early postwar period, many Japanese sincerely believed they were not just working for money but to rehabilitate Japan in the eyes of the world and create a decent life for themselves. The home, the home they wanted more than the one they actually got, and the family (with the same proviso) were the fulfillment of dreams. But the 1973 oil shock dashed many of these dreams and younger Japanese especially became more cynical, as expressed in bestsellers like *Indefinitely Crystal, End of the World* and *Hard Boiled Wonderland* which, according to social psychologist Munesuke Mita, expressed the 'non-reality, unnaturalness of the times.' However, prosperity returned, and with it a more worldly-wise attitude, this time more for women than men. They were into everything that was 'cute, smart and beautiful.'[8] The bursting of the 'bubble' resulted in another breath of reality, but one that seems to be affecting the men more than the women who still shop until they drop.

Another trend has been a gradual loss of interest in the basic social institutions. There is clearly little love of the nation as an abstract entity, which is not surprising given the abuse of that concept during the war. But the new focus of life, the company, is also being downgraded. According to an Economic Planning Agency survey, more than 67 per cent of those aged 65 and over, and 64 per cent of those in their early sixties, saw the meaning of life in their work. Only 25 per cent of those in their twenties felt that way. Even compared to foreigners, young Japanese (aged 18–24) came in relatively low.[9] Young Japanese came in uncommonly low when asked whether they would take care of their aged parents, with only 23 per cent saying they would do 'whatever it takes' while 66 per cent affirmed they would help only 'in accordance with their means,' the most grudging response of 11 countries.[10] So much for filial piety.

Nor is Japan's youth much interested in society as a whole. Some 53 per cent, in responding to yet another poll by the

Management and Coordination Agency, said they felt greatly
or somewhat dissatisfied with Japanese society today. And less
than 2 per cent replied that they were willing to sacrifice themselves for the sake of society. These results were far lower than
for the population as a whole. What did youth want? The vast
majority opted for a lifestyle corresponding to personal pre-
ferences and hobbies, followed by those who wanted to lead
a relaxed life and those who wanted to become rich.[11] Once
again, young Japanese were distinctly more on the 'frivolous'
and 'self-centered' side than their elders.

This all betrays an upsurge of individualism, some would
even say egoism, and a me-first attitude that is supposedly alien
to the Japanese nature. This image is not limited merely to
opinion polls but readily observable in everyday life. Younger
Japanese definitely do put their interests first more than
their elders, although the constraints of society are such that
in practice they may do so secretly and unobtrusively so as
not to elicit criticism. For the moment, they still seem rather
tame compared to Western youths. But, they are headed in
the same directions and may be catching up.

When these trends are taken together, it becomes abund-
antly clear that the differences between the older and younger
generations never cease growing. They are creating not only
one but several generation gaps, each increasingly hard to
bridge (should the attempt even be made). This has become
particularly pronounced in recent years, with supposed 'generations' replacing one another not only every decade or two
but every few years and the youngest cohorts going out of
their way to distinguish themselves from previous ones. Whereas
once elders could confidently chide youngsters, they are now
getting it back with interest. This can be sensed from references to the 'old breed' and 'living fossils' or the quaint expression applied to elderly women of *obatarian*, itself derived
from the derogatory word for aging woman (*oban*) and the
name of the Zombies in the horror movie *Return of the Living
Dead*.

Naturally, many older people are upset by the trends and
wonder what the Japanese are coming to. Others, perhaps
overly optimistic, insist that this is just a passing phase, the
youngsters will grow up and become *shakaijin* (responsible
adults and members of society) like their parents. This may be

so, in the sense that they will grow up. But they will not be like their parents, any more than their parents are like the grandparents. As the trends continue, and are assimilated by each successive generation, they work their way through the whole population from bottom to top. If the trends are not positive, that will be felt.

And, so far, there is cause to fear that the trends are not the best. Nor does there seem to be a noticeable change in the directions. Thus, whatever social problems exist today could be considerably worse in another ten or 20 years.

Gone Is The Joy Of Youth

Japanese youngsters start off their lives in the freest, warmest and most pleasurable atmosphere they are likely to encounter for the rest of their lives. For children, young children, not knowing the demands of society nor having them imposed, are allowed to run about and play as they want, with their mothers (quite rarely, fathers) chasing after them and picking up things or apologizing to innocent bystanders who get shoved, trampled or dirtied by their offspring. Discipline is uncommonly lax, not only for Japan but for anywhere in the world. And Japanese children would be regarded as spoiled and rude in most other places.

However, it does not take long for that period to pass, and it does as soon as the children are absorbed in the education machine.[12] The age for this is increasingly young, working its way down to four and three for most. Life in kindergarten, once upon a time and with luck nowadays, can be fairly relaxed and pleasant, with more emphasis on socializing than learning. But more and more of the time is soon taken up with learning, and even the socializing has a larger learning content. By the time children reach primary school, they are expected to prepare for junior high school, and there to work more actively to enter senior high school, where the whole learning process is tilted toward cramming for college entrance exams.

From fun, school becomes a drag, and worse. Children have extremely busy schedules, increasingly busy as they rise through the system. First, there is the formal schooling, taking up six or seven hours a day, every day of the week and still largely on

Saturday. Then comes homework, which must not be neglected. And, for those preparing for exams, an ever bigger share of the total, there is private tutoring and cramming which can add anything from a few hours to ten or 20 hours a week to the time table. This goes on for the better part of the year, with 'free' Saturdays and sometimes Sundays and holidays given over to tutoring and cramming. Even the vacation is not reserved for relaxation, since pupils are given homework and projects that must be completed, and handed in for inspection, during the vacation period.

What school life consists of, and what it achieved, has already been mentioned in the section on education. Here, it must simply be added that schooling gradually overwhelms every other aspect of the children's existence. They wake up early, rush through breakfast, get dressed and hurry off to school. They have lunch at school. They may just come back for a snack in the afternoon, before doing homework or scurrying off to a tutor or *juku*. If not, they wolf down a quick bite between classes. Younger children do have dinner at home, those in the cramming routine frequently do not. Family life, such as it is, is limited basically to parts of the weekend and parts of the holidays or summer vacation.

This family life, as already intimated, does not consist of all that much pleasure either. The father is often away and, when he is around, he may be sleeping or grumpy and scold the kids for any trouble at school. The mother spends much more time with them, not overly much given their schedule, but sometimes more than is bearable. She exercises her role of 'education mama' to whatever extent she can, or will, and tends to neglect other aspects of training that are no less important. Most children are not taught to do chores around the house, especially the boys, for they are too busy with more urgent things. Nor can they get a 'job' babysitting or delivering newspapers or the like, for the same reasons.

Meanwhile, many parents tend to spoil their children. They are given all sorts of gifts, from video games to interactive television, from tape recorders to motor-cycles and cars, with a pair of Air Jordan sneakers for the boys and frilly dresses and jewelry for the girls. In addition to the gifts, children receive hefty allowances for which most provide no counterpart. Some children do not even have to worry about ready cash, since they have cash cards and credit cards. Whereas once much of this came from the parents, eager to compensate for being too strict, the grandparents now shower the younger generation with gifts and money, also in the hope of buying love.

For those who deny that Japanese society has changed, nothing could be more instructive than the efforts parents and grandparents now make to get on good terms with their progeny. For, in the not so distant past, the primary responsibility (sometimes almost a legal obligation) was to instill discipline. That was largely the task of the father. But, with fathers hardly around these days, the task has fallen on the mothers who find themselves very ill-equipped to perform it. The result has been a noticeable lack of discipline among the younger generations, with each new cohort apparently laxer than its predecessor.

The problem of discipline has therefore passed to the schools, since they cannot function without some degree of obedience and conformity. Pupils and students are expected to follow a strict dress code, sometimes wearing the school uniform not only at school but in the neighborhood. They must not let their hair grow too long, nor cut it too short, and they usually carry their books in a standard satchel. They must arrive on time, hand assignments in and naturally behave in class. They are taught not only to look up and talk up to their teachers and school administrators, but superiors in general, this including even their schoolmates in higher grades. They must tidy their desks and clean the classroom, including scrubbing the classroom floor. They must follow the rules and regulations, so many one can hardly keep track of them all, and formally (and abjectly) apologize for any infringements. Even if this becomes a bit much, they cannot object without appearing insolent and unruly.

As the children go about the grim business of 'learning,' they have little enough time or energy for anything else. They spend most of their free time watching television, reading comics, playing video games and shopping. The boys and girls create a personal dream world, for the boys with a lot more action and violence, for the girls with cute, cuddly toys that they keep to an amazingly late age. They seem to be lost in time as they cling to the remnants of childhood and mature at a much older age than their peers abroad. This is called the 'Peter Pan syndrome' among the Japanese. It may be just as well since their parents are usually in no position to explain things like 'the birds and the bees.'

Traditionally, Japanese youngsters could balance the restraints of dealing with parents, teachers and other authority figures with socializing among boys and girls of their own age. But this is ever less prevalent. Due to school and cramming, they have less time to see friends and many of their schoolmates are seen as rivals for exams. They do not attend parties or picnics, they certainly do not 'date' or go to dances and they do not even engage much in team sports. In fact, young Japanese have actually forgotten (if they ever knew) the traditional games and pastimes. Thus, according to the 1990 White Paper on Youth, most Japanese have superficial acquaintances but hardly any close friends with whom they can share their inner thoughts and feelings. And half of them have never joined in community events.[13]

If Japanese children do not confide in their friends, indeed, do not have many friends to begin with, where do they turn for advice? According to a 1985 youth survey by the Management and Coordination Agency, it is not the parents. Only 19 per cent looked to their fathers and 37 per cent to their mothers as counsellors. It is no longer to their teachers. Once a respected source of authority, now only 5 per cent would turn to them. Even fewer, a mere 4 per cent, would seek help from superiors at work. Schoolmates and work colleagues were more likely candidates, with 15 per cent. When asked what the biggest influences on their thinking about events and society were, TV and radio came out on top with 43 per cent.[14] Probably the strongest single influence is one of the popular magazines, each of which targets and caters to a specific age and sex group, and each of which generates a different type of personality that can almost be distinguished by the naked eye.

Many youngsters, with no clearcut views or social links, feel an emptiness which they try to fill one way or another. Sometimes their allegiance is transferred to the company, although that is ever less the case. Now many become attached to one of the 'new religions.' Coming mostly from families where the parents are either conservative or indifferent, they do not reason or show scepticism but throw themselves into groups they often wish to leave later but have trouble extricating themselves from. Since many young people already have accumulated or earn substantial sums, they are attractive to the more unscrupulous sects in particular. In them, they find not only comradeship, which they often lacked because of their intensive preparation for exams, but a new family and father figure. According to Professor Susumu Oda, the 'new cults have been serving as surrogate families for their adherents in the "fatherless" society of today's Japan.'[15]

Subject to so much pressure, with so few outlets of a constructive nature, and unable to turn to others for help, many Japanese children succumb to the system. This can happen in various ways, the more negative and unfortunate being the most noticeable. Physically, it is clear and easily ascertained that today's youngsters are weaker and less agile than their predecessors. The Ministry of Education regularly reports, on the occasion of Health-Sports Day, that teenage children are getting worse and worse at running, jumping, throwing, etc. Even sadder in a way, according to another poll, less than half of the teenagers have ever climbed a tree, flown a kite or gone fishing.[16]

Morally and psychologically, there are also negative signs and worrisome trends. In a comparative study of Japanese, Americans, Koreans and Taiwanese, the Japanese children had an uncommonly low self-image, with only 16 per cent saying their marks were good or very good at school. They also scored low in sports, popularity and personality.[17] Japanese children were also expressing anti-social feelings, to judge by one study of fifth- and sixth-graders. Their essays made repeated mention of wishes to be spoiled by their parents and unfulfilled desires. Some were outright alarming, such as 'I want to draw graffiti on the blackboard,' 'I want to rob a bank' and 'I will drop atomic bombs all over the world.'[18]

These inner feelings occasionally break through to the surface and there has been increasing open violence in a society which prides itself on avoiding, or at least repressing, aggressivity. More and more children are breaking the school rules and regulations, whether by flaunting the dress code or smoking on the premises. There has been a notable increase in truantism, quarrels in the classroom, and hazing behind the teachers' backs, or in front of them. Juvenile delinquency, including petty crime, is spreading. But what shocked the public most is *ijime* or bullying, with children sometimes being beaten quite brutally, robbed or forced to bribe their tormentors.[19] Despite all efforts, and much public clamor, it has been impossible to stop this bullying, with about one-third of the high schools reporting it in 1992.[20]

Bullying does occur in other countries as well. But it has some specific traits in Japan. It results less from children forming groups, or gangs, and fighting one another than a dominant group picking on just one or two victims. Most often, these are older children hazing younger ones who did not show due respect or brighter pupils whose success irked them. Although it is widely known who is being bullied, very few other children intervene to stop the violence, let alone help the weaker party. They do not even report this to the teachers. And the bullied children usually also hide it from their teachers and parents. This is perhaps the most visible case of nails that stick out being hammered in while society looks on and does nothing.

It is not surprising that, aside from truants and dropouts, most children keep in their fears and urges. But the negative feelings do not disappear, they gnaw at the person's innards. One consequence has been a rise in the incidence of ulcers among school children. There are also more signs of nervous tension and mental disorder. Indeed, according to a study team of the Ministry of Health and Welfare, as many as one out of five junior high school students are affected by some form of mental depression.[21] Worse, there have been more and more cases of suicide, since children simply could not stand the pressure of 'examination hell' or the humiliation of bullying. It might be noted that those who suffered most were the 'good' students, those who followed the rules, who studied hard and who sought to succeed in the Japanese rat race but just didn't have the fortitude or stamina.

Anti-social actions and total despair, admittedly, only affect a minority of the Japanese children, although this seems to be a sizeable and growing minority. The majority, or so it might be thought, is faring much better. Still, what is the meaning of better? Even the best are burdened with excessive studying, this consisting mainly of rote memory, and rarely enjoy their education. As noted, they do not play or relax much and, when they do, it does not take very constructive forms. They do not have many friends, they do not confide in their parents, they do not have much respect for their elders and superiors.

They do not show much interest in society and rather prefer going their own way, at their own pace and leading the kind of life that, most often, is beyond their reach.

They are individualists, but a special kind of individualists, very different from what many understand under that heading. They are not rugged individualists, they are not assertive or aggressive individualists, they are not creative individualists. They do not state openly that they dislike established society, that they want to change the world or that they seek to demolish existing institutions and replace them with something better. They do not even behave or dress very differently from others, with the exception of small groups of supposed 'punks' and dropouts. Rather, they are relative loners, sticking to a few close friends, if they have any, and otherwise withdrawing into the limited privacy of their room or the much vaster privacy of their mind.

Various Japanese observers have described the younger generation in various ways. Most place stress on a growing tendency to go it alone. 'They are very isolated because they stick indomitably to their own ideas and conclusions, excluding interaction with others. . . . This self-centeredness and isolation are based on a will and desire to be independent when facing any circumstances.'[22] That may explain why this generation 'naturally evades any kind of friction expected in life,' be it in personal relations or with regard to politics or company contacts.[23] Since the Japanese love to label everything, this cohort has been dubbed the 'dolphin generation.' Like dolphins, they are neat, clever and refined, but they avoid competition and prefer taking it easy. According to Tatsuo Inamasu of Hosei University, 'they have a general tendency to want to avoid being "excessively unique." They want to display enough individuality to be called interesting, but don't want to stand out from the group. . . .'[24] This is a rather dull and tame sort of individualism, seemingly nowhere as bothersome as earlier forms.

What is interesting is that this generation of youngsters consists of children whose parents may have participated in the radical and student movements of the 1960s. Then there was little thought of conforming to societal norms and no hesitation to generate friction. Thus, unlike their parents, younger Japanese are mistakenly regarded as practical, steady and amenable to the wishes of the establishment. Outwardly, perhaps they are. Inwardly, however, there is ample room for doubt. And it is the sizeable, but unmeasurable and uncertain gap between external appearances and inner desires, between *tatemae* and *honne*, which is most ominous. In the end, these cohorts may prove harder to shape, or even absorb, than their parents who had some spunk and knew what they wanted.

For a growing share of the population, there is one last stage on the path to adulthood, namely college. We already know that the students do not devote much time or effort to studying. What do they do instead? Most wake up late, having gone to bed late, attend a class or two, mainly to see their friends with whom they retire to a coffee house or the like. Considerable time is spent in clubs, of every possible sort, and which get priority over classes. When they are alone, or with friends, they read comics or watch TV. They may also travel a bit. But the pace is relaxed and easygoing, no strong passions, no excessive efforts, no great curiosity. Some do drink too much, others may take drugs, there is some dating and sex. But, on the whole, this experience is innocuous and vacuous, a means of recuperating from the rigors of 'examination hell.' The students regard it as a 'moratorium' and feel they have a right to drop out for a while and their professors, who saw them crushed in body and soul as freshmen, tend to agree. For, when they become seniors, they know they must enter the fray again as company employees and bureaucrats. Still, while those who passed the exams may have a 'right' to this break, it should be remembered that those who failed go directly from high school to the office or factory.

In Japan as elsewhere, youth is preparation for adulthood and young Japanese are also supposed to shape up and become responsible adults. But this is a rather odd preparation. For the losers, it consists mainly of intensive schooling followed immediately by absolute absorption in work. For the winners, there is this interruption in the never-never land of college, which is the complete opposite of high school and company life. If it contributes to anything, it is a last chance to make friends and get to know oneself. Otherwise, growing up has been a largely dull and dismal affair and has not contributed much to character building or socialization. Young Japanese are comparatively naive, relatively solitary and increasingly suspicious of those in authority. Anyone who thinks that, like their parents, and grandparents, and ancestors, they will grow into 'typical' Japanese is sorely mistaken. For, despite all the talk of tradition, the process of growing up in the late 20th century is totally different from that of early postwar Japan, let alone the prewar period.

Men: No Longer What They Were

Traditionally in Japan, as in any number of other countries, the man was the 'lord and master.' This status, and the related sex roles, were clearly defined during the Tokugawa era. Not only were men superior to women, women usually walked several steps behind. The distance between the two was shortened during the Meiji era and, with the postwar constitution, equality of the sexes was formally adopted. But the constitution, and assorted laws and regulations, could not immediately or completely erase the accumulated distinctions of the ages, although formal pronouncements and guidelines could help.

The biggest impact on the status and position of men came from the company and the family. It was the company which shaped its employees and gave them their principal role, which was as a servant of the company, and kept them from fulfilling what had earlier been their principal role, namely as the head of the family. Nothing has had a greater effect on emerging generations of Japanese men than the partial (sometimes nearly complete) withdrawal of the father from the home. This meant that, for the first time in Japanese history, children – boys as well as girls – were brought up largely (sometimes solely) by the mother. There was no problem with this in some respects, since mothers could feed, clothe and educate the children. But there was one thing she could not do, not in Japanese society as then constituted, namely turn the boy into a man.

Due to the still prevailing distinctions, and the considerable, if gradually lessening adherence to sex roles, a man is essential to bring up boys properly. A boy must learn 'manly' behavior, he must learn how to deal with women, whether older or younger, as different and admitted inferiors. He must, above all, learn to speak like a man. He must know which masculine words and expressions to use, which forms to apply and so on. That he can only acquire from another man, preferably his father. Without it, as soon as he opens his mouth, he would sound womanish, or neutered or simply odd. While most of the affectations of manly bearing can be foregone, until the language is changed thoroughly, a man must sound like a man.

Lack of a father as a role model has had an effect as more and more young men have become softer, weaker, more effeminate if you will. Some of this is doubtless to the good, since Japanese were too masculine in olden days. But not all: many young men have quite simply become confused as to what their behavior should be. And the results can range from a toned-down but still impressive manliness to varying degrees of femininity. Young men use more cosmetics, dress more elegantly, pay copious attention to their looks. They read fashion magazines and keep up with the fads. Older Japanese have noticed this and speak of the younger generation as androgynous. In more extreme cases, some have become outright feminine, with a recent craze for cross-dressing among male college students and a turn toward homosexuality.

The trend for men to become less masculine, if not outright feminine, has another basic cause, this time inflicted by the schools and companies. It derives from the contrived social distance between the sexes. In earlier times, the sexes were largely separated until marriage, although prior to that young men were at least able to meet and see young women. If need be, and they had the money, they could purchase the services of prostitutes. Now, schoolboys spend more of their time studying for examinations and do not get to know girls even though they may sit at the next desk. Even in college, there is limited dating and men often tend to congregate with men, and women with women. Still, at least there is some mixing.

The next stage is work at a company which keeps a very tight rein on its male employees. They are not only expected to work long hours, they have to give their all for the company. This means putting in overtime but also socializing with the other men in the office, not the women. Becoming too friendly with, say, the OL who serves them tea every day, would be a very unwise move and could destroy a career. Company socializing is often so extensive that young salarymen can only manage to see girls once or twice a week. Since they live at home, and this lacks all privacy, or in a company dormitory, which is constantly supervised, relations with any girlfriend may remain rather platonic unless they resort to one of the 'love hotels.' Oddly enough, while having a girlfriend is quite difficult, it sometimes happens that company socializing, especially company trips and parties, include a night with a prostitute.

This is hardly a proper atmosphere in which to seek a mate or have a healthy relationship with one's wife, a matter already dealt with under the heading of family. For individuals thus deprived, it is not surprising that many men remain unusually shy and withdrawn. Some have wild fantasies, often more violent than tender, as expressed in the sexually explicit comic books they read. When they actually do date women, they may suffer from impotence which is increasingly prevalent. For young men in their twenties and thirties, the causes are more psychological than physical and many men apparently have sex for the first time during the honeymoon. Later in life they may suffer from secondary impotence due to job stress or problems with their wife.

Something is obviously wrong. Actually, many things are probably wrong. This is how they are summed up by a Japanese specialist, Iwao Hoshi, in his section on 'shortcomings of Japanese men' in *The World of Sex: Sex and Marriage.*

Basically, Japanese men are unprepared to recognize women as equal partners in sex relations. Japanese mothers continue to indoctrinate their sons with the notion that they are the lords of creation. The boys imbibe this attitude of absolute male superiority with their mother's milk. This goes together with an extraordinarily intense relationship with their mothers. Hence, there are two basic expectations of the Japanese male, motherly catering to his physical needs and gratifications of sex impulses. . . . As a foreign woman put it, Japanese men want to relegate women to two simple positions, on their back or at the sink. In this way, the male can feel safe.[25]

Another reason why it is hard to find a wife is that men and women increasingly have differing views on marriage. With their job so important, men remain quite traditional in seeking the ideal marriage partner. The highest priority, according to a survey by the Prime Minister's Office, is a wife who is understanding about her husband's work and need to socialize with colleagues. This is followed closely by a wife who does the housework diligently, is good at bringing up children, and is willing to devote time and effort to helping with their education and, somewhat further down, who takes care of the aged parents. On these points, many women actually agree. But they differ on the matter of a career, more men expecting their wives to quit work after getting married and more women wanting to continue working.[26] Increasingly, it is hard to find a spouse who has the desired characteristics.

Thus, more and more men are getting married later or not at all. Some of them move into company housing which, for singles, is almost like an army barracks, crude in style and under the watchful eye of a supervisor. Others prefer staying with their parents. The mother may nag about their not getting married, and the father may insist they should be more 'independent,' but this is the easiest, most comfortable alternative. No wonder so many men seem immature and never quite grow up.

Fortunately for them, in the company men still reign supreme. Despite the two-track system which replaced earlier, crasser discrimination, women have been firmly put in their place. Aside from those who insist on a career, but rarely get one, most women are in clearly subordinate positions. They remain on the assembly line indefinitely while the men become supervisors, or they serve as 'office ladies' while the salarymen rise to managers and directors. It is usually possible to speak down to them, not only because they are women but because they are subordinates. One can even curse or spit and watch them cover their mouths and giggle. One might even crack an off-color joke, or poke a behind, since mild sexual harassment is almost standard practice.

Being tough with females, subordinate females at least, should not lead one to assume that salarymen, or factory supervisors, or bureaucrats for that matter, are tough with one another, proudly displaying their manly qualities. Most men do not rise by being tough, or smart, or dynamic or even hardworking. They reach the top mainly by being patient and getting along with others. A survey of employees of listed companies by Fukoku Life Insurance showed that, far from being individualists at work, 34 per cent wanted to be 'just like everyone else' and only 15 per cent wanted to be 'different from the others.' A good 44 per cent said they 'would not express different opinions' at company meetings and fully 62 per cent would 'feel reluctant to leave the office when their colleagues are putting in overtime.'[27]

If the men can exercise the remainder of any lingering superiority in the company, it is quite different in the home, as was already mentioned. There the wife reigns supreme and men are increasingly sidelined and ignored. Men have to pay in their salaries and then receive a modest allowance from their wives, although some keep a secret stash for emergencies. Meanwhile, the wife runs the family finances, consulting duly on major items, but doing much as she will for the rest. If the money runs out, rather than his complaining that she should control costs better, he is more likely to be informed that he does not earn enough. Naturally, and as also mentioned earlier, the wife is basically in charge of raising the children and looking after their education.

For some men the home has become such a hostile environment that, even when they can see their family, they avoid it. They invent work to finish at the office, find every possible excuse to go drinking with customers or colleagues, read comics in a coffee shop or play pachinko for hours before finally heading home. Even then, some purposely miss their station and ride to the end of the line and then back again, just to put off the moment of return. There is apparently a phobia spreading among salarymen which keeps them from going home.[28] And others are quite happy when they are stationed abroad or in distant prefectures and cannot take their family along. They have given up entirely on the family and home but fear ending up alone, and thus do not actually suggest a divorce.

Few men would regard themselves as superior to their wives, indeed 'henpecked' might be a better description. The fact that they are earning a livelihood and bringing home their salary no longer gets them much credit. Some have made a success of their family life, and have a close and warm relationship with their wife, with whom they get along better than their parents did. But this form of union remains elusive for all too many. So, they live alongside the woman of their life, who may well be treading a very different path.

Yet, although they get less and less thanks from the wife and kids, Japanese men really are sacrificing themselves for the family. Factory workers have to show up early, get their things ready, and then start work, often without much if any break, until the short lunch period, and then on again until closing time. This is not always respected and overtime, paid or unpaid, may be required as well as attendance at a pep talk or participation in a Quality Control Circle. During the whole day, they work at a frantic pace, under the eagle eye of the supervisors, and produce whatever quota has been assigned them, often without their consent. This pace, whatever it is, is more rapid than the year before and will be speeded up in coming years. Still, they have to smile and remain cheerful, move about in a sprightly way and bow modestly when any superior passes.

The white-collar employees usually work at a much slower tempo and find countless, apparently justifiable reasons to slack off, whether this entails consulting with clients or discussing policy with colleagues. But they put in even more hours. They awake early, swallow a quick breakfast, trudge to the train station and commute anywhere from one hour to two, usually standing, packed into the train or subway like herrings. They arrive at work early, break for lunch after noon and return early, then work again until closing time, when they do not leave. Instead, they sit around and discuss the events of the day or go off for an evening of socializing with colleagues, superiors, subordinates or customers. This they do nearly every week in the year, aside from some holidays and a vacation, half of which they usually do not take.

Most of the men can keep this up while they are young but, as they age, they find it a bit much. Also, as they age, they move into supervisory and managerial positions in which they come under considerable pressure. The stress and strain are such that many become worried they may meet with 'sudden death' or 'death from overwork' (*karoshi*). Once beyond lower managerial positions, they also agonize about whether they will make it to the top or be transferred to some lesser office or sent to a subsidiary or supplier. If they are passed over for promotions, they do not know when they may get a tap on the shoulder and a pointed request to seek early retirement.

Mention has been made of socializing.[29] Lest there be any mistake, this is not what it sounds like. Although it often takes place in fancy bars and restaurants, or on the golf course, this is not just a chance to meet people and enjoy themselves. It is part of the company's campaign to get employees working as a team and consists of discussing business-related matters, often concerning personnel and personal relations. Anyone who does not socialize is looked at askance by his colleagues and, more serious, may miss out on promotions. Thus, off they go, for an evening or weekend of eating and drinking, especially the latter. For, under the influence of alcohol, some of the barriers will fall and men can finally speak frankly. Then, sometimes stone drunk, they stagger to the subway station or are dumped in a taxi and sent home, perhaps puking on the way.

This is hardly fun and games. And it is no wonder that the salarymen are sometimes referred to as company 'warriors.' Still, for the first postwar generations, this was often an exciting and challenging period, certainly better than fighting a losing war. They helped launch new products, open new factories, conquer new export markets and so on. For this they were generously rewarded since, as the company grew, promotions and improved remuneration were possible. Later generations had a less exhilarating time. Competition was more intense and there were fewer victories. Too many employees contended for too few managerial posts and wages stagnated. Many could not work up much enthusiasm and their jobs quickly became routine, if not tedious. Yet, for the family, they soldiered on.

It is thus sad that when they finally return from the wars, rather than the honor and glory they had hoped for, the company warriors meet with relative indifference at best. Many have not had time to form close links with their family. The wife has drifted away, evolving in different directions, while the husband was frozen in time by company life. The children of the *moretsu gata* are 'my home' and 'new family' types who wonder why he sacrificed all. And the grandchildren are part of the new, or new new, or new new new human race who just cannot comprehend the old breed. Meanwhile, society as a whole has altered its values and forgotten its debts. There is little recompense to be expected and, being old-fashioned enough to endure, many retirees ask for relatively little, and frequently get even less.

Women: The Weaker Sex Wins

In Japan, as every survey shows, the distinctions between the roles of men and women are lessening, but certainly not disappearing. And the gap between the situation in Japan and other advanced countries remains enormous.[30] Thus, in a Public Opinion Survey Regarding Equality of the Sexes undertaken by the Tokyo Metropolitan Government, some 56 per cent of the respondents agreed with the proposition that 'the husband should be the breadwinner and the wife should stay home.' The progress on the Japanese side paled against that in the West, where only 13–25 per cent agreed. In another international comparison, about half of the Japanese women in their twenties were in favor of the sexual division of roles as against 10–20 per cent in the West. And as many as 78 per cent agreed that, 'all things considered, women's happiness lies in marriage, so it's better for women to marry.'[31]

There are also distinct differences on how girls and boys should be brought up, educated and inserted in society. According to one oft repeated poll, most fathers (51%) felt that boys should be brought up specifically to be 'men' and girls to be 'women,' although many mothers (44%) felt that both boys and girls should be brought up similarly to some extent. Both parents thought it was more important for boys to get a good education, including college. They hoped that the boys might eventually become bureaucrats, professional sportsmen or doctors while the three most-favored occupations for girls were kindergarten teacher, school teacher and nurse. And more parents hoped their sons would grow up to be respected members of society than was the case for daughters (38% against 9%) while a majority (57%) thought it was most important for their daughters to live happily and in harmony with those around them.[32]

Still, starting at lower levels and rising gradually, there has been some equalization. More and more women are going to college, already outnumbering the men, although many of them attend junior colleges that are little more than finishing schools and take 'girly' courses. The share of female managers remains uncommonly low, a mere 8 per cent according to a survey by the International Labour Organisation compared to 30 per cent in the United States and 19 per cent in Britain.

There are more women entering politics and winning elected posts, but not many. In fact, even now only about 7 per cent of the Diet members and 3 per cent of the prefectural assembly members are women, placing Japan in the 110th place out of 130 countries in a United Nations study of women's presence in elected legislatures.[33] Japan has finally gotten around to appointing some female ambassadors and there have been several ministers.

To accelerate the trends, and avoid losing face in international organizations, just after the International Women's Decade, the government enacted the Equal Employment Opportunity Law. This was followed up with a formal plan to create a society in which men and women would participate equally at all levels by the year 2000. But, aside from publishing reports, it did almost nothing to achieve this goal which appears patently unrealistic as the deadline approaches.

Thus, any progress has been slow, partial and grudging and many of the appointments to higher posts were 'token' and made to show foreigners that Japan was, indeed, enlightened. Compared to the progress achieved over the same period in other advanced countries, the record is particularly bleak. Women are not duped and, when asked if they are being unfairly treated compared to men, many complain of inequality. In one government study, 63 per cent of the women said they were unfairly treated in the workplace, 62 per cent with regard to social mores and people's sentiments, 46 per cent at home and 37 per cent by laws and institutions. While ever more men conceded that their wives should be allowed to work, pitifully few are willing to help with the housework and child-rearing and the contribution of those who do is usually minimal.[34]

Unlike contemporary men, the women apparently have less trouble adjusting to their expected role in society and adopting the appropriate comportment and language. This they can learn from their mother, who is hovering around all the time and with whom they interact more than the boys. On the other hand, with the father away so much, many girls and women do not quite know how to relate to men and, in general, to figures of greater authority.

This they may learn in school or college, where there are male teachers and professors. But it seems that the company has to reeducate them after they are hired. They must learn to speak polite language, showing due respect to men in general and displaying suitable deference to superiors, officials and customers, the former being mainly men. They have to behave demurely, even timidly, and bow low as befits their station. Females are more often expected to wear the company uniform and reflect favorably on the company. Many are chosen at least partly for their looks and become the 'flowers of the office.'

Aside from that, women have much less trouble at being feminine than men at being masculine. If anything, they seem to overdo it and have become progressively more feminine than their mothers and grandmothers, most of whom led hard and rough lives. They play with dolls and cute things into their late teens and early twenties and the adjective 'cute' is always on their tongues. They dress in frilly clothes when young then slavishly follow the latest fashions, switching from one exotic or extravagant fad to another. They do not stint on costs and, what they cannot afford to buy, they gladly accept from their parents or grandparents. Japanese women make considerable use of cosmetics, wash their hair and bathe frequently, and increasingly engage in cosmetic surgery to look better, not sexy but cute.

For many, these pursuits are not even interrupted when they take up a job or 'career.' Most high school graduates need a job and many college graduates want one, whether they need it or not, since work is preferable to staying home and has certain compensations. Customarily, the high school grads were gladly accepted and put into the assembly lines. The college grads graced the offices, where they became 'office ladies.'[35] There most of them stayed, doing supportive and subordinate tasks, and rarely advancing. With the Equal Employment Opportunity Law, some have been allowed to enter a career track, but most apparently accept being OLs indefinitely.

All too often, for women employment is just an interlude between education and marriage and, even while working, the women show considerably less commitment to the company. In a study by the Tokai Bank, about 40 per cent more men than women agreed that 'I work hard to earn money and improve my standard of living' and 'I gain fulfillment from my work.' Whereas, according to a Lake Company survey, three-quarters of the male white-collar employees took work home if it could not be finished in the office, 70 per cent of the women, in a Daiyasu Company survey, said they forgot about work entirely when not on the job.[36]

Here, it is essential to distinguish between different categories of women. High school grads, with more limited scholastic credentials and often enough lower-class or rural, usually work very hard to earn their pay, certainly as hard as most men. And they throw themselves into quality control activities and the like with surprising enthusiasm. College grads, who really pursue a career, have to work twice as hard as men to be accepted, and three times as hard to get promotions. They almost always have to become surrogate men, behaving and talking like them, and putting in endless hours which preclude a normal family life and children in many cases. They are the true heroines of the struggle for women's equality, but they seem to be followed or admired by ever fewer younger women.[37]

One of the rare trends which has reversed over the past decade or so is the resolve with which women seek a career as opposed to a job, no matter what they may say. Many women accept outright the second, general track, and others just cannot keep up the slog. If men don't want them to be part of the team, if men don't want them to be equals, fine. They will keep on working and earning a salary, but that is all. And the number of OLs in this category has grown as ever more give up on a career and ever more stay with the company for longer periods, ten, 20, 30 years, since they marry and have children later or not at all.

Many of these OLs continue living at home, partly because the company does not like them to live alone, partly because they can save money on room and board. With quite limited expenses, they can put aside nearly everything they earn and, in the earlier years, they earn as much as a man and even later on quite substantial amounts. Some of this money can be put away in savings, perhaps for marriage or old age, although apparently rather little. The rest can be spent in any way they want. And it is spent lavishly on cosmetics, clothing, accessories, visits to the beauty parlor, sports and leisure. This has made the OLs the biggest spenders of all Japanese aside from the very rich, and a juicy segment of the market.

The OLs like to socialize, not forced company socialization which they can do without, but socializing with friends from college or the office, preferably of their own age group so they do not have to use stilted language. After work, rather than return home, they may meet friends and go shopping together, take in a movie or go to a disco, or have a nice meal in a fancy restaurant and wash it down with beer or wine. Indeed, whereas women were once not expected to drink much, and certainly not in public, they are quickly catching up with the men. Women also love to travel, usually with girlfriends, whether to a local ski resort or on a trip abroad. In fact, women in their twenties and early thirties account for nearly a fifth of all overseas travel. Less expected, the latest fad is gambling, not only by playing pachinko but also betting on horse races.

What about sex? Women certainly have more time for this than men and, since they get away from the company more readily, they also have more opportunities. In addition, the fashionable magazines for young women have been running increasingly explicit articles on the subject, teaching their readers everything they need to know and then some. The problem is that most of the men of their age are unavailable most of the time. Apparently, according to the media and gossip, the gap is filled with foreigners, older men and one another. Sometimes this is for 'love,' sometimes for pleasure and sometimes for money. For many of the hostesses in bars and clubs are college girls or OLs, and even married women, trying to earn more to support their lifestyle. Yet, an amazing share of bachelors, two out of five according to one survey, were not dating anyone.

This has turned the OLs into the most visible and envied class of the 'bachelor aristocrats' for which reason they have been dubbed the *OL-kizoku* or 'office lady nobility.' They lead the life they want, and they profit to the full. They have completely overturned the traditional order of priorities between work and leisure, with only 3 per cent of the women in their twenties regarding work as important and 38 per cent feeling they should enjoy leisure as much as possible.[38] What a contrast with their parents, with whom they continue to live and to whom they ordinarily pay rather little for the privilege, let alone the males they may date or eventually marry!

Leading the good life, which they do not want to give up, it is primarily this category of women which does not seek marriage, or wish to raise children, and revert back to the lowly station of a more traditional married woman. In fact, only 20 per cent of the young women in a recent survey wanted to become a housewife as opposed to having a career and participating in social activities.[39] This may signify that they will never grow up, in the old-fashioned sense of having a husband and children, but they do not mind. They can fill their time with shopping, dining out, dancing, traveling and socializing. And, when that runs out, they can take every possible sort of lesson from tea ceremony to flower arrangement, from English language to French cooking, from calligraphy to golf. This is part of their so-called 'bridal training' (*hanayome shugyo*), although that is increasingly a misnomer.

With all this to lose, women are growing very picky about whom they are willing to marry. For them, the third narrow gate after a 'good' college and a 'good' company is a 'good' match. Gone are the days when family background and social status were predominant, gone at least for the 'love' marriages. For Tokyo women working in major companies, the OL crowd, according to one poll the desired qualities are tolerant and sympathetic attitudes, the ability to make quick decisions and to act fast, and kind and humane tendencies. Academic background is also important. So is wealth as most want to live in expensive neighborhoods. (This is part of the three Hs: higher education, high income and height.) Alas, most of the women admitted they only had a 50 per cent chance of finding such a partner.[40] And thus many remained unmarried or settled for less.

While waiting for Mr Right, unlike their counterparts in the West, nearly all Japanese young (and older) ladies continue living at home. This is known as the 'snapping-turtle syndrome' since, like said turtles, they hang on stubbornly. And their parents, worried about being left alone or trying to compensate for earlier behavior, strongly approve. The pampered daughters may, or may not, make small contributions to household expenses and for rent. They may, on occasion, invite their parents out for dinner or take them on a trip. But many keep all their money for themselves and others actually receive additional sums, as gifts and the like, from their parents. The same quite often applies to male bachelors. This is, indeed, a reversal in Japanese tradition, with the young getting much more than they give.

Although not as readily as before, most women eventually do get married. And most of those eventually beget one or more children. For them, the routine is soon as frantic as for the men, having children, raising children, helping the children get an education, preparing them for exams, getting them into a 'good' college and then a 'good' company if possible. Cleaning the house, cooking for a husband who doesn't come home, having meals alone, going to bed without waiting, and then being woken up when he stumbles in. Unpleasant and dull as this may be, child rearing does not usually take up all their time and it only lasts for about 20 years while looking after the home takes ever less time.

Thus, today's housewives have many hours of leisure during their thirties and forties and can visit with friends, do some personal shopping, read a book or watch TV, even take a lesson or two. Later they can return to work, admittedly accepting rather lowly chores, but at least doing this purely for money with no real commitment to the company, and therefore free to behave as they will outside. With this money, they can engage in even more of the above leisure and probably afford a nice meal from time to time and occasionally even a trip to a local hot springs or abroad. In their fifties, with the children grown up (sort of), even if they may still be tending the home, the women have nearly all their time to themselves. Most have forgotten about their husband as a companion and found friends or hobbies they would rather devote themselves to. They do not quite form an aristocracy, but it is certainly a better life than that of the aging worker or salaryman.

During the past half-century the relationship between men and women, and their respective statuses, have both changed and remained amazingly static.[41] The men have been feminized somewhat; the women have adopted some coarser habits. But the man is still, by and large, the bread-winner who goes out and works while the woman stays at home. While more women than before work, they have not gotten very far and by now many do not even mind. This side is quite different from the West where not only do more women have real jobs, more of them make it to the top, and there is more equality in every respect. However, while holding on to their bastions, Japanese men have played a trick on themselves. For the women no longer care and have adjusted as best they could, often in ways that give them a superior lifestyle. The women no longer walk several paces behind, nor do they walk side-by-side, they are off at an angle somewhere, but definitely out front.

And Then You Are Old

Traditionally, old age was a time of difficulty for the elderly and their family, especially the first-born son (*chonan*) who was supposed to look after them. But it was not normally a time of distress. Living in the countryside, peasants had no trouble finding a corner for their parents, enough food for additional mouths, and also useful tasks for the aged (and then aged meant perhaps 50 years old) to earn their keep or at least maintain some self-respect. The same could be done by artisans and merchants, to say nothing of the upper classes. Of course, if the family were very poor, it may not have been able to provide much care and in some cases the elderly were disposed of. But, with the combined weight of Confucian filial piety and Tokugawa stress on family ties, a way could usually be found.

Now, several centuries later, an infinitely richer and more developed Japan is encountering serious problems. The primary causes are the vast demographic changes already referred to, namely the shift to nuclear families, the aging of the population and the decreasing birthrate. Where they all come together most alarmingly is for the aged, roughly counted as those 65 and older but with an upper level of 80, 90 or more. Already today, some 14 per cent of the population is 65 and over. More than 12 per cent of all households are headed by such persons. And the number of elderly people living alone exceeds two million, the majority of them being women.[42]

But that is nothing compared to what is coming. In the year 2025, not that very far away as such things go, this aged population should rise to some 32 million or over a quarter of the population. Those needing nursing care should be over five million, 3.5 million of whom may be bed-ridden and two million senile. Some 12 per cent of the men will be living alone and 22 per cent of the women. This human burden will be carried by fewer young people than ever, with only 18 million under 15 years of age. (Figure 8.1)

Figure 8.1. *Share of Population Aged 65 Years or Over by Country, 1900–2025*

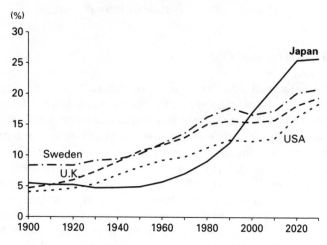

From the youngest to the oldest population
structure in only a century.

Source: Institute of Population Problems, Ministry of Health
and Welfare, *Jinko no doko* (Population Trends).
Credit: *Facts and Figures of Japan*, 1995, p. 14.

It will be necessary to provide for these people somehow.
The most obvious measures to relieve the financial load are
adequate social security, pensions and health care. The Liberal Democratic Party, under the muted pressure of the voters
and urged on by the OECD, introduced all of the various
plans and schemes popular in the advanced world back in
the 1960s and 1970s. They were expanded somewhat in the
1980s and there is vague talk of doing more in the 1990s. Yet,
the safety net would seem to be grossly inadequate. Of all
the advanced countries, Japan has the lowest expenditure on
social security and welfare. In 1988, social security payments
only represented 14.4 per cent of national income in Japan
compared to 16.2 per cent in the United States, 29.1 per cent
in Germany and 40.7 per cent in Sweden. Its companies, which
talk of caring for the workers, do not offer particularly brilliant benefits either.

The Japanese can now count on a modest pension, the
amount varying considerably with the size of the company or

organization and the number of years worked. It also varies with
the type of scheme, more generous for corporate employees,
less so for the self-employed, and markedly worse for those
who have never worked or not achieved a minimum of 20
years. Toward the top would be a male company employee,
with 35 years seniority, who would receive ¥213,000 a month,
supposedly about 68 per cent of his average monthly salary but
only 50 per cent if you calculate in the bonuses. Considerably
further down would be a self-employed person, with 25 years
in the scheme, who would get ¥60,000 a month. Down at the
bottom would be people who have not paid in anything and
receive a state pension of ¥31,000 a month, most of these
being women.

This hardly seems adequate. Calculations have been made of
the minimum living expenses of the aged, one estimate being
about ¥300,000 monthly according to a study of the Institute
of Life Insurance. Alas, not many Japanese thought their living costs would be covered by the national pension fund, only
about a quarter, in fact.[43] Thus, as much as they could, they
have made other arrangements. Nearly all households have
already taken out life insurance policies. Most have considerable savings and some could sell the house or other assets. Yet,
even then, the general feeling among Japan's aged is that they
will not have enough money and a fair number could not
possibly survive on what they have or receive.

Most elderly persons also have health problems. Medical care
at least seems to be adequately provided for. But the system is
rather poorly run, with hospitals not particularly comfortable
or efficient and doctors more interested in earning money
than curing patients. Thus, they prescribe drugs, the more the
better, and the more expensive the better since many doctors
double as pharmacists. Meanwhile, hospitals keep patients
longer than necessary to fill empty beds. But that kind of 'treatment' is useless for old people. And there are few doctors,
nurses or hospitals geared to the need of the aged. Nor are
there enough old age homes. So, the burden of caring for the
elderly falls increasingly on the family, mainly the women.

If the system is inadequate now, it can be expected to
become more inadequate as time goes by. Social security and
old age pensions are only partly financed by contributions, the
rest comes from the state, and the Japanese government is in

no position to increase its share given the financial constraints. Yet, the costs could double and triple over the coming decades as the number of elderly rises and the number of working persons falls (from 6.3 per pensioner in 1995 to 2.1 in 2025). The health system is even worse off since it is already heavily subsidized by the state and costs could skyrocket. The only solution is to shift more of the burden to the people who, as we saw, already have trouble making ends meet.

It is claimed that the Japanese bureaucrats are particularly far-sighted. Well, it did not take much foresight to realize that the costs would mount and the money run out. There have already been dozens of reports and thousands of newspaper articles to that effect. Indeed, in 1994, the Ministry of Health and Welfare projected that social security, welfare and medical costs would rise from 15 per cent of national income to 30 per cent by 2025. Yet, it has not managed either to cut costs sensibly and humanely or increase revenue by imposing reasonable contributions and taxes. All it achieved was to have patients pay more of their medical expenses and raise the pension eligibility age from 60 to 65 to postpone the crunch. For themselves, they had little worry, the bureaucrats have the best pension scheme of all. (Figure 8.2)

The government, explicitly entrusted with ensuring the health and happiness of the population, has clearly not been up to the task. The LDP introduced many of the schemes to steal a march on the socialists and, when there was plenty of money around, raised the benefits without considering whether they could be afforded when the time came to pay. When the revenue became inadequate, and something had to give, the politicians gradually whittled away at the benefits. It would have been more purposeful to increase the funding so that the elderly could be taken care of properly. Still, the people must also share the blame. They wanted a more comfortable old age, but they were not willing to pay for it, and resisted any increase in their own contributions and taxes.

As for the companies, the business leaders who had so many bright ideas about how to solve various social and economic problems only had one fixed idea with regard to aging: don't increase their costs. Don't make them provide bigger pensions, don't make them pay higher taxes, for that would be ruinous and sap the strength of the Japanese economy. With-

Figure 8.2.   *Social Security Expenditures*

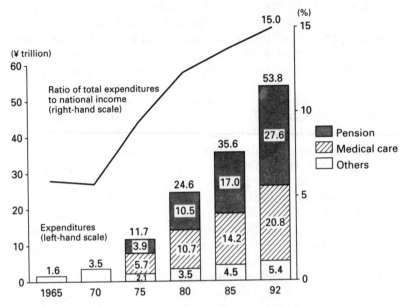

Welfare costs skyrocket. Where will all the money come from?

Source: Ministry of Health and Welfare, *Kosei hakusho*
(White Paper on Health and Welfare).
Credit: *Facts and Figures of Japan*, 1995, p. 74.

out mentioning it, there was also an underlying fear that by
doing too much for the aged, they would be weakening the
work will and dependence on the company and importing
the 'advanced country disease.' Yet, as is perfectly obvious, the
present system is patently inadequate. And, as is equally obvious, social costs are much lower in Japan than elsewhere, just
24 per cent of total labor costs over against 28 per cent in the
United States and about 44 per cent in Europe. The companies could afford to do more, but they do not even want to try.

Having failed to provide general solutions for a broad social
problem, the government tried to slough it off on the population. Already, in the mid-1980s, it was announced that the
family would have to look after the aged more than before.
Unfortunately, as we saw, this was no longer the traditional
family but one beset by all sorts of trouble even in the best of
times. More families than ever were nuclear and more aged

couples were living alone. Many had lost their children, or had no children to begin with, or had children who were too busy or too poor or did not care. According to a *Mainichi* survey, only 30 per cent of the respondents said it was the children's 'duty' to look after aged parents (down from 57 per cent in 1986) while 12 per cent actually regarded this as a bad custom (up from 4 per cent).[44]

Even if the children were good and giving, which was less frequently the case, there was a limit to what they could do. As noted, millions of elderly would be ill, bed-ridden, senile. Family members, without suitable training, could actually worsen their condition. Yet, not only were there not enough nurses and welfare workers, it was hard to recruit more for such poorly paid and unpleasant jobs. The Gold Plan budget to establish special clinics and homes was grossly insufficient and the facilities would never meet the projected needs. And, even when personnel and establishments existed, they were too expensive for many.

This failure further accentuated the growing division between the haves and have-nots, the rich and the poor, the forming social classes. Some could afford an affluent lifestyle while they were younger and still have a comfortable old age. Others would work their whole lives and scrimp and save just to get by. The less fortunate, no matter what they did, could not possibly put aside enough money or round it out with the limited social security and pension. After endless years of hard work, probably harder than most, they could face a terribly impoverished old age. And perhaps not even that. As one old man suggested, the government was asking them to go into the mountains and die.

Thus, despite talk of a 'silver age' and an 'age of welfare,' despite the Gold Plan and a dozen similar schemes, despite hundreds of promises and thousands of pronouncements, the Japanese are approaching a social and financial crisis of major proportions. They are also approaching a human disaster. And the old people are worried. In a survey of aging (53 years old) married salaried workers living in Tokyo, only about one-third of the respondents were optimistic about the future and more than 40 per cent said they were uncertain about their 'second lives.'[45] In another poll, 55 per cent of Japanese adults felt anxious about growing old, fearing disease and declining health, the inadequacy of their pensions or retirement allowances and a possible shortage of savings.[46]

Aside from this, individual Japanese often have to cope with exceptional social and human problems. For the men, it is particularly traumatic to leave the company. It is not only a place of work where they spent untold hours, it is the place where they found human companionship. For the company, they forsook in many cases their family, their community, their religion. For the company they gave up their friends and made 'friends' of their colleagues. And now all this is gone and they feel empty. With little time, and also lacking foresight, many aging Japanese never cultivated alternative activities such as sports, hobbies, volunteer work, even just reading or listening to music. And they do not know what to do with themselves. Even the Economic Planning Agency had to concede that 'the lack of personal relationships at home or in the community, especially among grown men who have left their jobs,' has become a social issue.[47]

This partially explains why so many Japanese men continue working after the compulsory retirement age, presently around 62 for most. This work is usually unpleasant and poorly paid, but better than nothing. The main reasons given for accepting this are a wish to do something to make their lives 'worthwhile' or to remain healthy and active. The other cause is financial, they want 'to live comfortably' or 'to earn living expenses.' That the financial considerations may be uppermost, despite what they say, is indicated by the fact that the lower the men's pension the more likely they are to work. And, an ominous sign of the times, over the years the percentage of elderly workers has actually risen, reaching 72 per cent for men aged 60–64 and 59 per cent for men aged 65–69, figures substantially higher than in the West.[48]

For women, the biggest problem is often that they don't know what to do with their husband. They have spent 30 years and more looking after the kids or working. They have spent countless hours alone or with their own friends and acquaintances. In the 'love' marriages, the affection has probably long since dissipated and there are often no common interests or activities they might share. For them, a man around the house is the equivalent of *nure-ochiba* or damp, fallen leaves which stick to the floor and are impossible to sweep away. Rather than finally getting together, the period of retirement can lead to annoyance, friction and separation.

More and more women also have another headache. Given the lack of finances, and also the lack of facilities, it is the women of the household who have to care for the aged. And this may be not just once but many times over. They may have to look after their husband's parents, and perhaps their own parents, and also their husband who is older, and finally themselves. This initially just involves making an occasional friendly visit but gradually develops into much more. They may have to sit and talk with bed-ridden relatives and provide essential help for senile persons. They may also have to clean, clothe, feed and nurse these people. For this, the woman will have to sacrifice work, pleasure and socializing to a rather large extent.

As they themselves age, those approaching or passing retirement age become intensely worried about their own health and financial situation. They have more time and feel lonely. And they turn to their children. But that is not always so easy for many fathers neglected the children while the mothers may have been 'monsters.' Moreover, the children may live in a tiny home of their own with no room for others even if they wanted to take them in. As noted, filial piety is not what it used to be. Thus, more and more elderly people want to live with their children, but fewer and fewer actually do. And, more surprisingly, elderly Japanese see their children less often than Europeans and Americans, let alone Chinese and Koreans.

Recently, there has been a positive trend in this direction, sort of. More and more children, women but also men, continue living with their parents because they do not get married and move out. In other cases, married couples move in with the grandparents who have a larger house and may provide all sorts of financial incentives. But this can only go so far. For the unmarried children will have no one to look after them and the children in a three-generation household would hardly be able to look after their own children as well as their parents and their parents' parents.

While some elderly work out a reasonable solution, others despair. Life is hardest on single men who have lost their wives, then on single women who have no children and couples without children. But many couples with children receive very few visits and very little attention, sometimes because the distances are too great, sometimes because the children are simply too busy, and sometimes because they don't really care. Many aged just do not have enough money to live. The outcome has been anxiety and distress. But it can also result in suicide, which is occurring with greater frequency among the aged, who leave behind notes to the effect that they do not want to create 'family trouble' or be 'treated like a nuisance by family members.'

Like so many other problems, those of aging, old people and the aging society have not been solved. Measures have been adopted, almost always inadequate, but in some cases too generous. While the inadequacies are not being overcome the bits of generosity are quickly removed. So, when the crisis strikes, it is bound to begin with society's weaker elements who today are the elderly. Old Japanese know that, young Japanese sense that, even the establishment realizes it has not done enough. It is only foreign apologists who could possibly claim that these problems have actually been solved in Japan or propose Japan as a model for 'productive aging' or 'affordable health care.'[49]

9

The Future

(The Crisis That's Coming)

This, then, is the present state of Japanese society. Is it sufficiently bad to warrant the expression crisis? I think so. And
there is no shortage of concrete examples to support this view.
Moreover, many Japanese apparently agree, to judge by the
number of articles and books they write in which the term
crisis is used freely and frequently. Others, who do not write
books, know there is a crisis because they are out of work or
cannot afford a decent living. Or because they are unhappy and
frustrated. Or because they are looked down upon and dis-
criminated against. Still, not everyone would agree. Certainly
not the foreign apologists who find an excuse for everything
or, indeed, those Japanese in the middle or upper classes who
only suffer from inconveniences rather than actual hardship.

Another reason why some do not complain of a crisis, be
it social, political or economic, is that one gets accustomed so
quickly. Many things the Japanese would have regarded, in fact,
did regard as constituting a crisis when the initial *Japan: The
Coming Social Crisis* was written, are now regarded as acceptable or tolerable.[1] Thus, if 15 years ago one had asked a Japanese whether a severe slowdown of the economy would imply a
crisis, the answer would have been affirmative. If asked whether
widespread discontent among school children and bullying of
weaker ones would be a crisis, the answer would again have
been affirmative. Most certainly, if asked whether the collapse
of the ruling Liberal Democratic Party would signify a crisis,
the answer would have been a resounding Yes. Now that all
these things, and many more, have come to pass and the world
has not quite drawn to an end, crisis sounds a bit harsh.

Thus, a crisis is more of a comparative than an absolute
state and it can best be shown by the existence of many more

246

negative than positive trends over a long enough time to bring about far-reaching, and largely negative, changes. It is also comparative in another sense. If all other countries have faced similar trends then, even if there is a crisis, it is not specifically 'Japanese.' If, on the other hand, Japan also has gotten worse in certain ways while the others have not or if Japan has been moving in the wrong directions faster, then one can speak of a Japanese crisis.

Naturally, if it appears that the problems could be solved and the trends reversed, this would be just a temporary crisis, a nasty patch one has to get through. That has applied to many of the individual crises that litter Japan's recent history, be it the oil crises or the repeated yen crises. But most of the problems we have dealt with, in the schools, company, state, family, society and nation are not being solved. And neither the people nor the leadership seem in a position to solve them. Consequently, whatever crisis there is today, it could be very considerably worse in another decade or two. Then it would be extremely hard to deny the existence of a CRISIS, even if the toleration of such phenomena grows.[2]

Following The Trends

About half a century ago, with the help of its American victors, Japan put an end to one of the ugliest, most traumatic periods of its history. This was a crisis the likes of which it will hopefully never see again. And it started out in new directions which appeared infinitely more promising. During the initial period, substantial progress was made, admittedly much more in the economic than the social and political spheres. Yet, even for the economy, things began to turn sour by the 1970s and the trends gradually became less encouraging. That is particularly important here because economic growth was also the primary social goal, it being assumed that all sorts of other, seemingly lesser tasks would be automatically accomplished. Thus, if the economy weakens, the fundamental underpinnings for much of today's social cohesion will also weaken. More simply, if there is less money available, many social problems that could be readily solved in the past by throwing money at them or buying off some segment of the population, will continue to fester. To be specific, there will be less funds available for schools, salaries and pensions, homes and vacations, hospitals and old age homes, social security and health insurance and, for that matter, bribes and kickbacks.

As must be perfectly evident to all, Japan's economy has slowed down over the past few decades. It has slowed down fairly dramatically. It went from a growth rate of well over 10 per cent in the 1960s to a mere 5 per cent or so in the 1970s and then, aside from the 'bubble economy' when rates were artificially high, to just several per cent at present. Equally serious, tax revenues have ceased expanding regularly and almost effortlessly and taxes are taking a bigger bite out of incomes than ever. This means that both the individual Japanese and the state are no longer in a position to pay for as many of the things as they want or, sometimes, need. There have been cuts in personal spending on many items and the state, although it is still expanding some programs (while containing others) can only do so by running up debts that will have to be paid.

The economic crisis appeared gradually. The political crisis came like a bolt from the blue. No one expected it. Indeed, if asked not ten years before but ten days before it occurred, nearly all commentators would have insisted that the LDP would solve its internal problems and continue to rule (govern? go through the motions of governing?) Japan for many years to come. Now, instead of one familiar party, run by well-known and experienced politicians who, even if they did not actually produce legislation, could at least keep tabs on the bureaucrats who did, there is a multitude of parties. None of these parties has shown enough ability to take the lead. In fact, no one even knows how long any of them will be around in their present form. And shifting coalitions of such parties are certainly no improvement on the, admittedly, rather unsatisfactory situation that existed before.

The only reason that decisions can be reached on crucial matters and legislation adopted is that the bureaucrats are filling the gaps. But these are not the same calibre of bureaucrats who took charge after the war. They may be somewhat better educated and sometimes have greater technical competences, but they lack the drive and vision to run the country. They have become hopelessly bogged down in precedent. At best, they can keep things moving in the way they were before, but they cannot strike out in new directions. While they can handle ordinary business, they cannot take on anything new. And they cannot solve the existing problems in numerous sectors, let alone totally unexpected ones which have a nasty habit of cropping up.

Confusion among the parties and politicians, groupthink and fear of change among the bureaucrats, are a sure recipe for an ongoing political crisis that will have ramifications in every other sphere. This leaves Japan leaderless and rudderless, as the media repeatedly point out. And even the influential business community cannot put the government back together again. The *zaikai* can continue holding meetings, adopting declarations and circulating papers. It can certainly influence politicians and bureaucrats. But it cannot get them to take resolute or decisive action under such circumstances.

The only apparently positive trend here is that the people have finally done something. The electorate, which passively allowed politicians and bureaucrats to rule for decades with little concern as to what the public thought, have thrown out (some of) the old bunch of rascals. And they seem to be voting in newcomers who are more willing to do what the electorate wants. Alas, the people have not yet sorted out just what they do want – as opposed to what they don't want – and until they can agree on policies and programs, and then impose them on the political class, there is little hope for progress. Quite to the contrary, they are injecting greater uncertainty and instability which only exacerbates the political aspects of the overall crisis.

Obviously, an economic crisis conjugated with a political crisis are bound to aggravate the strictly social problems. One cluster can be found in the schools. It is becoming ever more difficult for teachers to teach and pupils to learn the formal curriculum, whatever its failings may be. Cramming and assistance in passing exams have become the primary task of education. Rote memory and mock tests are the principal tools. Thus, even if Japanese students do well on some comparative tests, especially for 'hard' subjects, they are better with the mechanical aspects than problem solving. And their knowledge of 'softer' subjects, be it humanities or language, is rather flawed. More worrisome, they are not learning to reason or think for themselves at a time when imagination and creativity are increasingly vital.[3] As for higher education, that is an ever bigger waste of time and effort.

The company is no longer what it used to be either. This does not mean that the harmonious company family ever existed or that management really cared for the workers. But even the cohesion and cooperation that once prevailed is gradually dissolving as the core shrinks and the periphery grows. If the company will no longer guarantee extended employment, even for the lucky elite, more employees will consider leaving the company. For the moment, few do. Yet, that could change. Anyway, it is evident that bungled attempts at imposing discipline and boosting performance will not reinforce this most important of social institutions.

Friction and frustration are growing in other bodies as well. The trade unions have patently failed their members on what matters most: working hours, vacations and pay. They may not even be able to ensure job security any more. If all they can do is hold rallies, their membership will doubtlessly fall. And if temples and shrines cannot provide something more than periodic ceremonies and good luck charms, they should not be surprised if more tourists come than actual believers. The 'new religions,' which are more assiduous both at recruiting and holding on to followers, offer them more. But with new ones popping up all the time many are bound to be ephemeral.

Meanwhile, what once was and should still be the most vital cell, the family, has come on very bad times. Countless families have been fragmented or crushed by companies that make such overwhelming demands on their (male) employees that it is difficult to be a father. It is almost as hard to be a normal mother if one accepts the need to prepare the children for exams. And 'examination hell' keeps the children from participating in whatever may remain of the family. This is not only tearing apart existing families, through divorce or separation, it is discouraging men, and especially women, from getting married to begin with. Meanwhile, more new couples are having second thoughts about raising children. Here the trends are easiest to follow, as the divorce rate rises and the birthrate sinks.

While each of the basic social institutions has been weakening, they remain strong enough to undermine society as a whole.

Employees are tied to their company so effectively that, as noted, they cannot even become full-fledged members of their family, let alone their neighborhood, or Japan. Adepts of new religions, more even than old, are expected to devote themselves thoroughly to the cause. Politicians, bureaucrats and business leaders are kept so busy doing their job that they have no energy to expand their horizons and consider the good of the whole nation.

All this while, the Japanese have been further segmented by age. Each new cohort thinks of itself as a new generation, somehow different from its predecessors and soon also its successors. The differences from one batch to the next may be relatively marginal. But the gaps between seniors and juniors, bosses and rank-and-file workers, parents and children, have become immense. The gulf between men and women, which once seemed to be closing, is now growing wider than ever. Even youngsters don't mix much and older couples often find it hard to remain together. To this can be added the increasing distinctions of class, wealth and, not to be forgotten, racial or social origin.

With this, the nation's leaders have moved ever further from the bulk of the population. Almost by definition, due to seniority, leaders are rather old and their ideas are increasingly outdated, even antiquated. They have a different educational background, not only that they are university educated, but that they attended the 'good' universities. And more and more of them are rich, having made money in business, or politics, or through *amakudari*. Now this elite is passing on wealth and status to its offspring, and an upper class is emerging which knows and cares little of the lower class or even the supposedly massive middle classes.

While more and more things divide the Japanese, fewer and fewer hold them together. Religion, to the extent they actually practice one, is splintered among so many mainline groups and lesser sects that there is limited agreement on precepts and values. There is no ideology that binds large numbers, again because so many half-baked ideologies have been absorbed, and also because one of the most widespread, Marxism, has subsided. Old-fashioned nationalism has largely faded, only to be replaced by a still tame cult of Japaneseness. While this does remind the Japanese of what they have, or it is claimed they have, in common, its main thrust comes from insisting that this distinguishes them from foreigners. And any gains to internal Japanese cohesion must be weighed against the losses of international understanding.

These trends are, on the whole, negative. But they are more so because most have been so rapid that people could not adjust adequately. In just half-a-century, Japan has gone from overwhelmingly rural to overwhelmingly urban. It has gone from the extended family with five or more members to the nuclear family with three or less. It has gone from having families as the primary cell to their replacement by the company. And the father has passed from head of the family to just a temporary visitor. The number of students cramming for exams, and the time spent cramming, has expanded swiftly. An elite has arisen, and grabbed much of the money and power, in little time. And it should take even less for a lower class and even underclass to develop now that the economy has slowed down.

Surely, this should be enough to justify the claim that Japan is immersed in a crisis in many sectors and that these specific crises are gradually merging into a broader crisis for society. Once solid social institutions have not ceased imploding even if there have been rather few spectacular collapses, such as that of the LDP and the family structure as well as many companies and most unions. Meanwhile, more and more people have less and less to do with any acknowledged institution. So the self-destruction has spread further and faster than expected, although it often takes the form of decay and degeneration that cannot be readily perceived on the surface.

Hardly Number One

Still, even conceding that there is a crisis, if things are no better elsewhere, the Japanese are perhaps not so much to blame. This is what many of them believe. And that is not surprising. For most Japanese know very little about life in the outside world and what they 'know,' or think they know, is provided by Japanese media which go out of their way to show how poorly other countries are doing. The Japanese also tend to make comparisons not with the best, but the worst, of foreign countries. Thus, they boast about how much better their schools are than American ones (while conveniently overlooking those in Singapore or Europe). Or they exclaim at how lazy European workers have become (and say nothing about how much harder Koreans or Chinese work). And they look down on impoverished developing countries (rather than up at more comfortable advanced ones). Still, going through the various sectors, it does appear that Japan has done poorly enough that this can qualify as a 'Japanese' crisis.

The tendency toward rote learning, cramming and excessive competition to get into higher schools has cropped up in all the 'Confucian' countries, Korea, China, Taiwan, Singapore. But, in Korea, at least the government is taking measures to control these abuses and, among the Chinese, there is certainly more imagination and creativity. Graduates from these countries are often superior to Japanese graduates at all levels. Even in Europe, where cramming and 'examination hell' are attenuated, students usually get a better education, perhaps less intensive on math but certainly better on humanities, and they master one, two or three foreign languages. They are also taught to reason and develop more common sense. While weaker at lower levels, the United States has some of the world's best colleges and graduate schools.

Although not widely known, job security is almost as entrenched in larger American and European multinationals and there is little job-hopping in parts of Europe, although nobody would think of promising lifetime employment. True, the likelihood of getting fired is greater. On the other hand, the chances of finding another job, one that is equally good or better, are much greater as well. Foreign managers do not go out of their way to make employees feel good, and they cannot afford many frills that hurt the bottom line. Yet, according to poll after poll, foreign workers are happier with their jobs than the Japanese.

The family is obviously under tremendous stress in the West. The number of divorces has risen dramatically, there are more broken families and single mothers than ever. Compared to this, Japan's difficulties are modest. But Western societies have also adjusted to different types of families and made life easier for those concerned, including the children. Asian countries, despite several decades of rapid growth, have preserved family unity far better, largely because (aside from Korea) the company has not become as intrusive. Family members see much more of one another and relations are far closer.

To say the French and Germans, or Chinese and Koreans, are not nationalistic would be erroneous. But they are more spontaneously so. They do not presently have the urge to concoct a national philosophy based largely on their differences with others. And thus they find it easier to get along with other countries, joining or forming more organizations and participating much more actively than the Japanese. Not only the Oriental countries, but also most Western ones, managed to preserve their mainline religions more successfully. Not only do they exist, believers actually know what their precepts are and attend services. Having learned to reason, Westerners found it much easier to evaluate, accept, reject or merge the many ideologies they encountered.

Japan's biggest failure has been the inability to find a useful role for the individual, something most Western countries would not even regard as a task. Even in parts of Asia, the individual enjoys greater respect, and can shape his or her life more freely, than in Japan. This can be done more openly as well so it is better known what people want. Naturally, this facilitates politics. True, there are still many dictatorships. But, among the advanced countries at least, the democracies deserve that name more than Japan. In addition, politicians tend to have policies, parties tend to have programs and voters tend to have specific demands. The politicians and parties run the government, the bureaucrats by and large only executing laws, and businessmen who do more than just lobby are likely to get into trouble.

Of course, Japan has had its successes. None was more brilliant than its economic growth. But that has slumped substantially, to a point where it is hardly growing faster than other advanced countries, while it has been overtaken by an increasing number of newly industrialized countries. Moreover, it never had much to show for its rapid growth, since its people had to work harder and content themselves with rather mediocre housing, amenities and leisure compared to the West. With sluggish growth nowadays, it will never be able to create a social safety net and social security system such as is already commonplace in Western Europe. And, with the unravelling of the family and weakening of society there is little hope it can generate enough private concern or voluntarism to fill the gaps.

The Next Fifteen Years

Is that it? Has Japan reached the nadir of its social crisis and can we now expect it to react and gradually turn the situation around? Or is there more to come?

I would tend toward the latter response. The social crisis, which has been worsening over the past 15 years, and had already been deepening before, will continue getting worse. The present situation, which is already rather uncomfortable for many Japanese, will become considerably more painful and people will think back with nostalgia on the 1990s.

One reason to expect this is that, despite the heightened awareness of severe problems, so little has been done. Over the past decades, reform movements have been launched in a multitude of sectors: educational reform, management reform, anti-corruption drives, administrative reform and deregulation, improvement of the quality of life to create a lifestyle 'superpower,' upgrading of social security, urban reform, tax reform and so on. Yet, pitifully little has been accomplished by any of these movements and they are all stymied at present. Why?

For one, the Japanese have to cope with all sorts of reflex reactions, mind sets and vested interests that work almost blindly against reforms and changes, whatever they may be. The decision-making process is exceedingly slow. It is necessary to bring in too many participants, some only marginally concerned, and to require too much agreement among them. The consensus is not only slow in forming, it is achieved at such a low common denominator that any measures are terribly feeble. The Japanese claim that they are slow to decide but, once the decision is taken, action is rapid. That is just another *tatemae.* Because one decision calls for another, and another. The decision to boost social security implies a decision to raise money, and perhaps increase taxes, and then to set up new bureaucracies to dispense the money, and so on. Until all those decisions are made, nothing much can happen.

Once upon a time, just after the war or under energetic or

ambitious prime ministers like Tanaka and Nakasone, the process could be accelerated somewhat. Leadership at the top could make a difference. But such relatively dynamic leaders are being replaced by follower leaders, men who have gotten where they are haltingly and cautiously, by following instructions and not taking initiatives. What can be expected of them? Not very much. And there is even less chance that the people will impose action on the leaders, given the prevailing streak of fatalism best expressed by the plaintive whine of *shikataganai* or 'it cannot be helped.'

Meanwhile, the older generation is becoming ever older. And the views of the leaders, such as they are, are becoming ever more remote from those of rising generations of Japanese. The biggest urge for change, for improvement, for reform, is among younger people. But they have the least input in any social institution due to the prevailing rule of seniority. And even the seniors cannot act freely. For they are bound by precedents, and there are precedents for everything, most of which preclude updated or innovative measures.

While the respect for precedents, the need for consensus, the complicated decision-making process and other customs hamper efforts at reform, they are not even the worst impediment. That is the relative distaste for rationality and the preference for more 'human,' Japanese methods. Carefully selected participants do not sit down, cooly analyse the situation, permit one another to openly express their views, devise possible compromises and then rationally examine each one until the best is found. Rather, they let all and sundry attend, but only listen seriously to those in stronger positions, and then judge the suggestions (usually rather woolly ones) more as a function of whom they came from than their inherent merits. While the stronger side wins, to avoid upsetting the others compensations may be provided. This is not a compromise, it is mere horse-trading. And the chances of adopting measures that actually work are considerably reduced.

For such reasons, there is little likelihood that Japan will solve its problems any time soon. There should not only be more of the same, there should be more of more of the same. Since we already know the trends, there is no need to delineate the future scenario in great detail. It might just be mentioned that in some cases, rather than just worsening, the

situation could reach the breaking point. This means there would be more implosions and society's self-destruction would continue and perhaps accelerate.

In the schools, pupils will cram more than before, and make more frantic efforts to get into a 'good' school. Once there, they will do even less. They will become neither particularly knowledgeable nor creative, but they will form the rising elite. In companies, ever fewer employees concentrated in the core will work ever harder and have ever greater responsibilities. Since they are only human, there should be more breakdowns and certainly less efficient companies. The political parties have not yet ceased fracturing and fissioning, reforming and merging. Goodness knows which ones will come out on top. But their members will probably still be too busy hunting for votes to bother with policy. Nor can the people really be expected to take charge. Thus, the burden of government will rest more heavily on the bureaucracy. As long as it can simply extend past measures into the future, it can get by. But Japan cannot survive in tomorrow's world on the basis of yesterday's legislation.

How much weaker can the family get? Unfortunately, if the trends hold, more so than at present. Certainly, there is cause to expect men and women to get married later, and women to have less interest than before in looking after a husband or children. In the existing families, the husband may actually become a more active member as working hours gradually sink and more opt out of being company men. But the children will still be too busy to think of anything but cramming. With an aging population, more wives than ever will have to look after sick and bed-ridden relatives and this is what may smother the family if the state does not provide more care for the aged.

There is good reason to expect young people to be more alienated than before. Schools will be an even more crushing experience, followed by yet laxer ways in college, then the abrupt regimentation of the company. In the future, managers will be even stricter, given the need to survive in tougher economic circumstances. There will not be much place for women, and even OLs will not have it as good. Again, to remain competitive, older employees will be squeezed out sooner. Where they can go is very uncertain. Surely, the age hierarchy will remain, with those boasting seniority bearing down on relative youngsters. And the gulf between men and women will persist in the company, political parties and other formal bodies, even if it narrows a bit in the family or among younger cohorts more informally.

Since the company and workplace will no longer meet the individual's inner needs, more will turn to other institutions. Once this would have implied political parties and movements, but they are in such ill repute that conventional ones will be rejected, although fringe groups are possible. There is not much chance that trade unions or the labor movement in general will attract more members, given their dismal record. There are rather few grassroots organizations left. Religions seem the most likely winner. But which religions? Less the mainstream ones than new, newer and newest sects, each trying to peddle a more spectacular and seductive formula, and avidly collecting and binding members so they will not leave. This may be fine for the religious leaders and gurus; it will certainly not help any broader community, be it the neighborhood or the nation. Nor will it encourage the Japanese to become more individualistic. They may just trade the company's tyranny for even more compulsive control by a religious hierarchy.

It can be expected that the segmentation of society will continue. Graduates of 'good' schools will still get relatively secure jobs with 'good' companies and in the bureaucracy while high school grads and dropouts are stuck with lesser ones. Most assuredly, coming from a 'good' family will make it easier to get into a 'good' school and a 'good' company. And the offspring of such families will meet more readily and intermarry. Since money still generates money more readily than doing an honest day's work, the rich will continue getting richer. That was the story of the 'bubble economy.' The story of slow growth is that the poor will get poorer. This will also contribute to the growing polarization. The only thing that can hold all these people together, rich and poor, elite and plebeians, is a feeling that Japan is somehow different and better. While it will still be different, the 'better' part of that myth should be getting rather threadbare by the 21st century, but not enough for the Japanese to suddenly become internationalists.

This is how things might evolve in the major social institutions we considered. Admittedly, what was done in each instance was to extend trends. It is just conceivable that some trends might reverse. As noted, men may become better family members. And the family might hold together somewhat more. Youngsters might just develop a healthier and more purposeful individualism. Goodness knows, one of the celebrities might turn out to be a genuine leader or, if not, at least make the right gestures and say the right words, and the bureaucracy could fill in the blanks. There could be reforms and improvements.

Alas, relatively unexpected occurrences could also work in the opposite direction. They could further worsen the situation and throw up unexpected, perhaps unsolvable problems. It does not take too much imagination to think of some rather unpleasant scenarios.

The most probable starts with the incontrovertible fact that the Japanese economy is slowing down and it is economic growth, more than anything, which permitted society to react as well as it did thus far. With slower economic growth, income will rise more slowly and it will become tougher for some segments to keep up. The poor will be hard pressed to cover even necessities. The middle class will be squeezed by heavy mortgage payments which must be made, come what may, and would cramp expenditures on other items. If it is only a matter of wages that grow less rapidly, or maybe even decrease, at least in real terms, most Japanese should be able to get by while they are still working. They can dip into their savings if need be. This would create a pretty morose population, and no one knows how it might vote, but the social and political reactions would be muted.

More serious is what happens to those who are not working. First, there are more and more retired persons, many of them living off rather meager pensions and savings and perhaps leaning on children or relatives in the previous category. They will definitely need more social security and welfare to scrape through. Since this is less likely to be forthcoming, in a time of economic stringency, they may be in trouble. They may suffer hardship as bad as, or worse than, after the war. But they have been brought up to endure and endure they will, without causing too much political fallout, although the social consequences could be disastrous.

If poor people lose their jobs, that is another matter. They may not have the skills to find other work, especially if they are manual laborers or ordinary factory workers and jobs continue migrating abroad. They may not have much savings to fall back on. Some will doubtlessly accept whatever work they can get, no matter how harsh, no matter how demeaning. Others may take to crime. Whatever the case, the fond illusion of an equalitarian society with a vast middle class and no lower class to speak of would be shattered. There would be more poor, and poverty would be inherited, since poor parents cannot buy their children as much education. Some segments of the poor could sink into a hopeless underclass with its own social ills which, like it or not, the state would have to worry about.

There is one last category, the most significant as every Japanese knows, and it could raise the most serious problems. These are fresh graduates from high school and college. For half-a-century they have been almost automatically enrolled in Japan's companies. Indeed, in past years, companies fought over them. Now, for the first time, not all graduates are finding work. This is most difficult for the women, but even male graduates cannot get the kind of job they like or, in some cases, any job. They can continue living with their family for some time, so they are not out on the street. And they may take courses and maintain the pretext of being students so they can apply for a job the following year, and the year after. But the most sacred, if tacit promise will have been broken and those who do not get jobs could become asocial and anti-social.

With more poor, and more unemployed, and more antagonistic elements, and youth in general dissatisfied with its limited say, the whole social code that has prevailed for decades would be undermined. Inevitably, there would be more persons who turned to crime just to eke out a living. They would not be professional gangsters, *yakuza* who are known to the police, but irregular, unaccountable thugs who might engage in more vicious crimes on occasion. Or, they might go into drug trafficking. After all, the pool of potential users would have grown and drugs are easy enough to come by. So are increasingly guns. More women may be forced into prostitution. With this burgeoning sex industry, there should also be more AIDS, and by ignoring the threat Japan only encourages further proliferation.

These are not just horror stories. They are very real possibilities. They may actually be probabilities given Japan's past behavior. And, even if they do not all materialize, some will. These will only add to the fairly predictable problems indicated by the many negative trends in various social institutions which have already been traced.

Closing Words

In writing about Japan, there are a number of conventions that most (politically correct, if not necessarily sycophantic) authors follow. One is to apologize for having perhaps overdone the criticism. Japan is, they say, fundamentally a very fine country although it does have some blemishes. They would thus not have their readers believe they exaggerated on the negative side.

I see no point to such a disclaimer. It is possible that I exaggerated. But, if I did, it was by accident and not on purpose. I have done my best to determine what is positive and what is negative and I have encountered considerably more of the latter than the former. If the picture I have painted is unattractive, unpleasant, ugly, that is because the reality I observed had the same characteristics. I did not overdo it to prove a thesis or sell more copies, I really believe Japan is in for serious trouble.

Moreover, I am not alone in having these views. While most of the literature by foreign writers remains fairly upbeat even now, most of the literature by Japanese writers is increasingly downbeat and dismal, just like mine.[4] I have no difficulty in quoting authors who say pretty much the same thing, and this without even seeking among the harsher critics, let alone iconoclasts and rebels. An interesting analysis is provided by the very official *Trade and Industry Policy Vision in the 1990s*, drawn up by the highly reputable Industrial Structure Council, an advisory body of MITI.

In the light of gross national product and scale of business, the Japanese economy has indisputably achieved excellent results. . . . On the other hand, people have come to ask themselves, 'Are we really rich?' They ask this because the formation of such social assets as houses and infrastructure has been delayed, because they work for too long hours and because women and the aged are given only scant opportunities or conditions for self-realization. People do not feel a sense of affluence in life, since the fruit of economic growth, the product of their toil and sweat, is not properly distributed among them.[5]

Another summary of Japan's problems was reproduced on the opinion page of the *Nihon Keizai Shimbun*, the leading business newspaper, and written by Masanori Moritani, a technology analyst who conceded that while technological progress has done a lot for economic strength, industrial growth and material wealth, it has not contributed much to enhancing social quality.

Despite its wealth, Japan has a pile of social problems: crowded commuter trains, clogged highways, a degraded environment, deterioration of beauty and a dearth of urban amenities. It is also lacking in the areas of education and medicine. The county may be rich in material wealth but it remains poor in lifestyle. . . .[6]

A particularly intriguing critique was made by Mariko Sugahara, presently cabinet councilor and head of the office for women's affairs in the Prime Minister's Office, again certainly an establishment figure, and a respected one. This was done in a widely read article on the 'Japanese disease.' The five symptoms she stressed, briefly summed up, are the following. First, 'the growing number of people who hate work.' Second, an 'excessive homogeneity and conformity,' one result of which is that 'thinking or behavior that is in any way out of the ordinary is viewed with scorn, suspicion, or distaste.' This causes the third symptom, 'a lack of creativity and vitality.' The fourth is 'the loss of ethics, public spirit, and civic morals,' which results in an 'emptiness of people's personal lives.' And the last is 'society's failure to tap the potential of women and senior citizens.'[7]

Moreover, it is not just opinion-leaders or intellectuals who are complaining. Ordinary people also have plenty of gripes. They appear openly in letters to the editor and personal conversations. They are even being recorded in public opinion polls. The latest one, taken by the Economic Planning Agency, found that 79 per cent of the respondents were worried by the increase in the number of 'irresponsible people' and its affect on the safety and order of Japanese society, 79 per cent felt that people were selfish and 75 per cent said that ethics and social justice were being eroded.[8]

Under these conditions, there is more cause to apologize for an overly positive and optimistic than an overly negative and pessimistic view. All the more so since, despite the fact that the precursor *Japan: The Coming Social Crisis* was often criticized as too strong, it turned out to be too weak as Japan's social crisis became far worse than even I had claimed.

A second convention is to end with an uplifting sentiment. This might be a reference to the well-known adaptability of the Japanese, or their superior performance in adversity, or their fabled ability to confound the critics by pulling off another miracle. Thus, the Japanese will somehow overcome these problems, no matter how daunting, and come out ahead. There is always a silver lining if only the author will search hard enough.

Obviously, I am not happy that Japan has gotten into such a mess and I would be very happy if it managed to extricate itself without too much unpleasantness. But, as I have gone to great pains to show, it is most definitely in a mess and there is no silver lining to be found anywhere. Moreover, no matter how bad the mess is today, it should be considerably worse tomorrow and the day after. This is unfortunate but, as far as I can tell, it is true. And my function is not to gush sentimentality but analyse the situation as best I can. I may be wrong. Still, the overwhelming weight of the evidence suggests that things are more likely to get worse than to get better.

In writing about any society, Japan's or another, it is extremely important to follow the trends. That is the only way of peering into the future, even if it is not perfect. Otherwise, you are stuck with anecdotal evidence and speculation. So, this book has devoted more space than most to defining and interpreting trends. Very few of them are positive. The vast majority are negative. There is no way of escaping this and, to be frank, no point to it either.

That is why I was particularly interested in the comments of Mariko Sugahara because, prior to her present post, until recently she was in charge of supervising many of the opinion polls and surveys that are quoted in this book. And she has worked intensively on the issues of young people, women and the elderly. It is thus worthwhile reading the opening paragraph to her article which shows just how grievously the Japanese social organism is afflicted.

The people and society of Japan are being ravaged, quietly but steadily, by an insidious ailment – a potentially lethal disorder that advances from within, attacking our vital functions at the very core before it displays its outward symptoms. This is a deep-rooted internal disorder, not some seasonal malady or external injury. The responsible agent has not been identified, nor has a specific remedy been found. It may be that we are predisposed to this illness by our lifestyle or genetic makeup. All that is certain is that the Japanese disease is gradually sapping us of our energy and the will to build our own future.[9]

The third convention, one that is almost always applied, is to proffer solutions to any problems and remedies for any social abuses. I have done a bit of that in the past. And even in this book, if not directly then certainly incidentally, I have mentioned possible solutions. But there is no point to going any further in that direction. The Japanese are aware of the problems, and they have even identified many of the solutions or can apply, with suitable variations, those used by other advanced countries, especially those which developed similar diseases earlier. The solutions are there. What is lacking is the will to implement them. And, as long as the will is lacking, it is a waste of time to propose solutions.

This is not a very pleasant note to end on. And I am not personally happy about it. I would very much have preferred apologizing for any tendency to overdo the criticism, then conjured up a silver lining and finally, in my wisdom, have counseled the Japanese on how to resolve their dilemma. It would have been nice for me. It might have been nice for them, who knows? But, given the circumstances, it would also have been futile and hypocritical. I have had my say and let us see whether I was right or wrong.

Notes

Chapter 1

1. The story of this attack can be found in D.W. Brackett, *Holy Terror, Armageddon in Tokyo.*
2. Brian Reading, *Japan, The Coming Collapse*, p. 299.
3. *Ibid*, p. 300.
4. *Journal of Asian Studies*, Spring 1990, p. 408.
5. Policy Speech by Prime Minister Ohira at the 87th Session of the National Diet, January 25, 1979.
6. Mikio Sumiya, *The Japanese Industrial Relations Reconsidered*, pp. 151–2.
7. *Keidanren Review*, No. 130, August 1991, p. 5.
8. Edwin O. Reischauer, *The Japanese*, p. 309.
9. Ezra F. Vogel, *Japan As Number One*, p. 235.

Chapter 2

1. See W. Dean Kinzley, *Industrial Harmony in Modern Japan, The Invention of a Tradition.*
2. Akio Morita, *Made in Japan*, p. 144.
3. Robert J. Ballon, *Doing Business in Japan*, p. 8.
4. On the role of women in the workforce, see the relevant books listed under Women in the Bibliography.
5. See Alice Lam (ed.), *Women and Japanese Management, Discrimination and Reform.*
6. See Jeannie Lo, *Office Ladies, Factory Women.*
7. See Norma J. Chalmers, *Industrial Relations in Japan: The Peripheral Sector.*
8. See James C. Abegglen, *The Japanese Factory.*
9. Ministry of Labor, *Basic Survey on Wage Structure*, annual.
10. *Ibid.*
11. Management and Coordination Agency, *Special Survey on Labor Force*, February 1990.
12. See Jon Woronoff, *Japan's Wasted Workers* and *The Japanese Management Mystique.*

13. Abegglen and George Stalk, Jr., *Kaisha*, p. 207.
14. *Financial Times*, December 16, 1991, p. VII.
15. Robert Ozaki, *Human Capitalism, The Japanese Enterprise System as World Model*, p. 8.
16. *Look Japan*, April 30, 1983.
17. *Nikkei Weekly*, December 19, 1994.
18. *Japan Economic Journal*, April 9, 1986.
19. *Tokyo Business Today*, September 1990, p. 12.
20. *Press Guide*, Foreign Press Center/Japan, March 1990.
21. *Nikkei Weekly*, November 22, 1993.
22. *Yomiuri*, February 14, 1992.
23. *Nikkei Weekly*, May 16, 1994.
24. Management and Coordination Agency, *Worldwide Survey on Consciousness of Youth*, 1994.
25. *Yomiuri*, March 29, 1991.
26. *Yomiuri*, February 14, 1992.
27. Jonathan Rice, *Doing Business in Japan*, p. 41.

Chapter 3

1. Edwin O. Reischauer, *The Japanese*, p. 167.
2. Ezra F. Vogel, *Japan As Number One*, p. 161.
3. The source for most of the data provided here is Ministry of Education, *Kyoiku shihyo no kokusai hikaku*, annual.
4. See Mamoru Tsukada, *Yobiko Life*.
5. *Far Eastern Economic Review*, March 12, 1992, p. 22.
6. Vogel, *op. cit.*, pp. 164 and 167.
7. *Tokyo Business Today*, February 1992, p. 54.
8. *Economic Eye*, Spring 1993, p. 16.
9. *Mainichi*, December 3, 1977.
10. They include Richard Lynn, *Educational Achievement in Japan*, Thomas Rohlen, *Japan's High Schools*, and Merry White, *The Japanese Educational Challenge*.
11. *The Economist*, April 21, 1990.
12. See Lisa Martineau, *Caught in a Mirror*.
13. *Wall Street Journal*, December 26, 1991.
14. See Jon Woronoff, *Japan As – Anything But – Number One*, p. 102.
15. *Tokyo Business Today*, February 1992, p. 55.
16. *Far Eastern Economic Review*, April 6, 1989, p. 70, and *Tokyo Business Today*, February 1992, p. 55.
17. *Mainichi*, November 3, 1990.
18. *Far Eastern Economic Review*, June 30, 1994, p. 50.
19. *Financial Times*, April 5, 1995.
20. *Tokyo Business Today*, January 1987.
21. *Tradepia International*, Summer 1989, p. 27.
22. *Economic Eye*, Spring 1993, p. 11.
23. *Far Eastern Economic Review*, June 30, 1994, p. 50.
24. *Yomiuri*, March 14, 1992.

25. *Yomiuri*, September 1, 1991.
26. See Leonard James Schoppa, *Education Reform in Japan, A Case of Immobilist Politics.*

Chapter 4

1. See Jon Woronoff, *Politics, The Japanese Way.*
2. Gerald Curtis, *The Japanese Way of Politics*, p. 249.
3. Phillip Oppenheim, *Japan Without Blinders*, p. 151.
4. See Junko Kato, *The Problem of Bureaucratic Rationality.*
5. See Masao Miyamoto, *Straitjacket Society*, pp. 73–92.
6. *Nikkei Weekly*, August 23, 1993.
7. *Wall Street Journal*, March 10, 1993.
8. On some of Japan's many scandals, see among others Peter J. Herzog, *Japan's Pseudo-Democracy*, William J. Holstein, *The Japanese Power Game*, Brian Reading, *Japan, The Coming Collapse*, Peter Tasker, *Inside Japan*, and Woronoff, *op. cit.*
9. *Financial Times*, August 5, 1993.
10. Ezra Vogel, *Japan As Number One*, p. 90.
11. See Chalmers Johnson, *MITI and the Japanese Miracle.*
12. See Johnson, *Japan, Who Governs?*
13. *Nikkei Weekly*, 'Letters,' December 6, 1993.
14. See Woronoff, *op. cit.*
15. See Christopher Wood, *The Bubble Economy.*
16. See Woronoff, *Japanese Industrial Targeting.*
17. See Miyamoto, *op. cit.*, pp. 157–60.
18. *Yomiuri*, February 25, 1991.
19. *Far Eastern Economic Review*, November 11, 1993, p. 30.
20. Naohiro Amaya, 'Rudderless bureaucrats need strong political captain,' *Nikkei Weekly*, February 14, 1994.
21. *Nikkei Weekly*, December 6, 1993.
22. Few serious works have been written specifically on the subject, although it is mentioned in passing in many of the critical books on politics. Of some abiding interest is Chitoshi Yanaga, *Big Business in Japanese Politics.*
23. See Michael Gerlach, *Alliance Capitalism*, and Leonard H. Lynn and Timothy J. McKeown, *Organizing Business*, as well as other books listed under Business Community in the Bibliography.
24. See Woronoff, *Politics, The Japanese Way*, pp. 150–74.
25. *Japan Update*, December 1993, p. 2.
26. See Karel van Wolferen, *The Enigma of Japanese Power.*
27. See among others Kent Calder, *Crisis and Compensation*, John Creighton Cambell, *How Policies Change*, Curtis, *op. cit.*, and T.J. Pempel, *Policies and Politics in Japan: Creative Conservatism.*
28. *Nikkei Weekly*, December 14, 1992.
29. *Financial Times*, April 5, 1993.
30. See among others Ichiro Miyake in Scott C. Flanagan et al., *The Japanese Voter*, pp. 226–66.

31. *Japan Update,* June 1995, back page.
32. Flanagen, *op. cit.,* p. 113.
33. See among others Leonard Schoppa, *Education Reform in Japan: A Case of Immobilist Politics,* and J.A.A. Stockwin et al., *Dynamic and Immobilist Politics in Japan.*
34. Stockwin, *op. cit.,* p. 2.
35. See among others David Apter and Nagayo Sawa, *Against the State, Politics and Social Protest in Japan,* and Kurt Steiner et al., *Political Opposition and Local Politics in Japan.*
36. See Tetsuya Kataoka (ed.), *Creating Single-Party Democracy,* and T.J. Pempel (ed.), *Uncommon Democracies.*

Chapter 5

1. Derek Massarella, 'The other side of the yen?,' *Far Eastern Economic Review,* March 5, 1982, p. 39.
2. These figures and most other demographic statistics are drawn from the National Census of the Management and Coordination Agency and various sources of the Ministry of Health and Welfare.
3. *Nikkei Weekly,* November 16, 1992.
4. *Japan Update,* Spring 1991, pp. 4–9.
5. See among others Theodore Bester, *Neighborhood Tokyo,* Ronald P. Dore, *City Life in Japan,* Jennifer Robertson, *Native and Newcomer,* and Ezra Vogel, *Japan's New Middle Class.*
6. Yasuhiko Yuzawa, *Japanese Families,* Foreign Press Center/Japan, 1994, pp. 40 and 63–8.
7. See Jane Condon, *A Half Step Behind, Japanese Women Today,* and Sumiko Iwao, *The Japanese Woman: Traditional Image and Changing Reality.*
8. *Yomiuri,* December 2, 1989.
9. Yuzawa, *op. cit.,* pp. 45–8.
10. *Nikkei Weekly,* June 20, 1994.
11. Yuzawa, *op. cit.,* p. 26.
12. *Yomiuri,* September 26, 1988.
13. *Nikkei Weekly,* November 6, 1995.
14. Yuzawa, *op. cit.,* pp. 28–9.
15. *Nikkei Weekly,* April 4, 1994.
16. *Nikkei Weekly,* May 16 and April 4, 1994.
17. *New York Times International,* February 17, 1991.
18. *Nikkei Weekly,* June 20, 1994.
19. *Japan Times,* May 30, 1980.
20. *Japan Economic Journal,* June 25, 1985.
21. *New York Times International,* February 17, 1991.

Chapter 6

1. Bank of Japan, *Kokusai hikaku tokei,* 1992.
2. Survey of Ministry of Education, *Nikkei Weekly,* July 25, 1994.

3. *Nikkei Weekly*, August 22, 1994.
4. Prime Minister's Office, *Public Opinion Survey on State and Society*, 1995.
5. Yomiuri Shimbun/Gallup Poll of September 1993, *Japan Update*, December 1994.
6. Prime Minister's Office, *Monthly Public Survey, Japan Update*, May 1995, p. 25.
7. See among others David E. Apter and Nagayo Sawa, *Aainst the State, Politics and Social Protest in Japan*, and Kurt Steiner et al., *Political Opposition and Local Politics in Japan*.
8. See books listed under Crime in the Bibliography.
9. See David E. Kaplan and Alec Dubro, *Yakuza: The Explosive Account of Japan's Underworld.*
10. Tele Suisse Romande, March 27, 1995.
11. *Nikkei Weekly*, April 3, 1995.
12. David Bayley, *Forces of Order*, p. 10.
13. Prime Minister's Office, *Class Perceptions of Japanese Households*, annual.
14. See Rob Steven, *Classes in Contemporary Japan.*

Chapter 7

1. Prime Minister's Office, *Public Opinion Survey on Society and State*, 1991 and 1995.
2. William H. Forbis, *Japan Today*, p. 95.
3. Ian Reader, *Religion in Contemporary Japan.*
4. The 'official' statistics on religion appear in the annual *Religious Almanac* of the Agency for Cultural Affairs. There is obviously much double and even triple counting and the figures for membership of the various religious groups cannot be verified. But they are considerably more reliable than those emanating from the religious groups themselves, which are very definitely on the high side.
5. See Helen Hardacre, *Shinto and the State*, and Stuart Pickens, *Essentials of Shinto.*
6. See among others Hardacre, *Lay Buddhism in Contemporary Japan*, and Dale Saunders, *Buddhism in Japan.*
7. See among others Hardacre, *Kurozumikyo and the New Religions of Japan*, and Harry Thomsen, *The New Religions of Japan.*
8. See Daniel Metraux, *The History and Theology of Soka Gakkai.*
9. Institute of Statistical Mathematics, *Study of the National Characteristics of the Japanese*, annual.
10. *Business Tokyo*, May 1992, p. 62.
11. Prime Minister's Office, *Monthly Public Survey*, January 1994.
12. See Chie Nakane, *Japanese Society.*
13. *Yomiuri*, March 28, 1991.
14. Mariko Sugahara, 'Five Fatal Symptoms of the Japanese Disease,' *Japan Echo*, Summer 1994, p. 72.
15. See Ruth Benedict, *The Chrysanthemum and the Sword.*
16. See Ian Buruma, *The Wages of Guilt.*
17. See among others Bruce Stronach, *Beyond the Rising Sun, Nationalism*

in *Contemporary Japan*, and Kásaku Yoshino, *Cultural Nationalism in Contemporary Japan*.

18. See Ross Mauer and Yoshino Sugimoto, *Images of Japanese Society*.
19. See George A. DeVos, *Social Cohesion and Alienation*, and DeVos and Hiroshi Wagatsuma, *Japan's Invisible Race*.
20. See Peter N. Dale, *The Myth of Japanese Uniqueness*.
21. See Nakane, *op. cit.*
22. See Takeo Doi, *The Anatomy of Dependence* and *The Anatomy of Self*.
23. See Emiko Ohnuki-Tierney, *Rice as Self*.
24. See Merry White, *The Japanese Overseas*.
25. On a comparison between Japanese and German attitudes toward their wartime conduct, see Buruma, *op. cit.*
26. See Ichiro Ozawa, *Blueprint for a New Japan*.
27. Michael Dobbs-Higginson, *Asia Pacific*, London, Longman, 1993.

Chapter 8

1. *Japan Times*, October 27, 1985.
2. *Nikkei Weekly*, February 13, 1995.
3. Institute of Statistical Mathematics, *Study of the National Characteristics of the Japanese*, annual.
4. *Wall Street Journal*, February 20, 1992.
5. *Nikkei Weekly*, April 24, 1995.
6. *Japan Update*, September 1992, p. 11.
7. Seiko Tanabe, 'Prodigal Children, Impoverished Parents,' *Japan Echo*, Vol. XVII, 1990, pp. 61–63.
8. See Munesuke Mita, *Social Psychology of Japan*.
9. *Financial Times*, November 13, 1993.
10. Management and Coordination Agency, *Worldwide Survey on Consciousness of Youth*, 1994.
11. *Yomiuri*, December 25, 1991.
12. See Lois Peak, *Learning to Go to School in Japan*.
13. *Yomiuri*, June 12, 1991.
14. *Yomiuri*, January 15 and May 11, 1986.
15. Foreign Press Center/Japan, *Religion in Japan*, p. 35.
16. *Yomiuri*, May 31, 1989.
17. *Yomiuri*, December 19, 1988.
18. *Yomiuri*, February 8, 1984.
19. See Ken Schoolland, *Shogun's Ghost, The Dark Side of Japanese Education*.
20. *Financial Times*, December 15, 1994.
21. *Wall Street Journal*, December 26, 1991.
22. Yusuke Takatsuka, 'Identity Crisis for Japan's youth,' *Nikkei Weekly*, September 19, 1995.
23. *Nikkei Weekly*, September 4, 1995.
24. *Nikkei Weekly*, December 10, 1993.
25. Iwao Hoshi, *The World of Sex: Sex and Marriage*, p. 197.
26. Prime Minister's Office, *Monthly Public Opinion Survey*, May 1994.
27. *Yomiuri*, June 12, 1991.

28. Noriko Okifuji, 'Men Who Can't Go Home,' *Japan Echo*, Vol. XVII, 1990, pp. 48–52.
29. See Nicholas Bornoff, *Pink Samurai*, and Masao Miyamoto, *Straightjacket Society*, pp. 53–72.
30. See Prime Minister's Office, *Japanese Women in the World Today, The Present Status and Policies*, annual.
31. *Japan Update*, February 1995, p. 18.
32. Yasuhiko Yuzawa, *Japanese Families*, Foreign Press Center/Japan, pp. 41–2, and *Nikkei Weekly*, May 16, 1994.
33. *Nikkei Weekly*, September 27, 1993.
34. *Mainichi*, March 25, 1989, and *Nikkei Weekly*, May 30, 1994.
35. On the very differing career paths of these two categories, see Jeannie Lo, *Office Ladies, Factory Women*.
36. Takada Masatoshi, 'Woman and Man in Modern Japan,' *Japan Echo*, Vol. XVI, 1989, p. 40.
37. See among others Alice Cook and Hiroko Hayashi, *Working Women in Japan*, and Alice Lam, *Women and Japanese Management*.
38. *Japan Update*, May 1992.
39. *Nikkei Weekly*, January 2, 1992.
40. *Yomiuri*, May 13, 1989.
41. See Sumiko Iwao, *The Japanese Woman: Traditional Image and Changing Reality*.
42. Most of the population figures come from the Ministry of Health and Welfare and most of the social security costs come from the Ministry of Labor, *Basic Survey on the Life of the People* and *Basic Survey on the Administration of Social Welfare*.
43. *Nikkei Weekly*, February 20, 1995.
44. *Economic Eye*, Summer 1994, p. 25.
45. *Nikkei Weekly*, March 22, 1993.
46. *Yomiuri*, September 11, 1990.
47. *Financial Times*, November 13, 1993.
48. *Nikkei Weekly*, March 22 and August 9, 1993.
49. John Creighton Campbell, *How Policies Change, The Japanese Government and the Aging Society*, p. 395, and Scott A. Bass, *Productive Aging and the Role of Older People in Japan*, and Victor Rodwin, *Japan's Universal and Affordable Health Care*.

Chapter 9

1. To follow these trends over a longer period, and see how poorly Japan was doing even 15 years ago, it would not hurt to read Jon Woronoff, *Japan: The Coming Social Crisis*.
2. For further examples, see Woronoff, *Japan As – Anything But – Number One*.
3. See W.O. Lee, *Social Change and Educational Problems in Japan, Singapore and Hong Kong*.
4. For some examples in English translation, see Tadashi Fukutake, *Japanese Society Today* and *The Japanese Social Structure*, Rokuro Hidaka,

The Price of Affluence: Dilemmas of Contemporary Japan, Satoshi Kamata, *Japan in the Passing Lane,* Takako Kishima, *Political Life in Japan, Democracy in a Reversible World,* and Masao Miyamoto, *Straitjacket Society.*

5. Industrial Structure Council, MITI, *Trade and Industry Policy in the 1990s,* January 1993.
6. *Nikkei Weekly,* May 17, 1993.
7. For an English translation of the article, see Mariko Sugahara, 'Five Fatal Symptoms of the Japanese Disease,' *Japan Echo,* Summer 1994, pp. 68–74.
8. *Financial Times,* February 23, 1996.
9. Sugahara, *op. cit.,* p. 68.

Bibliography

1. Company and Management

Abegglen, James C., *The Japanese Factory*, Glenco, Free Press, 1958.
——, *Management and Labor, The Japanese Solution*, Tokyo, Kodansha International, 1973.
Abegglen, James C., and Stalk, George, *Kaisha, The Japanese Corporation*, New York, Basic Books, 1985.
Alletzhauser, Albert J., *The House of Nomura*, New York, Harper, 1990.
Ballon, Robert J., *The Japanese Employee*, Tokyo, Tuttle, 1969.
—— (ed.), *Doing Business in Japan*, Tokyo, Kodansha International, 1971.
Beck, John C., and Martha N., *The Change of a Lifetime: Employment Patterns Among Japan's Managerial Elite*, Honolulu, University of Hawaii Press, 1994.
Chalmers, Norma J., *Industrial Relations in Japan: The Peripheral Sector*, London, Routledge, 1989.
Clark, Rodney, *The Japanese Company*, New Haven, Yale University Press, 1979.
Cole, Robert E., *Work, Mobility, and Participation*, Berkeley, University of California Press, 1979.
Hamabata, Matthews Masayuki, *Crested Kimono: Power and Love in the Japanese Business Family*, Ithaca, Cornell University Press, 1990.
Hanami, Tadashi, *Labor Relations in Japan Today*, Tokyo, Kodansha International, 1979.

Hayashi, Shuji, *Culture and Management in Japan*, Tokyo, University of Tokyo Press, 1989.

Kamata, Satoshi, *Japan in the Passing Lane*, New York, Random House, 1980.

Kinzley, W. Dean, *Industrial Harmony in Modern Japan, The Invention of a Tradition*, London, Routledge, 1991.

Lincoln, James R., and Kalleberg, Arne L., *Culture, Control and Commitment*, Cambridge, Cambridge University Press, 1990.

Morita, Akio, *Made in Japan, Akio Morita and Sony*, New York, E.P. Dutton, 1986.

Ozaki, Robert, *Human Capitalism, The Japanese Enterprise System as World Model*, Tokyo, Kodansha International, 1991.

Rohlen, Thomas P., *For Harmony and Strength*, Berkeley, University of California Press, 1974.

Sumiya, Mikio, *The Japanese Industrial Relations Reconsidered*, Tokyo, Japan Institute of Labor, 1990.

Woronoff, Jon, *Japan's Wasted Workers*, Tokyo, Lotus Press, and New York, Rowman & Allenheld, 1981.

———, *The Japanese Management Mystique*, Burr Ridge, Irwin Professional Publishing, 1992.

2. Economy (Recent)

Emmott, Bill, *The Sun Also Sets, Why Japan Will Not Be Number One*, London, Simon & Schuster, 1994.

———, *Japanophobia: The Myth of the Invincible Japanese*, New York, Times Books, 1993.

Reading, Brian, *Japan, The Coming Collapse*, London, Weidenfeld and Nicolson, 1992.

Wood, Christopher, *The Bubble Economy: Japan's Extraordinary Speculative Boom of the '80s and the Dramatic Bust of the '90s*, London, Sidgwick & Jackson, 1992.

———, *The End of Japan Inc. and How the New Japan Will Look*, New York, Simon & Schuster, 1994.

Woronoff, Jon, *Japan: The Coming Economic Crisis*, Tokyo, Yohan, 1979.

———, *The Japanese Economic Crisis*, London, Macmillan, and New York, St. Martin's Press, 1993.

3. Education

Beauchamp, Edward R. (ed.), *Windows on Japanese Education*, New York, Greenwood Press, 1991.

Cummings, William, *Education and Equality in Japan*, Princeton, Princeton University Press, 1980.

Duke, Benjamin, *The Japanese School*, New York, Praeger, 1986.

———, *Education and Leadership for the Twenty-First Century: Japan, America and Britain*, New York, Praeger, 1991.

Goodman, Roger, *Japan's 'International Youth,' The Emergence of a New Class of Schoolchildren*, New York, Oxford University Press, 1990.

Lee, W.O., *Social Change and Educational Problems in Japan, Singapore and Hong Kong*, New York, St. Martin's Press, 1991.

Leestma, Robert, and Walberg, Herbert J., *Japanese Educational Productivity*, Ann Arbor, Center for Japanese Studies, 1992.

Lynn, Richard, *Educational Achievement in Japan. Lessons for the West*, Armonk, M.E. Sharpe, 1988.

Nagai, Michio, *Higher Education in Japan: Its Take-Off and Crash*, Tokyo, University of Tokyo Press, 1971.

Peak, Lois, *Learning to Go to School in Japan, The Transition from Home to Preschool Life*, Berkeley, University of California Press, 1991.

Rohlen, Thomas P., *Japan's High Schools*, Berkeley, University of California Press, 1983.

Schoolland, Ken, *Shogun's Ghost, The Dark Side of Japanese Education*, New York, Bergin & Garvey, 1990.

Schoppa, Leonard James, *Education Reform in Japan: A Case of Immobilist Politics*, London, Routledge, 1991.

Shields, Jr., James J., *Japanese Schooling, Patterns of Socialization, Equality and Political Control*, University Park, Pennsylvania State University Press, 1993.

Tsukuda, Mamoru, *Yobiko Life: A Study of the Legitimization Process of Social Stratification in Japan*, Berkeley, Institute of East Asian Studies, 1991.

White, Merry, *The Japanese Educational Challenge: A Commitment to Children*, New York, Free Press, 1987.

4. Politics and Politicians

Abe, Hitoshi, Shindo, Muneyuki, and Kawato, Sadafumi, *The Government and Politics of Japan*, Tokyo, University of Tokyo Press, 1994.

Allinson, Gary, and Sone, Yasunori (eds.), *Political Dynamics in Contemporary Japan*, Ithaca, Cornell University Press, 1993.

Apter, David E., and Sawa, Nagayo, *Against the State, Politics and Social Protest in Japan*, Cambridge, Harvard University Press, 1984.

Calder, Kent E., *Crisis and Competition: Public Policy and Political Stability in Japan, 1949–1986*, Princeton, Princeton University Press, 1990.

Curtis, Gerald L., *Election Campaigning Japanese Style*, New York, Columbia University Press, 1971.

——, *The Japanese Way of Politics*, New York, Columbia University Press, 1988.

Flanagan, Scott C. et al., *The Japanese Voter*, New Haven, Yale University Press, 1991.

Hayao, Kenji, *The Japanese Prime Minister and Public Policy*, Pittsburgh, University of Pittsburgh Press, 1993.

Herzog, Peter J., *Japan's Pseudo-Democracy*, New York, New York University Press, 1993.

Holstein, William J., *The Japanese Power Game*, New York, Charles Scribner's Sons, 1990.

Ishida, Takeshi, and Krauss, Ellis S. (eds.), *Democracy In Japan*, Pittsburgh, University of Pittsburgh Press, 1989.

Kataoka, Tetsuya (ed.), *Creating Single-Party Democracy*, Stanford, Hoover Institution Press, 1992.

Kishima, Takako, *Political Life in Japan, Democracy in a Reversible World,* Princeton, Princeton University Press, 1992.

Kyogoku, Jun-ichi, *The Political Dynamics of Japan,* Tokyo, University of Tokyo Press, 1987.

Masumi, Junnosuke, *Contemporary Politics in Japan,* Berkeley, University of California Press, 1995.

McCormack, Gavan, and Sugimoto, Yoshio (eds.), *Democracy in Contemporary Japan,* Armonk, M.E. Sharpe, 1986.

Nestor, William, *The Foundation of Japanese Power,* London, Macmillan, 1990.

Ozawa, Ichiro, *Blueprint for a New Japan, The Rethinking of a Nation,* Tokyo, Kodansha International, 1994.

Pempel, T.J., *Policy and Politics in Japan, Creative Conservatism,* Philadelphia, Temple University Press, 1982.

—— (ed.), *Uncommon Democracies: The One Party Dominant Regimes,* Ithaca, Cornell University Press, 1991.

Richardson, Bradley M., *The Political Culture of Japan,* Berkeley, University of California Press, 1975.

Richardson, Bradley M., and Flanagan, Scott C., *Politics in Japan,* Boston, Little, Brown & Co., 1984.

Rothacher, Albrecht, *The Japanese Power Elite,* London, Macmillan, 1993.

Steiner, Kurt, Krauss, Ellis S., and Flanagan, Scott C. (eds.), *Political Opposition and Local Politics in Japan,* Princeton, Princeton University Press, 1980.

Stockwin, J.A.A. et al., *Dynamic and Immobilist Politics in Japan,* Honolulu, University of Hawaii Press, 1988.

Tasker, Peter, *Inside Japan: Wealth, Work and Power in the New Japanese Empire,* London, Sidgwick & Jackson, 1987.

Thayer, Nathaniel B., *How the Conservatives Rule Japan,* Princeton, Princeton University Press, 1969.

van Wolferen, Karel, *The Enigma of Japanese Power,* New York, Alfred A. Knopf, 1989.

Woronoff, Jon, *Inside Japan, Inc.,* Tokyo, Lotus Press, 1982.

——, *Politics, The Japanese Way,* Tokyo, Yohan, London, Macmillan, and New York, St. Martin's Press, 1987.

5. Bureaucracy

Campbell, John Creighton, *Contemporary Japanese Budget Politics,* Berkeley, University of California Press, 1976.

Johnson, Chalmers, *MITI and the Japanese Miracle,* Stanford, Stanford University Press, 1982.

——, *Japan, Who Governs?,* New York, W.W. Norton, 1995.

Kato, Junko, *The Problem of Bureaucratic Rationality, Tax Politics in Japan,* Princeton, Princeton University Press, 1994.

Keehn, Barry E., *Ministries and Information in Japan,* London, Macmillan, 1995.

Kim, Hyung-Ki, and Yamamura, Kozo (eds.), *The Japanese Civil Service and Economic Development,* New York, Oxford University Press, 1994.

Kubota, Akira, *Higher Civil Servants in Postwar Japan: Their Social Origins, Educational Background and Career Patterns*, Princeton, Princeton University Press, 1969.

Miyamoto, Masao, *Straitjacket Society*, Tokyo, Kodansha International, 1994.

Park, Yung H., *Bureaucrats and Ministers in Contemporary Japanese Government*, Berkeley, Institute of East Asian Studies, 1986.

Shibata, Tokue, *Japan's Public Sector: How the Government is Financed*, Tokyo, University of Tokyo Press, 1993.

Tsuji, Kiyoaki (ed.), *Public Administration in Japan*, Tokyo, University of Tokyo Press, 1984.

Woronoff, Jon, *Japanese Industrial Targeting, Successes, Failures, Lessons*, London, Macmillan, and New York, St. Martin's Press, 1992.

6. Business Community

Dodwell Marketing Consultants, *Industrial Groupings in Japan*, Tokyo, Annual.

Gerlach, Michael L., *Alliance Capitalism: The Social Organization of Japanese Business*, Berkeley, University of California Press, 1992.

Johnson, Hazel J., *The Banking Keiretsu*, Chicago, Probus, 1993.

Lynn, Leonard H., and McKeown, Timothy J., *Organizing Business, Trade Associations in America and Japan*, Washington, D.C., American Enterprise Institute, 1988.

Yanaga, Chitoshi, *Big Business in Japanese Politics*, New Haven, Yale University Press, 1969.

7. Society

Allison, Anne, *Nightwork: Sexuality, Pleasure, and Corporate Masculinity in a Tokyo Hostess Club*, Chicago, University of Chicago Press, 1994.

Bester, Theodore, *Neighborhood Tokyo*, Stanford, Stanford University Press, 1990.

Bulletin of Concerned Asian Scholars, *The Other Japan*, Armonk, M.E. Sharpe, 1988.

Dore, Ronald P., *City Life in Japan: A Study of a Tokyo Ward*, Berkeley, University of California Press, 1958.

Fukutake, Tadashi, *Japanese Society Today*, Tokyo, University of Tokyo Press, 1981.

——, *The Japanese Social Structure*, Tokyo, University of Tokyo Press, 1982.

Hendry, Joy, *Understanding Japanese Society*, London, Routledge, 1987.

Hidaka, Rokuro, *The Price of Affluence: Dilemmas of Contemporary Japan*, Tokyo, Kodansha International, 1984.

Lebra, Takie, *Japanese Social Organization*, Honolulu, University of Hawaii Press, 1992.

Martineau, Lisa, *Caught in a Mirror, Reflections of Japan*, London, Macmillan, 1993.

Mita, Munesuke, *Social Psychology of Modern Japan*, London, Kegan Paul International, 1992.

Mouer, Ross, and Sugimoto, Yoshio, *Images of Japanese Society*, Kegan Paul International, 1986.

Murakami, Yasusuke, and Patrick, Hugh T., *The Political Economy of Japan: Cultural and Social Dynamics*, Stanford, Stanford University Press, 1992.

Reingold, Edwin M., *Chrysanthemums and Thorns, The Untold Story of Modern Japan*, New York, St. Martin's Press, 1992.

Reischauer, Edwin O., *The Japanese*, Cambridge, Harvard University Press, 1981.

——, *The Japanese Today*, Cambridge, Harvard University Press, 1988.

Robertson, Jennifer, *Native and Newcomer, Making and Remaking a Japanese City*, Berkeley, University of California Press, 1991.

Steven, Rob, *Classes in Contemporary Japan*, Cambridge, Cambridge University Press, 1983.

Upham, Frank K., *Law and Social Change in Postwar Japan*, Cambridge, Harvard University Press, 1987.

Ui, Jun (ed.), *Industrial Pollution in Japan*, Tokyo, United Nations University Press, 1992.

Vogel, Ezra F., *Japan's New Middle Class*, Los Angeles, University of California Press, 1967.

——, *Japan As Number One*, Cambridge, Harvard University Press, 1979.

Woodiwiss, Anthony, *Law, Labour and Society in Japan: From Repression to Reluctant Recognition*, London, Routledge, 1991.

Woronoff, Jon, *Japan: The Coming Social Crisis*, Tokyo, Yohan, 1980.

——, *The Japan Syndrome*, Tokyo, Lotus Press, and New Brunswick, Transaction Publishers, 1985.

——, *Japan As – Anything But – Number One*, Tokyo, Yohan, London, Macmillan, and Armonk, M.E. Sharpe.

8. Crime

Bayley, David, *Forces of Order: Police Behavior in Japan and the United States*, Berkeley, University of California Press, 1976.

Hamilton, Lee, and Sanders, Joseph, *Everyday Justice*, New Haven, Yale University Press, 1992.

Kaplan, David E., and Dubro, Alec, *Yakuza: The Explosive Account of Japan's Underworld*, Reading, Addison-Wesley, 1986.

Miyazawa, Setsuo, *Policing in Japan*, Albany, SUNY Press, 1992.

Parker, Craig, *The Japanese Police System Today*, Tokyo, Kodansha International, 1984.

9. Religion

Brackett, O.W., *Holy Terror, Armageddon in Tokyo*, Tokyo, Weatherhill, 1996.

Davis, Winston, *Japanese Religion and Society: Paradigms of Structure and Change*, Albany, SUNY Press, 1992.

Hardacre, Helen, *Lay Buddhism in Contemporary Japan: Reiyukai Kyodan*, Princeton, Princeton University Press, 1984.
——, *Kurozumikyo and the New Religions of Japan*, Princeton, Princeton University Press, 1986.
——, *Shinto and the State, 1868–1988*, Princeton, Princeton University Press, 1991.
Metraux, Daniel, *The History and Theology of Soka Gakkai*, Lewiston, Edwin Mellon Press, 1988.
Mullins, Mark R., Shimazono, Susumu, and Swanson, Paul L. (eds.), *Religion in Modern Japan: Selected Readings*, Berkeley, Asian Humanities Press, 1993.
Picken, Stuart, *Essentials of Shinto*, Westport, Greenwood, 1994.
Saunders, Dale, *Buddhism in Japan*, Tokyo, Tuttle, 1972.
Thelle, Notto R., *Buddhism and Christianity in Japan*, Honolulu, University of Hawaii Press, 1987.
Thomsen, Harry, *The New Religions in Japan*, Englewood Cliffs, Prentice-Hall, 1963.
Reader, Ian, *Religion in Contemporary Japan*, Honolulu, University of Hawaii Press, 1990.

10. Nationalism

Benedict, Ruth, *The Chrysanthemum and the Sword*, Tokyo, Tuttle, 1954.
Buruma, Ian, *The Wages of Guilt*, New York, Farrar, Straus, Giroux, 1993.
Dale, Peter N., *The Myth of Japanese Uniqueness*, London, Routledge, and New York, St. Martin's Press, 1986.
Ishihara, Shintaro, *The Japan That Can Say No, Why Japan Will Be First Among Equals*, New York, Simon & Schuster, 1991.
Ohnuki-Tierney, Emiko, *Rice as Self*, Princeton, Princeton University Press, 1993.
Stronach, Bruce, *Beyond the Rising Sun, Nationalism in Contemporary Japan*, New York, Praeger, 1995.
Yoshino, Kasaku, *Cultural Nationalism in Contemporary Japan*, London, Routledge, 1995.

11. The Individual

Craig, Albert M., and Shively, Donald H. (eds.), *Personality in Japanese History*, Ann Arbor, Center for Japanese Studies-University of Michigan, 1995.
DeVos, George A., *Social Cohesion and Alienation: Minorities in the United States and Japan*, Boulder, Westview Press, 1992.
DeVos, George A., and Wagatsuma, Hiroshi, *Japan's Invisible Race: Caste in Culture and Personality*, Berkeley, University of California Press, 1971.
Doi, Takeo, *The Anatomy of Dependence*, Tokyo, Kodansha International, 1971.
——, *The Anatomy of Self, The Individual versus Society*, Tokyo, Kodansha International, 1986.
Hane, Mikiso, *Peasants, Rebels, and Outcastes*, New York, Pantheon Books, 1982.

Johnson, Frank A., *Dependency and Japanese Socialization, Psychoanalytic Investigations into Amae*, New York, New York University Press, 1992.

Koschmann, J. Victor, *Authority and the Individual in Japan: Citizen Protest in Historical Perspective*, Tokyo, University of Tokyo Press, 1978.

Krauss, Ellis S., *Japanese Radicals Revisited*, Berkeley, University of California Press, 1977.

Leupp Gary P., *Servants, Shophands and Laborers in the Cities of Tokugawa Japan*, Princeton, Princeton University Press, 1992.

Martineau, Lisa, *Caught in a Mirror: Reflections of Japan*, London, Macmillan, 1993.

McKean, Margaret A., *Environmental Protest and Citizen Politics in Japan*, Berkeley, University of California Press, 1981.

Naff, Clayton, *About Face: How I Stumbled onto Japan's Social Revolution*, Tokyo, Kodansha International, 1994.

Najita, Tetsuo, and Koschmann, J. Victor (eds.), *Conflict in Modern Japanese History: The Neglected Tradition*, Princeton, Princeton University Press, 1983.

Nakane, Chie, *Kinship and Economic Organization in Rural Japan*, New York, Humanities Press, 1967.

———, *Japanese Society*, Berkeley, University of California Press, 1970.

Taylor, Jared, *Shadows of the Rising Sun*, New York, William Morrow, 1983.

Turner, Christina L., *Japanese Workers in Protest*, Berkeley, University of California Press, 1995.

Ueda, Atsushi (ed.), *The Electric Geisha: Exploring Japan's Popular Culture*, Tokyo, Kodansha International, 1994.

White, Merry, *The Japanese Overseas: Can They Go Home Again?*, New York, Free Press, 1993.

———, *The Material Child, Coming of Age in Japan and America*, New York, Free Press, 1993.

12. Women

Bornoff, Nicholas, *Pink Samurai, The Pursuit and Politics of Sex in Japan*, London, Grafton Books, 1991.

Brinton, Mary C., *Women and the Economic Miracle*, Berkeley, University of California Press, 1992.

Coleman, Samuel, *Family Planning in Japanese Society*, Princeton, Princeton University Press, 1991.

Condon, Jane, *A Half Step Behind, Japanese Women Today*, Tokyo, Tuttle, 1991.

Cook, Alice, and Hayashi, Hiroko, *Working Women in Japan: Discrimination, Resistance and Reform*, Ithaca, Cornell University Press, 1980.

Hunter, Janet E. (ed.), *Japanese Women Working*, London, Routledge, 1993.

Iwao, Sumiko, *The Japanese Woman: Traditional Image and Changing Reality*, New York, Free Press, 1993.

Lam, Alice, *Women and Japanese Management, Discrimination and Reform*, London, Routledge, 1992.

Lo, Jeannie, *Office Ladies, Factory Women*, Armonk, M.E. Sharpe, 1990.

Ministry of Labor, *White Paper on Women's Labor*, Tokyo, Annual.

Roberts, Glenda S., *Staying on the Line: Blue-Collar Women in Contemporary Japan*, Honolulu, University of Hawaii Press, 1994.

Saso, Mary, *Women in the Japanese Workplace*, London, Hilary Shipman, 1990.

13. Old Age and Welfare

Anderson, Stephen J., *Welfare Policy and Politics in Japan: Beyond the Developmental State*, New York, Paragon House, 1993.

Bass, Scott A., *Productive Aging and the Role of Older People in Japan: New Approaches for the United States*, New York, Japan Society, 1995.

Campbell, John Creighton, *How Policies Change: The Japanese Government and the Aging Society*, Princeton, Princeton University Press, 1992.

Kinoshita, Yasuhito, *Refuge of the Honored, Social Organization in a Japanese Retirement Community*, Berkeley, University of California Press, 1992.

Palmore, Erdman, *The Honorable Elders: A Cross-Cultural Analysis of Aging in Japan*, Durham, Duke University Press, 1975.

Palmore, Erdman, and Maeda, Disaku, *The Honorable Elders Revisited*, Durham, Duke University Press, 1985.

Rodwin, Victor, *Japan's Universal and Affordable Health Care: Lessons for the United States?*, New York, Japan Society, 1995.

Takayama, Noriyuki, *The Greying of Japan, An Economic Perspective on Public Pensions*, New York, Oxford University Press, 1993.

Index